Queer Indigenous Studies

Queer Indigenous Studies

Critical Interventions in Theory, Politics,

and Literature

Edited by
Qwo-Li Driskill, Chris Finley, Brian Joseph Gilley, and
Scott Lauria Morgensen

The University of Arizona Press   Tucson

The University of Arizona Press
© 2011 The Arizona Board of Regents
All rights reserved

www.uapress.arizona.edu

Library of Congress Cataloging-in-Publication Data

Queer indigenous studies : critical interventions in theory,
politics, and literature / edited by Qwo-Li Driskill ... [et al.].
     p.   cm.
   Includes bibliographical references and index.
   ISBN 978-0-8165-2907-0 (paper : alk. paper)
     1. Indians of North America—Sexual behavior.   2. Maori
(New Zealand people)—Sexual behavior.   3. Indigenous
peoples—Sexual behavior.   4. Queer theory.   5. Criticism
(Philosophy).   6. Sexual minorities—Social conditions.
7. Sexual minorities—Political activity.   8. Sexual
minorities—Intellectual life.   9. Gender identity.
10. Sex role.   I. Driskill, Qwo-Li.

   E98.S48Q84 2011
   305.8—dc22   2010035093

Manufactured in the United States of America on acid-free,
archival-quality paper.

16   15   14   13   12   11   6   5   4   3   2

All royalties from this book will be donated to the National Native
American AIDS Prevention Center (www.nnaapc.org) and the
Indigenous Women's Network (www.indigenouswomen.org)

Contents

Queer Indigenous Studies

Introduction

Qwo-Li Driskill, Chris Finley, Brian Joseph Gilley,
Scott Lauria Morgensen

> The imagining needs praise as does any living thing. We are
> evidence of this praise, and when we laugh, we're indestructible.
> No story or song will translate the full impact of falling,
> or the inverse power of rising up. Of rising up.
> —Joy Harjo[1]

This book is an imagining. It is an emergence story about the current work of activists, artists, and scholars to address the theoretical specificities of Indigenous gay, lesbian, bisexual, transgender, queer, and Two-Spirit (GLBTQ2) lives and communities.[2] These theories are arising in grassroots movements, in conversations between Indigenous and queer studies, and in the everyday lives of Indigenous GLBTQ2 people. This collection asks us to imagine what critical Indigenous GLBTQ2 theories look like, and what impact they have on our practices as scholars, activists, and artists.

This project arose from conversations that began at the 2008 Native American and Indigenous Studies Meetings on the coeditors' panel "Contesting Borders of Sexuality and Indigeneity." We came together with the help of conference organizers who, like us, wished to see a panel on sexuality and gender at the meetings, and we sensed a high energy around our work that drew us into further collaborations. We met just as two important new publications were appearing: a special issue of *Studies in American Indian Literatures* devoted to GLBTQ2 literatures, and a special issue of *GLQ: A Journal of Lesbian and Gay Studies* on intersections of Native and queer studies.[3] We took inspiration from these projects as we recalled our desires as teachers, scholars, artists, and organizers to see a scholarly collection in Native American and Indigenous studies that would arise from and respond to the lives, cultures, and social movements of Indigenous GLBTQ2 people.

After returning to our lives, and without designating a leader, we formed online environments to discuss what a book could and should be in its scope, composition, politics, and accountability to communities. We invited contributions from Native/Indigenous studies scholars and Indigenous community members and activists, and these participants informed how we collaborated. We assembled this text to answer our hopes for such a collection, and to address a set of open questions: How did a prior generation of anthropology and gay and lesbian studies define scholarship on gender, sexuality, and Indigenous people? How have old accounts been displaced by decades of Indigenous GLBTQ2 organizing and writing? How do we understand the cultures and politics that Indigenous GLBTQ2 people create, including the reclaiming of identities such as *fa'afafine, asegi,* and *takatapui*? How does current theory in queer and Indigenous studies inform our work, from queer theory's promotion of a "subjectless critique," to efforts in Indigenous studies to center Indigenous knowledges and critically investigate settler colonialism? We answer these questions by offering new scholarship to the transnational work of Native and Indigenous studies in the form of a conversation we call queer Indigenous studies. This book is intertwined with the simultaneous publication of a new anthology of creative works by Indigenous GLBTQ2 people, edited by Qwo-Li Driskill, Daniel Heath Justice, Deborah Miranda, and Lisa Tatonetti. Contributions to both books inform one another and highlight the array of creative and critical voices building theories and practices of Indigenous GLBTQ2 resistance. This collection contributes to this broader project by assembling critical studies of diverse claims by and about Indigenous GLBTQ2 people in transnational conversations crossing North America and the Pacific.

This text is an assembly of many voices, writing work that centers Indigenous GLBTQ2 people and theories. At times the text addresses Indigenous GLBTQ2 people as speakers and listeners. At other times the text invites a conversation across the many identities of the co-editors and contributors, which include Native, trans, straight, non-Native, feminist, Two-Spirit, mixed blood, and queer, to name just a few. Each time the text speaks from and to Indigenous GLBTQ2 people, it recognizes that allies are listening, among the contributors and readers, who witness and are held accountable to these acts. And each time the text invokes non-Indigenous and/or non-GLBTQ2 people, it reminds us of shared commitments to accountably respond to Indigenous GLBTQ2 people who center Indigenous lives and stakes as a core intervention this book invites.[4]

Indigenous GLBTQ2 identities are deeply complex. The issue of terminology always pushes at the limits of language. All of the available terms are to us equally ambiguous and contested. Our purpose here is not to assert an umbrella term for the countless identities that fall under categories such as queer, Two-Spirit, transgender, gay, bisexual, or lesbian. Each of these terms inevitably fails to reflect the complexities of Indigenous constructions of gender and sexual diversity, both historically and as they are used in the present. Nevertheless, we find both *queer* and *Two-Spirit* useful for a number of reasons. *Queer* carries with it an oppositional critique of heteronormativity and an interest in the ambiguity of gender and sexuality. *Two-Spirit* was proposed in Indigenous organizing in Canada and the United States to be inclusive of Indigenous people who identify as GLBTQ or through nationally specific terms from Indigenous languages. When linked, *queer* and *Two-Spirit* invite critiquing heteronormativity as a colonial project, and decolonizing Indigenous knowledges of gender and sexuality as one result of that critique. Our intention in articulating Indigenous queer critiques and/or Two-Spirit critiques is not to create a monolithic analytic lens. Rather, we hope to bring Indigenous-specific critiques of colonial heteropatriarchal gender/sexuality into broader conversations within queer and Indigenous studies that link queer Indigenous people within and across Indigenous nations, colonial borders, and global networks. These conversations are internally multiple and sustain differences. For instance, the many essays that examine the category *Two-Spirit* reflect the Anglophone North American contexts in which this book arose, but these are interwoven with essays that examine no comparable category and with essays concerning the Indigenous Pacific. As editors we engaged *Two-Spirit* as an Indigenous identity category that is important both historically and culturally to Indigenous communities inside and outside of the academy, yet we locate it as one site among many where the meanings of queer Indigenous critiques are debated. The connections across borders, history, language, and politics that this book invites do not immediately resolve to a single story but instead constitute a conversation.

Conversations in Native Studies

This project arises within Native American and Indigenous studies by centering Indigenous knowledges as a basis for social theory. Scholars in Native studies are displacing non-Native conversations about Indigenous people by building theories from the everyday knowledges and intellectual histories of Indigenous people across time, space, and culture. Robert Allen Warrior has argued that this decolonizing gesture is not ideological, but methodological.[5] No single politics defines it, other than the interruption of colonial authority over knowledge and a recognition of Indigenous people as central to all knowledge claims about themselves. In her book *Decolonizing Methodologies,* Linda Tuhiwai Smith critiques colonial authority by calling Indigenous people to create distinctive knowledge, both in what is said and how it is said. For Smith, "indigenous methodologies" represent the intellectual work Indigenous people can take up in order to decolonize both knowledge and the methods producing it.[6] A methodological turn to Indigenous knowledges opens up accounts to the multiplicity, complexity, contestation, and change among knowledge claims by Indigenous people. While any claim to knowledge has a power to restrict conversation, Warrior and Smith join many scholars in Native studies in arguing that a methodological turn to Indigenous knowledges will study differences and dissent, and the many ties that Indigenous people form amidst them. For instance, Andrea Smith argues for rejecting colonial legacies in research in her writing on Native Americans and the Christian Right. She locates "nonacademic activists as intellectuals" in an "intellectual ethnography," which shifts ethnography from "studying Native people so we can learn more about them" to working "to illustrate what it is that Native theorists have to tell us about the world we live in and how to change it."[7] Yet while she centers Native activist claims, she is attentive to the fact that political projects are internally multiple, identities "shifting and contingent," and all are capable of "reinscribing the power relations they seek to contest or possibly instilling new power relations, which can be oppressive."[8] Thus, for her and other scholars in Native studies, focusing on Indigenous knowledges marks their variety and notes how power can act within them as well as within colonial regimes. In the spirit of such claims, we center knowledges produced by Indigenous GLBTQ2 people in order to counter colonial representation, affirm Indigenous GLBTQ2 intellectual histories, and foreground multiplicity among Indigenous people to critically examine their production within power relations.

The methodological turn to Indigenous knowledges defines a recent generation of Native literary criticism that also informs accounts of GLBTQ2 Indigenous people. Native critics have worked to shift Native

literatures from colonial interpretation or adoption by settler multiculturalism by reading them and all Indigenous knowledges within frames
set by Indigenous conversations. In doing so, Native critics do not say
that Indigenous knowledges possess essential differences that need to
be separate from modes of thought linked to the history of colonialism. Instead, critics have argued that the full complexity of Indigenous
thought in the past and present should set a first frame for interpreting Indigenous knowledges. One model appears in the work of Jace
Weaver and Robert Warrior, who trace diverse Indigenous literatures
across time and examine their distinctions and connections.[9] Warrior
examines Indigenous "intellectual histories," while Weaver reads within
Indigenous literatures a theme of "communitism," or a shared commitment to assert community and mobilize activism for Indigenous survival. Both scholars take note of sexual diversity in Indigenous literary
traditions, as when Weaver keys Paula Gunn Allen's writing on Indigenous lesbians to communitism, or when Warrior opens *Tribal Secrets* by
calling Indigenous intellectuals to their "responsibility . . . for addressing such issues as economic and social class, gender, and sexual orientation within Indian life."[10] Alongside Warrior's and Weaver's work, a
linked project arose through Craig Womack's tribally specific theories of
Indigenous literatures, which Womack called "literary separatism" and
that he theorizes with Weaver and Warrior as "literary nationalism."[11]
Womack argues that a key method for decolonizing the study of Indigenous literatures would be to examine the tribally specific histories, cultures, and commitments to community that literatures reflect. Womack
and Daniel Heath Justice present national histories of Creek and Cherokee literatures, respectively, and both foreground queer presences and
critiques within those histories, notably in the work of Cherokee writer
Lynn Riggs.[12] Together, such works interrupt a twentieth-century history of non-Native scholars divorced from Native communities defining Native studies. Warrior traces that history to the small number of
Indigenous scholars who had been admitted to the field, and to how
rarely Indigenous intellectual histories were made a basis for the study of
Indigenous knowledges. All the noted scholars critique how non-Native
evaluations of Indigenous writing tended to hold it to standards defined
outside conversation with Indigenous intellectuals.[13] Their work instead
pursues Indigenous-centered conversations—in tribal frames of reference or among Indigenous writers across social and historical contexts—
as bases for building theory about Indigenous knowledge production.

Subsequent debates about communitist and literary nationalist work in Native studies have inspired deep reflection on the implications of defining knowledge about Indigenous people. In the recent collection by the Native Critics Collective, Christopher Teuton argues that a new generation of Native literary critics is "imagining the place of critical scholarship within Native communities . . . by providing terms that may be used to create a space for the articulation of Native epistemologies within academia but are accessible and informative to mainstream audiences."[14] Teuton quotes Womack in the same volume asking: "What is the relationship between our theories and the people we are theorizing about? Do the subjects of our theorizing see themselves in the same way as we describe them in books, journal articles, classroom lectures, and so on? How do we bring their self-representations into our theorizing?" Answering these questions by following the model of Warrior or Andrea Smith will create theory from Indigenous self-representation that reflects Indigenous people's complexity. Writing in conversation enables representing Indigenous lives in mulivalent contexts. Indeed, such writing may present Indigenous lives by not matching the self-representation of every Indigenous reader, but instead reflecting a core intention to argue that that diversity is crucial to writing for Indigenous audiences.

Centering relationships across difference in Indigenous knowledges also has led critics to ask what it means to center in Indigenous theories of the nation in scholarship. Lisa Brooks affirms tribally specific and nationalist criticism when she reflects on how Abenaki language suggests ways to think about the nation while questioning colonial definitions of that term. In her essay for the Native Critics Collective, Brooks explains that "to call myself 'Native' in Abenaki, I would use the term *alnôba*, or its long version, *alnôbawôgan*," a term that "is neither truly an adjective nor a noun" such as the English term "Native." Carrying a doubled meaning of "human nature" and "birth," *alnôbawôgan* translates as "the activity of 'being (or becoming) human.'" Brooks says that "this concept provides a striking contrast to the stereotypical European constructions of Native 'tradition' as static and potentially destructible (mortal)," in that Abenaki people use *alnôbawôgan* "in its active form" to mark "the transformations that constitute the ongoing process of 'being human' within a multifaceted world. . . . Therefore, 'Native' in the Abenaki language is not a term that is used to separate and distinguish us from other 'races' but is rooted in the recognition of relationship to other humans with whom we share common experience and common bonds. Identity is thus always relational, and grounded in a particular place and its history."[15] Brooks continues her reflections by considering how tribal belonging is imagined in Abenaki language: "The word for 'tribe' is *Negewet kamigwezo,* or 'those of one family.' The word for 'national,' however, is *Mizi Negewet kamigwezoi,* meaning 'families gathered together.'" Thus, the activity of nation building, in the Abenaki sense, is not a means of boundary making, but rather a process of gathering from within. This notion differs radically from colonial definitions of nationalism, including those projected onto Indigenous people and their activisms. Brooks promotes this point in her afterword to Weaver, Womack, and Warrior's *American Indian Literary Nationalism:*

> I have a different kind of nationalism in mind, which I hope lies in concert with the calls of those within: a nationalism that is not based on the theoretical and physical models of the nation-state; a nationalism that is not based on notions of nativism or binary oppositions between insider and outsider, self and other; a nationalism that does not root itself in an idealization of any pre-Contact past, but rather relies on the multifaceted, lived experience of families who gather in particular places; a nationalism that may be unlike any of those with which most literary critics and cultural theorists are familiar.[16]

Brooks uses a tribally specific reading of Abenaki language to show that a national frame for theory in Native studies can question colonial narratives and transform what the "nation" means on new and Indigenous terms.

Tol Foster also argues for studying tribally specific and nationalist knowledges and their internal diversity by centering their interdependence, through the method he calls "relational regionalism." Saying that "a regional framework . . . is not actually coherent without more specific tribal studies that serve to buttress and challenge it," Foster reminds us that interest in tribal perspectives calls us to ask how Indigenous communities are interdependent with differences that lie both outside and inside their bounds.[17] He argues for "the radical notion that tribally specific work is necessarily incomplete if it does not have multiple perspectives and voices within it and is even incomplete *if it does not acknowledge voices without as well.* Thus the regional frame is not necessarily ancillary to tribal specificity, but is actually at times the very center of a given tribal practice."[18] Foster offers a reading of the story of "Choffee, the rabbit trickster of the Creeks," who "stole fire from elsewhere and gave it to the Creek people," to suggest "that the very center of our culture was exchanged with (or taken from) some other people and place. Thus the center might be out there, among presumptive strangers."[19] Foster makes his claim in order to caution against a "danger" in "the tribally specific frame," if it

> leads us to close off voices that do not obviously seem to be part of the tribal community and to privilege the more conservative voices in that community. Worst of all might be the privileging of tribally specific values and attitudes merely because they are traditional, without asking whether or not they are useful or helpful. . . . Anywhere the story is simple, we can be assured that it is incomplete and that some crucial member of the community has been silenced.[20]

Foster's work offers a way to foreground the integrity of Indigenous knowledges while arguing that none can be understood without studying its relationship to differences.

The work in Native studies to frame Indigenous knowledges as conversations across differences also defines theories of political and intellectual decolonization and sovereignty. Robert Warrior proposes his thesis of "intellectual sovereignty" by asking how historical activism for national sovereignty informed theories of sovereignty in Native writing. He argues that "the struggle for sovereignty is not a struggle to be free from the influence of anything outside ourselves, but a process of asserting the power we possess as communities and individuals to make decisions that affect our lives."[21] His argument turns the category sovereignty away from establishing fixed boundaries in the past, and towards a present standpoint where Native people's creativity can be known. Thus, rather than equating to a defense against differences, sovereignty for Indigenous people can mark the power to "withdraw without becoming separatists, being willing to reach out for the contradictions within our experience and open ourselves to the pain and the joy of others. The decision to exercise intellectual sovereignty provides a crucial moment in the process from which resistance, hope, and, most of all, imagination issue."[22] Just as Warrior presents his claim as compatible with activism for national sovereignty, Indigenous feminists support sovereignty struggles when they argue that decolonization for Indigenous people will follow declaring sovereignty from the heteropatriarchal politics, economics, and cultures inherited from colonization.[23] Andrea Smith asserts, "It has been through sexual violence and through the imposition of European gender relationships on Native communities that Europeans were able to colonize Native peoples in the first place. If we maintain these patriarchal gender systems, we will be unable to decolonize and fully assert our sovereignty."[24] This call for feminist transformation invites all Indigenous people to proclaim sovereignty from colonial modes of thought, and from the idea that Indigenous traditions are incompatible with feminism. In contrast, they argue, Indigenous sovereignty struggles can engage feminism to question their own inequalities as part of critiquing colonial control. Indigenous feminist theories mean to free Native people from extending the power relations required by colonial regimes—which include heteropatriarchy—and to frame gender and sexuality as central to work for sovereignty and decolonization.

In such writing, Smith and Warrior ground Indigenous criticism and activism in embracing dissent that alters norms in Indigenous communities and fosters change that can serve all Indigenous people. Indigenous feminists have modeled dissent as a principle of their work as Indigenous activists, whose feminism works to strengthen collective struggles for sovereignty from locations within Indigenous communities and politics. In this sense, dissent from current leadership does not separate them as feminists from Indigenous communities but tries to mobilize those communities' capacity to dissent collectively from colonial regimes. Warrior considers such themes in his writing on his role as a scholar committed to the politics of sovereignty who also acts as a critic in such work.[25] He reflects on the legacy of his teacher Edward Said, whose unswerving commitment to Palestinian liberation was expressed in the life of a critic unafraid to defy Palestinian nationalist leadership, even to the point of being exiled in his late life from the PLO and Palestine. Warrior calls himself and other Indigenous critics to consider Said's stakes in defending the nation by holding all its forms of nationalism accountable to critical engagement. Warrior argues that this recognition in no way reduces his commitment to work as a nationalist and critic, but reminds us that these two commitments are not identical and remain in conversation across their differences.

These many directions in theory in Native studies inspire queer Indigenous criticism. A methodological turn to Indigenous knowledge affirms knowledges among Indigenous GLBTQ2 people as key to their lives and communities. Indigenous GLBTQ2 people appear as part of the diversity of their own nations and of Indigenous peoples generally, crossing many cultural, national, racial, gender, and sexual identities.

Respecting knowledge among Indigenous GLBTQ2 people honors their dissent from homophobia, transphobia, and misogyny, and their claim of belonging to Indigenous tradition and contemporary culture. Addressing Indigenous GLBTQ2 people inspires a variety of critically queer and indigenist accounts of Indigenous societies and settler colonialism. Recalling and defending Indigenous traditions of gender and sexuality makes Indigenous GLBTQ2 people a central part of the decolonization of Indigenous communities. Community and coalitional organizing allows both agreement and dissent to be part of decolonization.

Talking Back: Critical Interventions

To theorize from knowledges produced within Indigenous conversations, GLBTQ2 Indigenous people must interrupt the authority of anthropological knowledge and its many adaptations in non-Native sexual minority politics. Anthropology and sexual/gender-nonconforming activists share a long history of making definitive claims about Indigenous people by finding a "usefulness" in Indigenous people's divergences from western sex/gender norms. Anthropology foregrounded Native American gender and sexual diversity as an ethnographic cornerstone for the cross-cultural study of gender and sexuality, while this diversity has been cited as an inspiration for GLBTQ identities and politics across racial and national lines in the United States and elsewhere. These histories form part of the context in which Native American GLBTQ people proposed the community-based term *Two-Spirit*. *Two-Spirit* affirmed their belonging to cultural traditions by displacing anthropological terms—notably, *berdache*—thereby setting a new basis and method for Indigenous knowledge. After the term's proposal, scholars writing from within non-Native intellectual histories tended to understand that *Two-Spirit* replaced *berdache*, but most tended to miss how the term massively shifted the bases of knowledge production by interrupting anthropological authority to define Indigenous truth. Differences arose between Indigenous people producing knowledge in Two-Spirit organizing and academics theorizing in the anthropological tradition, raising questions that our book opens to discussion. Increasingly, however, these questions are answered when anthropologists and other scholars make the knowledges produced by Indigenous GLBTQ2 people—such as Two-Spirit identity—their ground for interpreting Indigenous identities and cultures today. The case of *berdache* and *Two-Spirit* is only one of many in the Americas and the Pacific where anthropologists and sexual minority activists have produced knowledge of Indigenous gender and sexuality at a distance from the stakes of Indigenous GLBTQ people and their Indigenous communities. We examine it as a key historical case illustrating the challenges and promises of Indigenous GLBTQ2 criticism.

The advent of the term *Two-Spirit* began a new era in the study of past and present Native American gender and sexual diversity. As a critique of anthropological writing based in colonial and western notions of gender and sexuality, the category Two-Spirit creates a distinct link between histories of diversity and Indigenous GLBTQ2 people today. Specifically, it revises the use of the term *berdache* and its assumptions in academic writing. Stories of the "berdache tradition" structured two moments of academic writing in the twentieth century. Initially, the word *berdache* entered academic literature through anthropological writing in the early century that studied the practices of sexual and gender "deviants," notably among gender-transitive males who had sexual and domestic relations with men in tribal societies. Anthropologists extrapolated *berdache* from its supposedly proper reference to Native American societies in order to explain roles in societies worldwide.[26] The berdache was deliberated again in the 1980s by anthropologists who tried to puzzle out its "status." The question of status arose in a moment when academic culture was opening to feminist interventions and beginning to question assumptions about constructions of gender and same-sex desire. Anthropologists in the United States became concerned with discovering the reasons why American Indians had "tolerated" same-sex sexuality and gender variance while Euro-Americans remained hostile, misogynist and heterosexist. Articles by Harriet Whitehead and by Charles Callender and Lee Kochems used the berdache as a vehicle to examine how sexuality was constructed by Indigenous people as secondary to an individual's role within community.[27] The argument that sexuality should not define a person's identity was taken up by Walter Williams in *The Spirit and the Flesh*. Williams used the question of status to praise American Indian tolerance of same-sex relations: "American Indian cultures have taken what Western culture calls negative, and made it a positive; they have successfully utilized the different skills and insights of a class of people that Western culture has stigmatized and whose spiritual powers have been wasted."[28] In drawing these connections Williams represents Indigenous cultures not on their own terms but as a critique of settler society that benefits its members. Nevertheless, these very connections between contemporary gay identities and practices and historic Indigenous cultures helped inspire the work of Indigenous GLBTQ activists in the 1980s to assert a relationship to Indigenous traditions.

Will Roscoe's book *The Zuni Man-Woman* represented a response to the 1980s anthropology of berdache even as it set a new direction. This study of Zuni gender systems was the first scholarly account to question correlations between contemporary GLBTQ identities and historic gender diversity and to foreground Indigenous cultural perspectives. By arguing that the Zuni Llhamana "represented a third possibility in the Zuni organization and representation of gender—a third status"— Roscoe presented historic gender diversity as less about sexual identity and more about the cultural categories of Indigenous communities.[29] Roscoe's work throughout the 1990s focused on the "multidimensional" aspects of historic Native gender constructions whereby bodily sex is "viewed as no less arbitrary than the sociocultural elaborations of sex in the form of gender identities and roles."[30] Roscoe's work had the effect of embedding a critique of sex/gender binaries in the analysis of Indigenous gender diversity traditions. A further effect of this analytical shift was the deemphasis of bodily sex and sexuality, in a move that also engaged Indigenous GLBTQ activists who rejected identity as "sexual minorities" by arguing their primary belonging to Indigenous communities and traditions.

While Indigenous GLBTQ people in the 1980s actively adapted berdache literatures, the next decade witnessed a rapid expansion of writing after their proposition in 1990 of Two-Spirit identity mobilized their communities and reshaped academic work. Indigenous GLBTQ people at the Third International Gathering of American Indian and First Nations Gays and Lesbians in Winnipeg discussed their desire for a term that could displace *berdache* while naming, at once, their diverse lives and their sense of relationship to Indigenous traditions of gender/sexual diversity and spirituality.[31] *Two-Spirit* emerged from these conversations. Well before it gained traction in academic writing, *Two-Spirit* already circulated widely among GLBTQ Indigenous people on reservations/reserves and in urban areas, and many community organizations incorporated the term into their titles. Over time the term also found its way into social service usage and provided concepts that made AIDS prevention work more compatible with the lives and cultures of Indigenous GLBTQ people.[32] A first indication of the impact it would have in academia occurred in 1992, when Sue-Ellen Jacobs and Wesley Thomas joined Two-Spirit organizers in proposing an academic workshop gathering anthropologists (some of them Native) and Indigenous GLBTQ2 people (including at least one anthropologist) to revisit anthropological writing on berdache and decide how Two-Spirit people would respond. Two workshops in 1993 and 1994, sponsored by the American Anthropological Association and Wenner-Gren Foundation, brought Two-Spirit activists into anthropological space where they questioned academic claims about Indigenous histories and contemporary life, and anthropologists responded. These workshops became the basis for the text *Two-Spirit People: Native American Gender Identity, Sexuality, and Spirituality*.[33] In their contributions, activists and scholars reflected on the term *Two-Spirit* and demonstrated that the it had done exactly what its originators had intended, by becoming "an indigenously defined pan-Native North American term that bridges Native concepts of gender diversity and sexualities with those of Western cultures."[34] But even though *Two-Spirit People* in 1997 was the first academic anthology to focus on historical Indigenous gender/sexual diversity or Indigenous GLBTQ2 people today, it did not yet reflect the shift in methods of knowledge production in Indigenous activisms and Native/Indigenous studies. Many non-Native contributors to the book adopted *Two-Spirit* as a replacement term for *berdache*—or reacted to the thought that this was what they were asked to do. But the new term's complexity ensured that its use as an anthropological category would lead to intellectual conundrums and yet miss its theoretical potential as an Indigenous methodology, as we discuss below. In turn, despite *Two-Spirit People* questioning anthropological authority over Indigenous people, its format seemed to reproduce it, in that the opening and closing sections highlighted non-Native anthropologists doing academic theory, while most interventions by Two-Spirit people appeared in between or were bracketed as personal narratives rather than as scholarship. Thus, while the book portrayed anthropologists admitting that they did not control discourse on Indigenous sexuality and gender and showed Two-Spirit people organizing in the halls that once spoke for them, *Two-Spirit People* did not yet present a clean break from the history of anthropological knowledge production about GLBTQ2 Indigenous people.

The troubles the term *Two-Spirit* presented to anthropology increased in the 1990s, as its success in Indigenous people's everyday lives was not reflected by academic scholars who grappled with its complexity. Multiple scholars took exception to the term's capacity to explain complex gender systems in specific tribal societies. Epple pointed out: "The synthesis of nadleehi and others into a single category has often ignored the variability across Native American cultures and left unexamined the relevance of gender and sexuality."[35] Goulet echoes this critique in arguing that scholars of gender diversity have failed "to consider indigenous constructions of personhood and gender."[36] Critiques of the application of pan-tribal concepts to highly specific local practices tended to focus on gender constructions unavailable to Indigenous GLBTQ people who used the term *Two-Spirit*. This fact, and scholars' work to represent historical Indigenous cultures apart from the desires of modern activists, positioned scholars as trying to reassert the critical distance of anthropology's writing on Indigenous culture, which now included distance from the contemporary intellectual histories of Indigenous GLBTQ2 people. As the 2000s approached, anthropological scholars largely had given up on *Two-Spirit* as an analytical category and instead deferred to analyzing its local usage and meaning.

Yet as Two-Spirit identity was cultivated and debated among Indigenous GLBTQ2 people, it engendered new thought across the differences in urban and rural, traditional and nontraditional, academic and popular writing that showed the term retained a capacity to do many forms of work. For instance, Two-Spirit and Indigenous AIDS organizers are among the activists who saw early on that after its proposal Two-Spirit gained popularity in intertribal and urban Indian organizing but was somewhat less common to rural or reservation communities. Yet regional and international gatherings, online and academic networking, and AIDS organizing became mediums in which the term traveled across these divisions and increased conversation among Native people about its meaning. In turn, Indigenous GLBTQ2 people debated the links to cultural tradition presented by Two-Spirit identity, which was understood variously as a term equal in meaning to tribally specific identities or as marking its own new and border-crossing community. Crucially, many Indigenous GLBTQ2 people define Two-Spirit identity as at once a point of continuity with tribal traditions and a statement of contemporary intertribal identity and politics, thus showing that the term cannot be drawn along an analytical distinction between "traditional" and "nontraditional."

In particular, the term *Two-Spirit* benefited from and inspired new Indigenous GLBTQ2 literatures that reflected the numerous differences just noted and many more. The work of creative writers had particular influence on building Indigenous GLBTQ2 identities and feminist theories, as in the work of writers such as Paula Gunn Allen, Beth Brant, Chrystos, and Janice Gould. Cherríe Moraga and Gloria Anzaldúa's *This Bridge Called My Back: Writings by Radical Women of Color* (1983) continues to be a defining moment for women of color feminisms in the United States.[37] The collection included several Native and Indigenous-identified Chicanas, helping to build a critical mass of Indigenous feminist thought and activism. Brant's 1983 special issue of *Sinister Wisdom*—later published as *A Gathering of Spirit: A Collection by North American Indian Women*—brought together creative and critical work by heterosexual and LBQ-identified Indigenous women for the first time.[38] Paula Gunn Allen's 1986 *The Sacred Hoop: Recovering the Feminine in American Indian Traditions* brought critical attention to articulating Indigenous lesbian and feminist theory.[39] Entwined with this wave of radical creative work by LBQ2 Indigenous women, Will Roscoe and Gay American Indians' 1988 *Living the Spirit: A Gay American Indian Anthology* brought artists and activists into critical conversation with the emergent work of anthropologists.[40] These legacies were cited and sustained by Indigenous GLBTQ writers in and after the 1990s who identified as Two-Spirit.[41] The creative qualities of such work meant that academics writing in the anthropological tradition often did not recognize it as theoretical or as scholarship, even though it formed a deep historical basis for Indigenous thought about the category *Two-Spirit*.

In these many ways, *Two-Spirit* marked and invited differences that informed its use as a basis for Indigenous community formation, a legacy that sustains us today. Any attempt to define the term based on its use in any one context will skew understanding of its meaning both within Indigenous conversations and beyond them. Our project hinges on foregrounding this multiplicity and tension within the term's current uses, as reflected in the at-times divergent claims of our contributors, even as we theorize the continuities that cross and do not erase that multiplicity.

Evaluating lines of tension in popular and scholarly engagements with *Two-Spirit* models the theoretical work that this book promotes. For instance, work by Two-Spirit organizers to define the term apart from non-Native theories of "sexual minorities," and to emphasize the integration of Indigenous GLBTQ2 people in traditional cultures, led some scholars to ask if this depoliticized analysis of sexuality in Indigenous communities. As Jacobs, Thomas, and Lang argued, using "the word 'two-spirit' emphasizes the spiritual aspect of one's life and downplays the homosexual persona. Homophobia may not be completely thwarted by using the term, but it may be held off in some instances."[42] In turn, scholars note that efforts by Indigenous GLBTQ2 people to distance themselves from definitions of "gay sexuality" also distanced them from markers used by heterosexual Indigenous people to discriminate and emphasized similarities with others in their Native communities. Downplaying a "homosexual persona" then could present *Two-Spirit* as a series of acts whereby one's cultural competency and socioreligious commitment to traditional cultural conservative ideals became primary.[43] These important concerns remind scholars of Two-Spirit communities to investigate critically all the cultural and political work that follows centering gender and spirituality in the term. At the same time, many Indigenous GLBTQ2 people testify to the erotic being central to their definitions and experiences of Two-Spirit identity, community, and spirituality. Driskill and Sophie Mayer have argued that a major theme of emergent Two-Spirit literatures is the decolonizing gesture of reclaiming the erotic.[44] Andrea Smith, Chris Finley, Scott Morgensen, and other scholars of Foucault in Native studies also remind that "sexuality" is a colonial discourse produced through biopower. In light of this critique, the erotic may invoke a relationship to "bodies and pleasures" that can displace the colonial power of "sexuality."[45] Two-Spirit-identified poets such as Brant, Chrystos, Driskill, and Scofield have formulated the erotic as part of decolonial resistance, while other Indigenous GLBTQ writers—Two-Spirit-identified and not—such as Deborah Miranda, Womack, and Justice also formulate radical erotics in their creative and scholarly work. In these ways, Indigenous GLBTQ2 writers and activists have argued not that the erotic is separate from Two-Spirit identities, but that it is a site of resistance and transformation for all Indigenous people, including GLBTQ2 people.

Another line of tension arises around how scholars perceive Two-Spirit identity's relation to Indigenous traditions. As noted, anthropologists found the new term difficult to apply if they read it as a pan-tribal descriptor of historical traditions, in which case its generality seemed unable to account for local differences, or to be too invested in telling a particular story of what those traditions were. Tension arose if Two-Spirit people positioned their identities within the realm of "tradition" in a manner that appeared to non-Native anthropologists to locate *Two-Spirit* as "beyond criticism." Legitimate questions ensued that led to conflict between Two-Spirit communities and the scholars who studied them. Did Indigenous GLBTQ people at times deploy Two-Spirit by conflating the qualities of their lives with their reimaginings of a distant past—perhaps by reproducing anthropological universals as Indigenous identities? Did definitions of Two-Spirit ever circulate in ways that failed to notice differences between GLBTQ Indigenous people who identify with traditional culture and those who do not? These and other questions can be asked to mark the fractures in personal and collective claims on Two-Spirit identity. *Two-Spirit* is similar to other identitarian terms for nationality or culture by being open to use in modernist modes as exclusive or authentic. But however important these factors might be for scholars to note, a critical history of *Two-Spirit* reminds us that the term arose to challenge prior investments in Indigenous authenticity by anthropologists. In the 1990s, anthropologists so longed for a scientific term that would accurately represent historical Indigenous gender and sexual diversity (what *berdache* never was, but many hoped it could be) that they grew frustrated if *Two-Spirit* seemed unable to do this work. *Two-Spirit*, however, was not proposed to satisfy a scientific desire for close correlation between analytical categories and Indigenous truth. Instead, it was designed as a logic and method to confound such desires. Displacing a prior generation's interest in anthropological authority, *Two-Spirit* became frustrating, complicating, and exciting by shifting the terms on which knowledge of Indigenous people would be produced and debated.

Between the late 1990s and into the first decade of the 2000s, *Two-Spirit*, as a critique of anthropology, largely disappeared from the academic literature except for the work of a few scholars. In the thirteen years between 1997 and 2010, the term emerged as a foundation of the community-based knowledges represented by Two-Spirit literatures, activism, and Native HIV/AIDS research. At the community level, *Two-Spirit* has come to be used variously to reference historical foundations of gender and sexual diversity in North American Indigenous societies, a contemporary interlinking of gender, sexuality, spirituality, and social roles, or a critique of heteropatriarchy in Native and non-Native communities. It is in the term's community-based usage and its critique of heteropatriarchy where we find our inspiration to reignite its power as an analytical tool. Community concepts of *Two-Spirit* laid the foundation for our ability to expand its critical edges within "queer Indigenous studies."

One way the category *Two-Spirit* denied anthropologists the authenticity they sought was by being proposed as a politically positioned identity, one that links historical traditions to contemporary life in a noncontra-dictory whole. In the wake of this term's political histories, academic scholars must ask if there is anything ideological in harboring a desire to produce knowledge that does not arise from a clear political positioning. *Two-Spirit* also joins theory in Native studies in suggesting no contra-diction between affirming the variety and contingency of identities and politics and claiming ties to nationality, tradition, and sovereignty. War-rior and Andrea Smith remind that as soon as such claims are made, the reality will appear that Indigenous people and knowledges are multiple and potentially contradictory or dissenting. This will continually open any claims on Indigenous collectivity to debate and change. But the dif-ference in such debates, like those defined by the interventions of Two-Spirit people, is that conversations will arise by centering Indigenous people before any non-Native intellectual history that would explain Indigenous people at a distance. We offer our book as an invitation into the multiplicity and complexity of these Indigenous conversations.

Linking Arms Together

This collection is an act of remembering and imagining. It articulates the ways in which the work of activists, artists, and scholars have already been weaving GLBTQ2 Indigenous critiques through decolonial activ-ism, art, and scholarship. It is through the work of activists, artists, and scholars who came before that we are able to dream and design practices and futures—both inside and outside of the academy—that can both re-member and create radical, decolonial GLBTQ2 Indigenous communi-ties. The goal of this volume is to continue weaving these critiques together into critical conversations. The book invites looking to Indigenous gen-ders and sexualities—both "traditional" and contemporary—for their potential to disrupt colonial projects and to rebalance Indigenous com-munities. Beginning to articulate and practice specific GLBTQ2 Indig-enous critiques is a way of continuing radical movements and scholarship that work for collective decolonial futures.

As scholar-activists in the academy, the editors and contributors to this book take the stance that GLBTQ2 Indigenous critiques can radically reshape Native studies, queer studies, trans studies, and Indigenous femi-nisms. The practice of such critiques entails shifting our methodologies and political frameworks by insisting on Indigenous GLBTQ2 movements as part of the "dissent lines" of decolonial work.[46] The models of dissent offered by Warrior and Indigenous feminists support the work of Indigenous GLBTQ2 critics to hold heteropatriarchal legacies accountable to change and thereby support the collective sovereignty of Indigenous people. Indigenous GLBTQ2 critics who engage struggles for sovereignty must be recognized as declaring not sovereignty from Indigenous communities—as in the image of non-Native GLBTQ politics, which defend sexual minorities as distinct from a social majority—but a sovereign alignment with and within Indigenous communities.

This book calls scholars and activists to pay attention to the ways that heteronormativity—the normalizing and privileging of patriarchal heterosexuality and its gender and sexual expressions—undermines struggles for decolonization and sovereignty and buoys the powers of colonial governance. Current Indigenous national struggles must question and challenge their relation to GLBTQ2 people. As many of our contributors argue, by disrupting colonially imposed and internalized systems of gender and sexuality, Indigenous queer and Two-Spirit critiques can move decolonizing movements outside dominant logics and narratives of "nation." We invite scholars, activists, and artists to imagine what Indigenous queer and Two-Spirit critiques can do to disrupt external and internalized colonialism, heteropatriarchy, gender binaries, and other forms of oppression.

An imagining of radical, decolonial Indigenous GLBTQ2 critiques demands centering Indigenous frameworks and experiences as sites inspiring theory and practice. Womack's notion of "code talking" as an interpretive tool to read the Cherokee queer contexts of Lynn Riggs's *The Cherokee Night*, for instance, offers an Indigenous-centered approach to interpreting queer Indigenous texts.[47] Similarly, Driskill has looked to Cherokee (and other southeastern) doublewoven baskets "as a model to articulate the emergent potential in conversations between Native studies and queer studies," while Miranda has used the Indigenous-rooted figure of La Llorona to theorize the impact of patriarchal colonization on the lives of Indigenous women and the entire world.[48] By bringing Native studies and queer/trans studies into dialogue, we Indigenous GLBTQ2 people continue to imagine and dream how Indigenous home-stories and home-practices can help articulate and theorize specifically Indigenous GLBTQ2 critiques. By asserting Indigenous people's right and power to invent and account for themselves, Warrior's thesis of "intellectual sovereignty" supports positions long argued by GLBTQ2 Indigenous people: to respect a sovereign ability to claim gender, sexual, and cultural identities and to promote the knowledges that Indigenous communities can reinvent to understand GLBTQ2 Indigenous practices, theories, and movements as decolonizing and sovereign acts.

Critiques drawn from Indigenous GLBTQ2 lives can radically open what indigeneity might mean to conversations across difference. GLBTQ2 identities claim and complicate relationships to national identities. GLBTQ2 Indigenous people's differences guarantee that any theory built from self-representation will be a theory of differences. Against cultural conservative efforts to reject queerness as a colonial quality, for instance, we can think with Brooks about how Indigenous knowledges demand acceptance. Brooks's reading of Abenaki language suggests that queerness could be defended on traditional terms: not because it can claim a unique tradition in Abenaki culture, but because decolonization calls the people to reject colonial insider/outsider binaries and asks how familial ties invite relationship across differences. Brooks's invocation of kinship recalls Rifkin's argument that kinship ties were targeted by colonial regimes to eliminate gender and sexual diversity. As a result, reimagining kinship presents a method for affirming that diversity without reinforcing heterosexist norms of family or nation in Indigenous communities.[49] In turn, with Foster and Powell, we can think more complexly about the nation's borders by asking whether GLBTQ2 Indigenous people are traditional not only by finding roots in Indigenous nations but also when forming border-crossing alliances—what Powell calls "alliance as a practice of survivance" with other Indigenous people.[50] An intertribal perspective could take note of tribally specific formations of gender or sexuality wherever they exist while also asking how they link or arise within broader connections, such as the GLBTQ2 networks today whose mobility can be read as part of the historical formation of Indigenous communities.

Foster's and Powell's claims reminds us that by engaging the lives of GLBTQ2 Natives in North America, we are already entering transnational conversations. Native North America has always been "transnational." Yet this book complicates those conversations by asking what happens if they link Indigenous Pacific and North American writers together. Immediately, globalization, transnational activism, and a multiplicity of colonial histories and legacies inform work by and for GLBTQ2 Indigenous people, which must account for its geographic, linguistic, and political locations in global conversations. The inspiration for this book arose among scholars and writers working in the United

States, a quality reflected in its primarily U.S. and North American pur-
view and the concentration of many contributions (including this introduction) on the histories, cultures, and politics of Two-Spirit people. Yet
the book accounts for this by linking texts that examine this specificity
precisely by *not* absorbing Indigenous Pacific GLBTQ claims (Driskill,
Gilley, Tatonetti, Rifkin, Scudeler) to texts that investigate histories
and contemporary politics of Indigenous Pacific gender, sexuality, and
GLBTQ identities (Erai, Taulapapa, Aspin) and their intersections with
Two-Spirit organizing (Morgensen).

These essays model multiple queer theories as decolonial work in
Native studies. Historically, queer theory separated from GLBT studies
by exchanging the promotion of GLBT people for critique of all sexual norms, heteronormative *and* homonormative. Contributors to this
book reframe this distinction by arguing that settler colonialism conditions sexual normativity and queer theory (Smith, Morgensen). Many
contributors then demonstrate that new queer theories within Native
studies will center the question of decolonization in ways that also
address GLBTQ2 Indigenous people. Chris Finley traces GLBTQ2 Indigenous resistance and demonstrates that colonization located Indigenous
peoples as queer to colonial heteropatriarchy. Her biopolitical analysis
suggests that decolonization will reimagine a queer erotic for Indigenous
communities. In turn, when Andrea Smith adapts queer theory's "subjectless critique" to Native studies—making Native studies a method to
critique colonialism rather than to describe Native people—she recognizes GLBTQ2 Indigenous people as inspirations and leaders in critiquing colonial heteropatriarchy and all that it conditions. In this light, we
can ask how Michelle Erai's questioning of the "legibility" of queerness
in the colonial archive, and her account of the queerness of mixed-race
children in colonial New Zealand, might link to Dan Taulapapa McMullin showing how the relationality of *fa'afafine* and their comrades dispels
any belief that heteropatriarchy traditionally defines Samoan culture.
For Taulapapa, respecting fa'afafine as queer Indigenous people actually
questions distinctions of "queer" from "normal" in Samoan society as
a colonial inheritance. How might this relate to how Erai suggests that
Maori peoples and mixed-race children became queer to settler rule by
living lives that precisely disturbed the boundaries of colonial heteropatriarchy? In turn, as Clive Aspin discusses, how do Maori GLBTQ people
defining their relationships as *takatapui* simultaneously assert unique
identities and shift sexual norms for all Maori peoples as a decolonial

act? Finally, June Scudeler, Mark Rifkin, and Lisa Tatonetti read how queer Indigenous writings portray GLBTQ Indigenous lives to critically theorize the normative power of nation, gender, and sexuality and open them to change. Thus, without forcing closure on differences between subject-focused and subjectless critique, this book models a variety of critically queer and Indigenous methods to trouble heteronormativity as colonial while highlighting engagement with the lives and critiques of GLBTQ2 Indigenous people.

This collection pushes us to imagine future potentials in Indigenous GLBTQ2 theories and practices. What are the differences and connections between "Two-Spirit critiques" and "queer Indigenous critiques"? What are the relations between contemporary GLBTQ2 Indigenous people and historical constructions of gender and sexuality? If tribally/nationally specific framings of gender and sexuality can further inform our questions, theories, and practices, what, for instance, do *mahu* critiques look like, as opposed to or in relationship to *hwame* critiques? How do these critiques relate to other Indigenous critiques and activisms? The tensions and connections among the answers to these questions will enter us further into the radical possibilities of critical thought and action. It is through the practice of these critiques that GLBTQ2 Indigenous people and allies can praise the imagination and work for a collective "rising up."

Rising Up

This book is divided into three sections that reflect our title by presenting critical interventions in theory, politics, and literature. Section I, "Performing Queer Indigenous Critiques," offers multiple pathways into the critical theoretical work of queer Indigenous studies. In "Decolonizing the Queer Native Body (and Recovering the Native Bull-Dyke): Bringing 'Sexy Back' and Out of Native Studies' Closet," Chris Finley argues for centering the erotic in Native studies through a queer reading of the colonization of Native peoples, which recognizes GLBTQ2 Natives who defy colonial heteropatriarchy as leaders in collective work for decolonization. Andrea Smith's essay "Queer Theory and Native Studies: The Heteronormativity of Settler Colonialism" takes stock of academic theory to argue that queer theory is challenged by anticolonial criticism in Native studies, even as Native studies can adapt queer theory's "subjectless critique" to act as a methodology for interrogating heteropatriarchy and all legacies of colonization. Michelle Erai engages a subjectless critique in "A Queer Caste: Mixing Race and Sexuality in Colonial New Zealand," by citing the queer locations of half-caste children in the colonial archive as a method to open to criticism the colonial heteropatriarchal control of Maori people and Maori–pakeha relationships. Dan Taulapapa McMullin's "*Fa'afafine* Notes: On Tagaloa, Jesus, and Nafanua" then creatively links history, memory, and cultural criticism from the lives of fa'afafine to defy anthropological description and to affirm queer relationalities in Samoan society that can inspire shared work for decolonization.

In Section II, "Situating Two-Spirit and Queer Indigenous Movements," contributors use history and ethnography to trace the theoretical and political implications of the work of GLBTQ2 Indigenous people creatively defining identity and culture in community organizing and political criticism. Qwo-Li Driskill's chapter, "**D4Ᏺ DᏰC** (*Asegi Ayetl*): Cherokee Two-Spirit People Reimagining Nation," traces how Cherokees creatively narrate GLBTQ2 identities and memories in relation to Cherokee history and sovereignty by reading in-depth interviews of Cherokee Two-Spirit and queer people adapting Cherokee language to regain a place in the nation. Clive Aspin's "Exploring Takatapui Identity within the Maori Community: Implications for Health and Well-Being" examines how the colonial control of Maori gender and sexuality is defied today by asserting *takatapui* as a descriptor of gender and sexual identity and relationship that facilitates health and community ties for Maori people. Brian Joseph Gilley's "Two-Spirit Men's Sexual Survivance against the Inequality of Desire" provides a new theoretical context for interpreting social and political conflict over sexuality and gender in Native American communities by explaining the epistemological construction of desire and Indigenous GLBTQ2 historical construction of a Native-specific eroticism. Scott Lauria Morgensen interprets the implications of Two-Spirit organizing for allied critics in "Unsettling Queer Politics: What Can Non-Natives Learn from Two-Spirit Organizing?" Tracing three "lessons" queer non-Natives can learn from Two-Spirit organizing, he names how queer politics will transform if it centers critique of settler colonialism from within accountable relationship to the leadership of queer Indigenous people and movements.

Scholars in Section III, "Reading Queer Indigenous Writing," analyze the cultural significance and theoretical and political implications of creative writing and cultural work by Indigenous GLBTQ2 people. Lisa Tatonetti in "Indigenous Fantasies and Sovereign Erotics: Outland

Cherokees Write Two-Spirit Nations" draws a genealogy of queer Indigenous writing for American Indian literature, which centers how recent works by Daniel Heath Justice and Qwo-Li Driskill theorize Indigenous nationhood and decolonization. Mark Rifkin's "The Erotics of Sovereignty" then interprets how Driskill's *Walking with Ghosts* proposes a "sovereign erotic" that can counter the formulas of property and blood that drive the colonial nation-state while proposing queer routes to renewing Native nationality. Finally, in "Gifts of *Maskihkîy*: Gregory Scofield's Cree Métis Stories of Self-Acceptance," June Scudeler interprets Gregory Scofield's framing of Cree Métis lives through concepts like *maskihkîy* (medicine) and *pawatew* (sacredness) that link to Two-Spirit identity and promote acceptance of gender and sexual diversity.

Together, the essays in this collection mark a turning point in queer Indigenous studies by building critical theories that intervene in many of the ways Indigenous GLBTQ2 people and histories have been talked about in academic scholarship, while building broader critiques that more complexly analyze the relationship between colonialism and heteropatriarchy. While these essays index an exciting moment in the building of critical queer Indigenous theories, they are embedded in larger dissent lines that activists, artists, and scholars have already built to make these discussions possible. We hope that this collection pushes deeper conversation, intervenes in colonial discourse, and contributes to more robust decolonial theories that place gender and sexuality at the center. Through this collection, we invite you to imagine with us the future of queer Indigenous studies as part of collective resistance.

Notes

1. Joy Harjo and Poetic Justice, "A Postcolonial Tale," in *Letter from the End of the Twentieth Century* (Boulder: Silver Wave Records, 1997).

2. Throughout our introduction, "Indigenous GLBTQ2" will be used to include Indigenous people who mark their genders and/or sexualities as outside of dominant heteropatriarchal Eurocentric constructions. This will include those who might disidentify with all of these terms, instead using terms from Indigenous languages to talk about their identities.

3. Daniel Heath Justice and James H. Cox, eds., "Queering Native Literature, Indigenizing Queer Theory," *Studies in American Indian Literature* 20, no. 1 (2008); Daniel Heath Justice, Mark Rifkin, and Bethany Schneider, eds. "Sexuality, Nationality, Indigeneity," *GLQ: A Journal of Lesbian and Gay Studies* 16, no. 1–2 (2010).

4. The co-editors took inspiration from our first meeting to prepare this book as a collaboration. Our names appear in alphabetical order to reflect our consistent efforts to think and work together. Each editor contributed to the introductory and concluding chapters, with the introduction being based on extensive writing by Driskill, Gilley, and Morgensen, and the concluding chapter being a composition by Finley with contributions by Driskill and Morgensen. Driskill coordinated the conceptualization of the book and its proposal; Gilley assembled the first manuscript for review; Finley facilitated the expansion of the book's contributors; and Morgensen coordinated editing of the final manuscript.

5. Robert Allen Warrior, *Tribal Secrets: Recovering American Indian Intellectual Traditions* (Minneapolis: University of Minnesota Press, 1994), 195.

6. Linda Tuhiwai Smith, *Decolonizing Methodologies: Research and Indigenous Peoples* (New York: Zed Books, 1999).

7. Andrea Smith, *Native Americans and the Christian Right: The Gendered Politics of Unlikely Alliances* (Durham, NC: Duke University Press, 2008), xxiv.

8. Ibid., xxi.

9. Warrior, *Tribal Secrets*; Jace Weaver, *That the People Might Live: Native American Literatures and Native American Community* (New York: Oxford University Press, 1997).

10. Warrior, *Tribal Secrets*, xiii.

11. Jace Weaver, Craig Womack, and Robert Allen Warrior, eds., *American Indian Literary Nationalism* (Lincoln: University of Nebraska Press, 2006); Craig Womack, *Red on Red: Native American Literary Separatism* (Minneapolis: University of Minnesota Press, 1999).

12. Daniel Heath Justice, *Our Fire Survives the Storm: A Cherokee Literary History* (Minneapolis: University of Minnesota Press, 2006).

13. Jace Weaver, "Splitting the Earth: First Utterances and Pluralist Separatism," in *American Indian Literary Nationalism*, ed. Jace Weaver, Craig Womack, Robert Allen Warrior (Albuquerque: University of New Mexico Press, 2006); Craig Womack, "A Single Decade: Book-Length Native Literary Criticism between 1986 and 1997," in *Reasoning Together*, ed. Native Critics Collective (Norman: University of Oklahoma Press, 2008); Craig Womack, "The Integrity of American Indian Claims (or, How I Learned to Stop Worrying and Love My Hybridity)," in *American Indian Literary Nationalism*, ed. Jace Weaver, Craig Womack, and Robert Allen Warrior (Lincoln: University of Nebraska Press, 2006).

14. Christopher Teuton, "Theorizing American Indian Literature: Applying Oral Concepts to Written Traditions," in *Reasoning Together*, ed. Native Critics Collective (Norman: University of Oklahoma Press, 2008), 204.

15. Lisa Brooks, "Digging at the Roots: Locating an Ethical, Native Criticism," in *Reasoning Together*, ed. Native Critics Collective (Norman: University of Oklahoma Press, 2008), 237, 241.

16. Lisa Brooks, "Afterword," in *American Indian Literary Nationalism,* ed. Jace Weaver, Craig Womack, Robert Allen Warrior (Lincoln: University of Nebraska Press, 2006), 244.

17. Tol Foster, "Of One Blood: An Argument for Relations and Regionality in Native American Literary Studies," in *Reasoning Together,* ed. Native Critics Collective (Norman: University of Oklahoma Press, 2008). 269.

18. Ibid., 272 (original emphasis).

19. Ibid.

20. Ibid., 270–71, 272.

21. Warrior, *Tribal Secrets,* 123–24.

22. Ibid., 124.

23. Andrea Smith, *Conquest: Sexual Violence and American Indian Genocide* (Cambridge, MA: South End Press, 2005); Andrea Smith, J. Kehaulani Kauanui, "Native Feminisms Engage American Studies," *American Quarterly* 60, no. 2 (2008).

24. Smith, *Conquest,* 139.

25. Robert Allen Warrior, "Native Critics in the World: Edward Said and Nationalism," in *American Indian Literary Nationalism,* ed. Jace Weaver, Craig Womack, and Robert Allen Warrior (Albuquerque: University of New Mexico Press, 2006).

26. Clellan Ford and Frank Beach, *Patterns of Sexual Behavior* (New York: Harper, 1951); Alfred Kroeber, "Psychosis or Social Sanction?" *Character and Personality* 8 (1940).

27. Charles Callender and Lee Kochems, "The North American *Berdache,*" *Current Anthropology* 24, no. 4 (1983); Harriet Whitehead, "The Bow and the Burden Strap: A New Look at Institutionalized Homosexuality in Native North America," in *Sexual Meanings: The Cultural Construction of Gender and Sexuality,* ed. Sherry Ortner and Harriet Whitehead (Cambridge: Cambridge University Press, 1981).

28. Walter Williams, *The Spirit and the Flesh: Sexual Diversity in American Indian Culture,* 2nd ed. (Boston: Beacon Press, 1986), 3.

29. Will Roscoe, *The Zuni Man-Woman* (Albuquerque: University of New Mexico Press, 1991), 22.

30. Will Roscoe, "How to Become a *Berdache:* Towards a Unified Analysis of Gender Diversity," in *Third Sex, Third Gender: Beyond Sexual Dimorphism in Culture and History,* ed. Gilbert Herdt (New York: Zone Books, 1993), 341–42.

31. Wesley Thomas and Sue-Ellen Jacobs, "' . . . And We Are Still Here': From *Berdache* to Two-Spirit People," *American Indian Culture and Research Journal* 23, no. 2 (1999).

32. Lester B. Brown, ed., *Two-Spirit People: American Indian Lesbian Women and Gay Men* (New York: Harrington Park Press, 1997).

33. Sue-Ellen Jacobs, Wesley Thomas, and Sabine Lang, eds., *Two-Spirit People: Native American Gender Identity, Sexuality, and Spirituality* (Urbana: University of Illinois Press, 1997).

34. Thomas, "'. . . And We Are Still Here'," 92.

35. Carolyn Epple, "Coming to Terms with Navajo Nádleehí: A Critique of *Berdache,* 'Gay,' 'Alternate Gender,' And 'Two-Spirit,'" *American Ethnologist* 25, no. 2 (1998), 268.

36. Jean-Guy A. Goulet, "The '*Berdache*'/'Two-Spirit': A Comparison of Anthropological and Native Constructions of Gendered Identities among the Northern Athapaskans," *Journal of the Royal Anthropological Institute* n.s. 2, no. 4 (1996): 683.

37. Cherríe Moraga and Gloria Anzaldúa, eds., *This Bridge Called My Back: Writings by Radical Women of Color,* 2nd ed. (New York: Kitchen Table Women of Color Press, 1983).

38. Beth Brant, ed., *A Gathering of Spirit: Writing and Art by North American Indian Women* (Rockland, ME: Sinister Wisdom Books, 1984).

39. Paula Gunn Allen, *The Sacred Hoop: Recovering the Feminine in American Indian Traditions* (Boston: Beacon Press, 1986).

40. Gay American Indians, *Living the Spirit: A Gay American Indian Anthology,* ed. Will Roscoe (New York: St. Martin's Press, 1988).

41. Chrystos, *Fugitive Colors* (Vancouver: Press Gang, 1995); Qwo-Li Driskill, *Walking with Ghosts: Poems* (Cambridge: Salt, 2005); Gregory Scofield, *Love Medicine and One Song/Sâkihtowin-Maskihkiy êkwa Pêyak-Nikamowin* (Wiarton, ON: Kegedonce, 2009).

42. Sue-Ellen Jacobs, Wesley Thomas, and Sabine Lang, "Introduction," in *Two-Spirit People: Native American Gender Identity, Sexuality, and Spirituality,* ed. Sue-Ellen Jacobs, Wesley Thomas, and Sabine Lang (Urbana: University of Illinois Press, 1997), 3.

43. Brian Joseph Gilley, *Becoming Two-Spirit: Gay Identity and Social Acceptance in Indian Country* (Lincoln: University of Nebraska Press, 2006).

44. Qwo-Li Driskill, "Call Me Brother: Two-Spiritedness, the Erotic, and Mixedblood Identity as Sites of Sovereignty and Resistance in Gregory Scofield's Poetry," in *Speak to Me Words: Essays on Contemporary American Indian Poetry,* ed. Janice Gould and Dean Rader (Tucson: University of Arizona Press, 2003); Qwo-Li Driskill, "Doubleweaving Two-Spirit Critiques: Building Alliances between Native and Queer Studies," *GLQ: A Journal of Lesbian and Gay Studies* 16, no. 1–2 (2010); Qwo-Li Driskill, "Stolen from Our Bodies: First Nations Two-Spirits/Queers and the Journey to a Sovereign Erotic," *Studies in American Indian Literatures* 16, no. 2 (2004); Sophie Mayer, "This Bridge of Two Backs: The Two-Spirit Erotics of Anthology/Documentary/Community," *Studies in American Indian Literature* 20, no. 1 (2008).

45. Scott Lauria Morgensen, "Settler Homonationalism: Theorizing Settler Colonialism within Queer Modernities," *GLQ: A Journal of Lesbian and Gay Studies* 16, no. 1–2 (2010); Andrea Smith, "Queer Theory and Native Studies: The Heteronormativity of Settler Colonialism" (this volume).

46. Smith, *Decolonizing Methodologies*, 13.

47. Womack, *Red on Red*.

48. Driskill, "Doubleweaving Two-Spirit Critiques: Building Alliances between Native and Queer Studies"; Deborah Miranda, *The Zen of La Llorona* (Cambridge: Salt, 2005).

49. Mark Rifkin, "Romancing Kinship: A Queer Reading of Indian Education and Zitkala-Sa's *American Indian Stories*," *GLQ: A Journal of Lesbian and Gay Studies* 12, no. 1 (2006).

50. Foster, "Of One Blood: An Argument for Relations and Regionality in Native American Literary Studies"; Malea D. Powell, "Down by the River, or How Susan La Flesche Picotte Can Teach Us about Alliance as a Practice of Survivance," *College English* 67, no. 1 (2004).

Section I
Performing Queer Indigenous Critiques

1
Decolonizing the Queer Native Body
(and Recovering the Native Bull-Dyke)
Bringing "Sexy Back" and Out of Native Studies' Closet
Chris Finley

> Whence the Freudian endeavor (out of reaction no doubt to
> the great surge of racism that was contemporary with it) to
> ground sexuality in the law—the law of alliance, tabooed
> consanguinity, and the Sovereign Father, in short, to surround
> desire with all the trappings of the old order of power.
> —Michel Foucault[1]

Thinking about how gender reifies colonial power has begun to be an important analytic in Native studies with the publication of special issues on Native feminisms in *American Quarterly* (2008) and *Wicazo Sa Review* (2009), and the three exciting panels on Native feminisms at the 2008 Native American and Indigenous Studies Conference in Athens, Georgia.[2] While gender is not a main theoretical framework in Native studies, discussions of gender occur more frequently than do those about sexuality. In Native studies, gender is not as scary a topic as sexuality, especially discussions of Native sexualities. This reaction should be reconsidered. An important analysis of colonial power for Native studies and Native nations can be found in Michel Foucault's theories of sexuality and biopower. He argues that the modern racial state comes into being by producing "sex" as a quality of bodies and populations, which get targeted for life or death as a method of enacting state power. He says that historically this "gave rise . . . to comprehensive measures, statistical assessments, and interventions aimed at the entire social body or at groups taken as a whole. Sex was a means of access to both the life of the body and the life of the species."[3] Scholars in Native studies increasingly argue that biopower defines the colonization of Native peoples when it makes sexuality, gender, and race key arenas of the power of the settler state.[4]

Histories of biopower deeply affected Native people's relationship to the body and sexuality. Natives, and lots of other folks, like sex but are terrified to discuss it. For many tribes, this shame around sex started in the boarding schools, and sexual shame has been passed down for generations. Throughout the imposition of colonialism in the United States, one of the methods Native communities have used to survive is adapting silence around sexuality. The silencing of sexuality in Native studies and Native communities especially applies to queer sexuality. While it does not differ from mainstream U.S. society, this attitude of silence has more intense consequences for Native peoples, because of the relationship of sexuality to colonial power. Sexuality is difficult terrain to approach in Native communities, since it brings up many ugly negative realities and colonial legacies of sexual violence. As Andrea Smith argues, sexual violence is both an ideological and a physical tool of U.S. colonialism.[5] Because of this reality, there is a high rate of sexual abuse in Native communities. Non-Native pedophiles target children in Native nations because there is little chance of perpetrators being brought to justice or caught by tribal police, since non-Natives on tribal lands are not bound to the same laws as Natives. Historically, and arguably in the present, Native women are targeted for medical sterilization. In some Native nations, tribal councils have adapted heterosexist marriage acts into their tribal government constitutions. All this proves that discussions of sexuality are happening in Native communities. Yet the relationship between colonial power and normalizing discourses of sexualities is not a part of these dialogues. Heterosexism and the structure of the nuclear family needs to be thought of as a colonial system of violence.

My goal here is to show how new and exciting work linking Native studies and queer studies can imagine more open, sex-positive, and queer-friendly discussions of sexuality in both Native communities and Native studies. This not only will benefit Native intellectualism but also will change the ways in which Native nationalisms are perceived and constructed by Native peoples, and perhaps non-Native peoples. How are queered Native bodies made into docile bodies open to subjugation by colonial and imperial powers? How does the queering of Native bodies affect Native sovereignty struggles? Can Native peoples decolonize themselves without taking colonial discourses of sexualities seriously? What might some of the results of a decolonizing revolutionary movement for Native people that challenged heteropatriarchy look like? How could a decolonizing movement that challenged biopower be constructed as a coalitional and community-building movement?

Heteropatriarchy, Biopower, and Colonial Discourse: Not So Sexy

Imagining the future of sexuality in Native studies and Native nations produces many stimulating possibilities for decolonization. One place where sexuality is discussed explicitly is in queer studies, yet this field only rarely addresses Native peoples and Native issues. The debates over the civil rights of queer peoples form one of the main topics of discussion in queer studies. Thinking about sovereignty and colonialism in relation to theory in queer studies would shift conversations of citizenship and subjectivity to rethinking the validity of the U.S. nation-state. Importantly, queer theory's critiques of heterosexism, subjectivity, and gender constructions would be very useful in the context of Native studies.

There are potential problems in intersecting queer studies with Native studies. For the most part, neither discipline has shown much interest in critically engaging the other.[6] It is my hope, along with other scholars in this collection, to change this relationship. I pursue that work here by: interrogating the queered colonial discourses that define Native people; critiquing the state for constructing Native people as nonheteronormative, since they do not conform to heteropatriarchy; and critiquing Native nation building that uses the U.S. nation-state as a model. In Native studies, discussions of sexuality, gender, and colonialism have the possibility of exposing heteronormative discourses of colonial violence directed at Native communities. Heteropatriarchy and heteronormativity should be interpreted as logics of colonialism. Native studies should analyze race, gender, and sexuality as logics of colonial power without reducing them to separate identity-based models of analysis, as argued by Andrea Smith in "Heteropatriarchy and the Three Pillars of White Supremacy: Rethinking Women of Color Organizing."[7] The simple inclusion of queer people or of sexuality as topics of discussion in Native studies and Native communities is not enough to effectively detangle the web of colonialism and heteropatriarchy. Taking sexuality seriously as a logic of colonial power has the potential to further decolonize Native studies and Native communities by exposing the hidden ways that Native communities have been colonized and have internalized colonialism. As Smith has argued, colonialism is supported through the structure of heteropatriarchy, which naturalizes hierarchies.[8] Heteropatriarchy disciplines and individualizes communally held beliefs by internalizing hierarchical gendered relationships and heteronormative attitudes toward sexuality. Colonialism needs heteropatriarchy to naturalize hierarchies and unequal gender relations. Without heteronormative ideas about sexuality and gender relationships, heteropatriarchy, and therefore colonialism, would fall apart. Yet heteropatriarchy has become so natural in many Native communities that it is internalized and institutionalized as if it were traditional. Heteropatriarchal practices in many Native communities are written into tribal law and tradition. This changes how Natives relate to one another. Native interpersonal and community relationships are affected by pressure to conform to the nuclear family and the hierarchies implicit in heteropatriarchy, which in turn, are internalized. The control of sexuality, for Native communities and Native studies, is an extension of internalized colonialism. As Foucault argues in the first volume of *The History of Sexuality,* simply talking about sex and having more deviant sex does not challenge power relations produced by sexuality. Instead, the "excitement" of sexuality discourses reifies their power.[9] Purposeful deconstruction of the logics of power rather than an explosion of identity politics will help end colonial domination for Native peoples.

Colonialism disciplines both Native people and non-Native people through sexuality. The logics governing Native bodies are the same logics governing non-Native people. Yet the logic of colonialism gives the colonizers power, while Native people are more adversely affected by these colonizing logics. The colonizers may feel bad, stressed, and repressed by self-disciplining logics of normalizing sexuality, but Native people are systematically targeted for death and erasure by these same discourses. Rayna Green discusses the intersecting logics of race, gender, and sexuality in her work to show the unequal power relationship between the colonizer and the colonized.

Green's "The Pocahontas Perplex: The Image of Indian Women in American Culture" argues that colonial discourses represent Native women as sexually available for white men's pleasure.[10] These images of Native women equate the Native female body with the conquest of land in the "New World." In other words, the conflation of the "New World" with Native women's bodies presents Native women's heterosexual desire for white male settlers as justifying conquest and the settlement of the land by non-Natives. I would like to consider this sexualization, gendering, and racialization of the land by providing a queer reading. First, the land is heterosexualized within the heteropatriarchal order through the discovery, penetration, and ownership of the land by white men.

Of course, this narrative erases the fact that Native peoples were living on and owning these lands. The conflation of Native women's bodies with racialized and sexualized narratives of the land constructs it as penetrable and open to ownership through heteropatriarchal domination. Becoming critically aware of the heterosexual construction of land while queering Native peoples would be a queer Indigenous studies approach to rethinking conquest, even as it would shift ideas of sovereignty, subjectivity, recognition, nationalism, and self-determination to include queer Indigenous readings of the land.

While I agree with Green's formulation, her focus on Native women's conflation with land erases the sexual desirability of Native men in the colonial matrix. Green states, "But the Indian woman is even more burdened by this narrow definition of a 'good Indian,' for it is she, not the males, whom white men desire sexually."[11] Here, I want to include Native men as well as Native women as having been sexualized, gendered, and racialized as penetrable within colonial and imperial discourses. In other words, it is not only Native women who are (hetero)sexually controlled by white heteropatriarchy, for Native men are feminized and queered when put in the care of a white heteropatriarchal nation-state. Importantly, heteropatriarchy is effective whether Native women are read as queer or heterosexual, because "deviant" queer Native women need to be disciplined and controlled by colonial sexual and gendered "norms." Nevertheless, heteropatriarchy is more effective if Native women are read as heterosexual, since they can fit neatly as mothers and wives into its power hierarchies. All sexualization of Native peoples constructs them as incapable of self-governance without a heteropatriarchal influence that Native peoples do not "naturally" possess.

Under the disciplining logics of colonialism, Native women need to be heterosexualized to justify conquest. The "creation" story of the U.S. nation carefully includes a Native woman named Pocahontas who chooses her love for John Smith, and later John Rolfe, over the interests of her Native family. According to these colonial logics, Native women need to be managed, because they lack control over their sexuality and therefore their bodies. Native women embody the reproductive position of receiver of the fertile white colonial heteropatriarch and the mother of the U.S. nation. Under the logics of patriarchy and white supremacy, when a Native woman reproduces with a white man the child of this union becomes a white inheritor of the land. The child, although racially half Native, through white supremacy and patriarchy becomes white, since inheritance under patriarchy is passed on through the father. Indigeneity, unlike blackness, is erased through miscegenation with whiteness, since colonizing logic stipulates that Native people need to disappear for the settlers to inherit the land. Then as soon as the Native mother gives birth, her indigeneity must disappear and die for her off-spring to inherit the land and replace her body. For this whole narrative to work, the Native woman must be heterosexual and desire to have her body sexually and reproductively conquered through her love of the white man. Her body, and therefore her land, would now be owned and managed by the settler nation.

If the Native woman were read as queer, her heterosexual desire for white settlers to invade her nation would not be for the universal truth of love, since the sexual desire for white men would not exist. The narra-tive of universal love covering for imperial expansion and colonial vio-lence would be exposed and destroyed. For this narrative to work, the Native woman *must* desire white heteropatriarchy through her desire of heteronormative sex and the love of white men. With a queer Native mother, the sex with the white settler may not have been consensual. In the absence of consent and the death of the mother sans the love story, conquest is revealed as a violent process with no regard for Native life. Colonialism naturalizes the heterosexual Native woman's desire for a white man to make conquest a universal love story.

In turn, in colonial narratives Native men must be queered as sexu-ally unavailable object choices for Native women. While Native women are necessary for the imaginary origin story for the U.S. nation, Native men are not. In fact, Native men's presence in that story is erased. They must disappear to allow the white male heteropatriarch to rule over Native women without competition from Native men. For this to occur, Native men are constructed as nonheteronormative and unable to repro-duce Native peoples. Native men are read as nonheteronormative because Native men do not correctly practice heteropatriarchy and govern Native women and children. Native gender norms and family structures, which vary from tribe to tribe, do not conform to Native men having control of the public space and the nuclear family or to caring for the land correctly. In other words, in a colonial reading, Native men "allow" matriarchal structures to govern society and extended families, while Native peoples do not make as much profit off the land as the settlers would. Native men are seen as sterile members of a dying race that needs a "genetically superior" white race to save it from the "unavoidable" extinction. Native men are constructed as nonheteronormative to justify the extinction of Native people. Since it is the father that gives the child the inheritance in patriarchy, white heteropatriarchy can slip in and "save" the Natives through the management of Native women and erasure of Native men.

Through the action of colonial discourses, the bodies of Native women and men are queered and racialized as disordered, unreproductive, and therefore nonheteronormative. By making Native bodies "disappear," the colonial logic of Native nonheteronormative sexualities justifies geno-cide and conquest as effects of biopower. On these terms, Native people are diseased, dying, and nonheteronormative, all of which threatens the survival of the heteronormative U.S. nation-state. Native people are elim-inated discursively or actually killed to save the heteronormative body politic from possible contamination by Native nonheteronormativity. Yet through death and disappearance, nonheteronormative Natives are transformed into heteronormative spirit/subjects in discourses told by the colonizer to appropriate the land and culture of Native peoples while building a heteropatriarchal nation.

Nation-Building: Native Feminist Critiques and Decolonization as Foreplay for Sexy Native Nations

Taiaiake Alfred, a Mohawk Native, offers a decolonizing challenge to Native people. He does not center his construction of indigeneity in apolitical identity politics or solely on genealogy. Instead, he wants Native people to recreate the relations between themselves and their land base. He advocates fighting colonialism through regaining the spiri-tual strength and integrity colonialism has stolen from Native commu-nities (as well as the hope Native people have given away to colonialism). This is a beautiful conception of sovereignty and self-determination. Alfred writes:

> Wasáse, as I am speaking of it here, is symbolic of the social and cul-tural force alive among Onkwehonwe dedicated to altering the balance of political and economic power to recreate some social and physical space for freedom to re-emerge. Wasáse is an ethical and political vision, the real demonstration of our resolve to survive as Onkwe-honwe and to do what we must to force the Settlers to acknowledge our existence and the integrity of our connection to the land.[12]

Alfred wants freedom for Native people that can come only from decolonizing Native communities. For him, this is a political project that
involves Native communities *and* the colonizing settlers. Alfred does
not discuss how colonialism impacts Native women specifically or how
colonial discourses of sexuality dispossess Native people from the land
and from capacity for governance. Yet his alternative construction of
sovereignty can be used to include sexuality as part of politics and land
management.

Jennifer Nez Denetdale is one of the few Native scholars overtly discussing the politics of sexuality, gender, and Native nationalisms in her
work. Denetdale's work exposes homophobia as part of modern Native
nation building. To critique masculinist discourses working within Navajo
nationalism, Denetdale, along with other Native feminists, has found it
necessary to critique traditionalism in Native communities. This is an
important intervention, because Native peoples are often read as existing outside of homophobic discourse or as more accepting of trans and
queer people in Native communities because of traditional Native ideas
regarding gender and sexuality. Denetdale writes: "With the imposition
of Western democratic principles, Navajo women find themselves confronted with new oppressions in the name of 'custom and tradition.'"[13]
Here, tradition is invoked to justify heteropatriarchy and male leadership
in the Navajo Nation (as in other Native nations) by discouraging or for-
bidding Native women from taking leadership roles, on account of this
being constructed as untraditional. Ironically, as Denetdale points out,
Navajo women are allowed to participate in the Navajo Nation beauty
pageant but not to hold a position on the tribal council. Denetdale supports Native sovereignty, but she also believes Native traditions should be
historicized so that traditions are not abused and used to support forms
of oppression, such as antiblack racism and heteronormativity. She writes:

> While it is necessary for Native scholars to call upon the intellec-
> tual community to support and preserve Indigenous sovereignty, it
> is crucial that we also recognize how history has transformed tradi-
> tions, and that we be critical about the ways tradition is claimed and
> for what purposes. In some cases, tradition has been used to disen-
> franchise women and to hold them to standards higher than those set
> for men. Tradition is not without a political context.[14]

Denetdale explains that traditionalism is used in Native communities
to silence women and to disenfranchise them from possessing political

power. She does not dismiss Navajo traditions when she asks critical questions about whether certain traditions emerge in a historical trajectory or how Navajo men benefit by defining traditionalism in a historical vacuum. Her critique denaturalizes heteropatriarchal traditionalism by placing it inside histories of heteropatriarchal discourse instead of outside of modern constructions of power.[15] Native nations should be self-critiquing of Native constructions of nationalisms.

Native nations' use of heteronormative citizenship standards also disallows nonheteronormative identity formations from belonging in Native nations. Denetdale discusses this matter further when she also takes on the Diné Marriage Act passed by the tribal council of the Navajo Nation, in her paper entitled, "Carving Navajo National Boundaries: Patriotism, Tradition, and the Diné Marriage Act of 2005."[16] Denetdale examines how the intersection of heteropatriarchy, militarism, and homophobia strengthened the Navajo Nation in the post–9/11 moment. She criticizes her tribe for participating in oppressive colonial nation building by trying to enforce heteronormative marriage practices on Diné people. This sort of homophobic nationalism is similar to the U.S. nation-state's use of hyped-up homophobic nationalism and militarism in this time of war. Nationalism that is dependent on the exclusion of queer people has many consequences for Native communities. Denetdale tells how some Navajo youth left the Navajo Nation to move to urban areas and to find a queer community because of the backlash against nonheteronormative Navajos. This is a loss to the Navajo Nation. As Denetdale successfully argues, Native nations that mirror the U.S nation-state by relying on homophobia and heteropatriarchy to establish national belonging and exclusion are not ideal models to further Native sovereignty. She forcefully argues, "Critically examining the connections constructed between the traditional roles of Navajo warriors and present-day Navajo soldiering for the United States, as well as the connections made between family values and recent legislation like the Diné Marriage Act, are critical to our decolonization as Native peoples."[17] Denetdale, like many other Native scholars, advocates looking for a construction of sovereignty and Native nation building other than the model of the U.S. nation-state. She does not want to reproduce the oppressive colonial methods that exclude queers, women, and black Natives. Instead, she, like Alfred, challenges us in Native studies to conceptualize a more harmonious construction of sovereignty and Native nationhood. Native people and Native studies need to understand how discourses of colonial power operate within our communities and within our selves through sexuality, so that we may work toward alternative forms of Native nationhood and sovereignty that do not rely on heteronormativity for membership.

Centering discourses of sexualities in Native studies engages gender, sexuality, and indigeneity as enmeshed categories of analysis, since examining gender is an important part of deconstructing sexualities and exposing colonial violence. Andrea Smith writes, "The very simplified manner in which Native women's activism is theorized prevents Native women from articulating political projects that both address sexism *and* promote indigenous sovereignty. In addition, this framework does not show the complex way in which Native women organizers position themselves with respect to other coalition partners."[18] I build my ideas upon the work of Indigenous feminist theorists whose ideas and articulations of indigeneity could transform other fields of study, such as white feminist and white queer theories. The scholarly work of Indigenous feminisms centers Native women and critiques white heteropatriarchy, colonialism, sexual violence, and the U.S. nation-state model of nationalism. I want to take this a step further, as some Native feminists have done, and add the intersection of these power relations with sexuality to reveal colonizing logics and practices embedded in constructing Native peoples as hypersexual and nonheteronormative. It is time to bring "sexy back" to Native studies and quit pretending we are boring and pure and do not think or write about sex. We are alive, we are sexy, and some of us Natives are queer. Native nationalisms have the potential to be sexy (and are already sexualized), but to be sexy from a Native feminist perspective, they need to be decolonizing and critical of heteropatriarchy.

Conclusion

Critical theory of biopower exposes the colonial violence of discourse on Native nonheteronormativity being used to justify Native genocide and the "disappearance" of Native people. Deconstructing Native sexualities within a biopolitical analysis has the ability to further unlock the closet of Native studies and expose how colonial power operates in Native nations. The silence in Native studies around issues of sexuality, even heterosexuality, does not benefit the work of decolonizing Native studies or articulating it as a project of freedom for Native people. Silence around Native sexuality benefits the colonizers and erases queer Native people from their communities.[19] Putting Native studies and queer studies in dialogue creates further possibilities to decolonize Native communities. Doing so will expose colonial violence in discursive practices that construct the Native body as hypersexualized, sexually disordered, and queer while presenting Native people as incapable of governance on Native land. Centering a queer studies framework within Native studies also calls Native communities to confront heteropatriarchal practices that have resulted from internalizing sexual colonization.

In response to Justin Timberlake's song "Sexy Back," the artist Prince stated, "Sexy never left."[20] The same can be said for Native studies and Native communities, because sex is always there, but Native sexualities are just beginning to be theorized. Sexuality discourses have to be considered as methods of colonization that require deconstruction to further decolonize Native studies and Native communities. Part of the decolonizing project is recovering the relationship to a land base and reimagining the queer Native body. What does this look like? We will have to imagine this and build this together. I want to imagine that Native peoples have a new bright future full of life and the spirits of our ancestors.

Notes

1. Michel Foucault, *The History of Sexuality,* vol. 1, *An Introduction* (New York: Vintage Books, 1978), 150.

2. Mishuana Goeman and Jennifer Nez Denetdale, eds., "Native Feminisms: Legacies, Interventions, and Sovereignties," *Wicazo Sa Review* 24, no. 2 (2009): 9–187; Andrea Smith and J. Kehaulani Kauanui, eds., "Forum: Native Feminisms without Apology," *American Quarterly* 60, no. 2 (2008): 241–315.

3. Michel Foucault, *The History of Sexuality,* vol. 1 : *An Introduction* (New York: Vintage Books, 1978), 146.

4. See, for example: Andrea Smith, "Queer Theory and Native Studies: The Heteronormativity of Settler Colonialism" (this vol.).

5. Andrea Smith, *Conquest: Sexual Violence and American Indian Genocide* (Cambridge: South End Press, 2005).

6. This is changing rapidly and some Native studies scholars are engaging queer theory and queering indigeneity. See, for example: Daniel Heath Justice and James Cox, eds. "Queering Native Literature, Indigenizing Queer Theory" *SAIL: Studies in American Indian Literature* 20, no. 1 (2008); Daniel Heath Justice, Mark Rifkin, and Bethany Schneider, eds., "Sexuality, Nationality, Indigeneity: Rethinking the State at the Intersection of Native American and Queer Studies" *GLQ: A Journal of Lesbian and Gay Studies* 16, no. 1–2 (2010).

7. Andrea Smith, "Heteropatriarchy and the Three Pillars of White Supremacy: Rethinking Women of Color Organizing." *The Color of Violence: Incite Women of Color against Violence,* ed. INCITE Women of Color Against Violence(Boston: South End Press, 2006), 66.

8. Ibid., 72.

9. Foucault, *The History of Sexuality,* 4. I am certainly not discouraging the practice of deviant sex, which is such a broad category, anyhow.

10. Rayna Green, "The Pocahontas Perplex: The Image of Indian Women in American Culture," *Massachusetts Review* 16, no. 4 (1975).

11. Ibid., 703.

12. Taiaia Alfred, *Wasáse,* (University of Toronto Press, 2005) 19.

13. Jennifer Nez Denetdale, "Chairmen, Presidents, and Princesses: The Navajo Nation, Gender, and the Politics of Tradition," *Wicazo Sa Review* 21, no. 1 (2006): 10.

14. Ibid., 20–21.

15. Traditionalism is seen as existing outside of discourse and existing before the invention of the law. By contextualizing tradition in history and heteropatriarchy, Denetdale disrupts the narrative of traditionalism as sacred and uncorrupted by modernity.

16. Jennifer Nez Denetdale, "Carving Navajo National Boundaries: Patriotism, Tradition, and the Diné Marriage Act of 2005," *American Quarterly* 60 (2008).

17. Ibid., 289.

18. Andrea Smith, *Native Americans and the Christian Right: The Gendered Politics of Unlikely Alliances* (Durham, NC: Duke University Press, 2008), 108.

19. Native people, who are racialized as being dead and gone, should be aware of the psychological damage erasure causes and be mindful not to do it to other people in our communities.

20. SFGate, "Prince Takes Swipe at Timberlake," August 31, 2006, http://www.sfgate.com/cgi-bin/blogs/dailydish/detail?blogid=7&entry_id=8455.

2

Queer Theory and Native Studies
The Heteronormativity of Settler Colonialism

Andrea Smith

Native studies and queer theorist Chris Finley (this volume) challenges Native studies scholars to integrate queer theory into their work. She notes that while some scholars discuss the status of gender-non-normative peoples within precolonial Native communities, virtually no scholars engage queer theory. This absence contributes to a heteronormative framing of Native communities. "It is time to bring 'sexy back' to Native studies and quit pretending we are boring and pure and do not think or write about sex," Finley insists. "We are alive, we are sexy, and some of us Natives are queer."[1] Furthermore, she notes, while there are emerging feminist and decolonial analyses within Native studies that point to the gendered nature of colonialism, it is necessary to extend this analysis to examine how colonialism also queers Native peoples. Thus, her charge goes beyond representing queer peoples within Native studies (an important project); it also calls on *all* scholars to queer the analytics of settler colonialism. Qwo-Li Driskill further calls for the development of a "two-spirit" critique that remains in conversation with, while also critically interrogating, queer and queer of color critique.[2]

Queer theory has made a critical intervention in GLBT studies by moving past simple identity politics to interrogate the logics of heteronormativity. According to Michael Warner, the "preference for 'queer' represents, among other things, an aggressive impulse of generalization; it rejects a minoritizing logic of toleration or simple political interest-representation in favor of a more thorough resistance to regimes of the normal." Native studies, however, has frequently intersected more with GLBT studies than with queer theory in that it has tended to focus on the status of "two-spirit" peoples within Native communities.[3] While this scholarship is critically important, I argue that Native studies additionally has more to contribute to queer studies by unsettling settler colonialism. At the same time, while queer theory does focus on normalizing logics, even those engaged in queer of color critique generally neglect the normalizing logics of settler colonialism, particularly within the U.S. context.

Queer theory and Native studies often do not intersect, because Native studies is generally ethnographically entrapped within the project of studying Natives. In her groundbreaking work *Toward a Global Idea of Race* Denise Ferreira da Silva argues that the western subject is fundamentally constituted through race. Through her exhaustive account of Enlightenment theory, Silva demonstrates that the post-Enlightenment version of the subject as self-determined exists by situating itself against "affectable others" who are subject to natural conditions as well as to the self-determined power of the western subject. The central anxiety with which the western subject struggles is that it is, in fact, not self-determining. The western subject differentiates itself from conditions of "affectability" by separating from affectable others—this separation being a fundamentally racial one. The western subject is universal; the racialized subject is particular but aspires to be universal.

Silva's critique suggests that Native studies often does not question the logics of western philosophy that are premised on the self-determined subject's aspirations to achieve universality. Consequently, Native studies often rests on a Native subject awaiting humanity. In other words, if people simply understood Native peoples better, Natives would then become fully human—they would be free and self-determining. Unfortunately, the project of aspiring to "humanity" is always already a racial project; it is a project that aspires to a universality and self-determination that can exist only over and against the particularity and affectability of "the other." Native studies thus becomes trapped in ethnographic multiculturalism, what Silva describes as a "neoliberal multicultural" representation that "includes never-before-heard languages that speak of never-before-heard things that actualize a never-before-known consciousness."[4] This representation, which attempts to demonstrate Native peoples' worthiness of being universal subjects, actually rests on the logic that Native peoples are equivalent to nature itself, things to be discovered that have an essential truth or essence. In other words, the very quest for full subjecthood implicit in the ethnographic project to tell our "truth" is already premised on a logic that requires us to be objects to be discovered. Furthermore, within this colonial logic, Native particularity cannot achieve universal humanity without fundamentally becoming "inauthentic," because Nativeness is fundamentally constructed already as the "other" of western subjectivity. To use Silva's phrase, ethnographic entrapment inevitably positions Native peoples at the "horizon of death."[5]

As a strategy for addressing ethnographic entrapment, many Indigenous scholars, such as Elizabeth Cook-Lynn, Sandy Grande, and Linda Tuhiwai Smith, while diverse in their concerns and methodologies, have all called for the development of a field of Native/Indigenous studies that is distinct because of its methodologies and theoretical frameworks and not just because of its object of study.[6] Their scholarly contributions call into question the assumption that Native studies should be equated with its object of study—Native peoples. Rather, their work suggests that Native studies could potentially have diverse objects of study that might be approached through distinct methodologies and theoretical formations that are necessarily interdisciplinary in nature. Robert Warrior has called such intellectual projects an exercise in "intellectual sovereignty."[7] Warrior understands Native studies as a field with its own integrity that can be informed by traditional disciplines but is not simply a multicultural add-on to them. As I discuss below, this reformulation of Native studies does not entail rejecting identity concerns but expands its scope of inquiry by positioning Native peoples as producers of theory and not simply as objects of analysis.

Warrior points out that intellectual sovereignty is not to be equated with intellectual isolationism. Many sectors of Native studies have often rejected engagement with other fields of inquiry such as ethnic studies, and postcolonial studies, by highlighting the tension between Native studies and other fields.[8] At countless Native studies conferences, I have heard Native studies scholars opine that they should not have to read Michel Foucault, Karl Marx, or Jacques Derrida, because "they are not Indian." Unfortunately, as Rey Chow so compellingly points out, ethnic studies and, by the same logic, Native studies often confine themselves and are confined to the realm of ethnic or cultural representation rather than positioning themselves as an intellectual project that can shape scholarly discourse as a whole.[9] Because Native studies scholars have often rooted their scholarship in a commitment to social and political justice for Native nations, it becomes all the more important for Native studies to develop its own intellectual project in conversation with rather than in isolation from potential partners. Alliances are necessary if Native scholars and activists are to build sufficient political power to enable the social transformation needed to ensure the survival of Indigenous nations. A critical Native studies must interrogate the strictures within which Native studies and ethnic studies find themselves.[10] Native studies can be part of a growing conversation of scholars engaged in diverse intellectual projects that do not dismiss identity but structure inquiry around the logics of race, colonialism, capitalism, gender, and sexuality. Native studies must be part of this conversation, because the logics of settler colonialism structure all of society, not just those who are Indigenous.

Queer theory provides a helpful starting point for enabling Native studies to escape its position of ethnographic entrapment within the academy. Warner contends: "Nervous over the prospect of a well-sanctioned and compartmentalized academic version of 'lesbian and gay studies,' people want to make theory queer, not just have theory about queers. For both academics and activists, 'queer' gets a critical edge by defining itself against the normal rather than the heterosexual, and normal includes normal business in the academy."[11] A queering of Native studies might mean that Native studies would move beyond studying Native communities through the lens of religious studies, anthropology, history, or other normalizing disciplines. Native studies would also provide the framework for interrogating and analyzing normalizing logics within disciplinary formations as well as academic institutions themselves.

Thus, Native studies can be informed by queer theory's turn toward subjectless critique.[12] As the coeditors of the *Social Text* special issue "What's Queer about Queer Studies?" state: "What might be called the 'subjectless' critique of queer studies disallows any positing of a proper subject *of* or object *for* the field by insisting that queer has no fixed political referent. . . . A subjectless critique establishes . . . a focus on a 'wide field of normalization' as the site of social violence."[13] A subjectless critique can help Native studies (as well as ethnic studies) escape the ethnographic entrapment by which Native peoples are rendered simply as objects of intellectual study, and instead can foreground settler colonialism as a key logic that governs the United States today. A subjectless critique helps demonstrate that Native studies is an intellectual project that has broad applicability not only for Native peoples but for everyone. It also requires us to challenge the normalizing logics of academia rather than simply articulate a politics of Indigenous inclusion within the colonial academy.

At the same time, however, Native studies also points to the limits of a "post-identity" politic or "subjectless" critique. Sarita See, Hiram Perez, and others who do queer of color critique in particular have argued that within the field of queer studies, this claim to be "post-identity" often retrenches white, middle-class identity while disavowing it.[14] For instance, in *Fear of a Queer Planet,* Warner concedes that queer culture has been dominated by those with capital: typically, middle-class white men. But then he argues that "the default model for all minority movements is racial or ethnic. Thus, the language of multiculturalism almost always presupposes an ethnic organization of identity, rooted in family, language, and cultural tradition. Despite its language of postmodernism, multiculturalism tends to rely on very modern notions of authenticity, of culture as shared meaning and the source of identity. Queer culture will not fit this bill . . . because queer politics does not obey the member/nonmember logics of race and gender."[15] He marks queer culture as free-floating, unlike race, which is marked by belonging and not belonging. To borrow from Silva's *Towards a Global Idea,* the queer (white) subject is the universal self-determining subject, the "transparent I," but the racialized subject is the "affectable other." But if queerness is dominated by whiteness, as Warner concedes, then it also follows a logic of belonging and not belonging. It also relies on a shared culture—one based on white supremacy. As Hiram Perez notes: "Queer theory, when it privileges difference over sameness absolutely, colludes with institutionalized racism in vanishing, hence retrenching, white privilege. It serves as the magician's assistant to whiteness's disappearing act."[16] To extend Perez's analysis, what seem to disappear within queer theory's subjectless critique are settler colonialism and the ongoing genocide of Native peoples. The analysis that comes from queer theory (even queer of color critique), then, rests on the presumption of the U.S. settler colonial state. Thus, this essay puts Native studies into conversation with queer theory to look at both the possibilities and limits of a post-identity analytic.[17]

The Disappearance of Indigeneity

Besides providing a helpful place from which to engage the politics of decolonization, a subjectless critique can further reveal how current scholarship reaffirms the assumption of settler colonialism. A subjectless critique helps highlight the ideological function of "the Native" even in works not ostensibly about Native peoples, thus expanding the intellectual reach of Native studies. In particular, Lauren Berlant's work on infantile citizenship provides some insights as to why the continuing colonization of Native peoples in the United States is normalized within critical theory. As she explains, the "abstract image of the future generated by the national culture machine also stands for a crisis in

the present: what gets consolidated now as the future model citizen provides an alibi or an inspiration for the moralized political rhetorics for
the present and for reactionary legislative and juridical practice. . . . Con-
densed into the image/hieroglyph of the innocent or incipient American,
these anxieties and desires are about whose citizenship—whose subjectivity, whose forms of intimacy and interest, whose bodies and identifications, whose heroic narratives—will direct America's future."[18] Her
analysis expands our analysis of genocide to include not just the physical
disappearance of Native peoples, but the ideological function of the figure of the Native within genocidal discourses. Ironically, however, while
a subjectless critique may highlight this ideological function, it may be
the case that within queer theory it obfuscates the manner in which the
"queer" subject is also a settler subject. That is, we can posit the Native as
the infantile "citizen" that enables the future of the white, settler citizen.

As many historians have noted, colonizers expected to find "Eden" in
the Americas, "a place of simplicity, innocence, harmony, love, and hap-
piness, where the climate is balmy and the fruits of nature's bounty are
found on the trees year round."[19] Many of the early colonial narratives
describe the Americas as an idyllic paradise. However, as Kirkpatrick
Sale argues, colonizers approached "paradise" through their colonial
and patriarchal lens. Consequently, they viewed the land and Indigenous peoples as something to be used for their own purposes; colonizers
could not respect the integrity of either the land or Indigenous peoples.
"The resulting tensions, then could be resolved . . . only by being played
out against . . . the natural world and its natural peoples. . . . the only way
the people of Christian Europe ultimately could live with the reality of
the Noble Savage in the Golden World was to transform it progressively
into the Savage Beast in the Hideous Wilderness."[20] Within this colonial
imaginary, the Native is an empty signifier that provides the occasion for
Europe to remake its corrupt civilization. Once the European is remade,
the Native is rendered permanently infantile (or as mostly commonly
understood, an innocent savage). She cannot mature into adult citizenship, she can only be locked into a permanent state of infancy—degener-
ate into brutal savagery or disappear into "civilization."

The Native as infantile citizen continues to exist not only in mainstream or conservative political thought but also within radical theory
and activism. It is the "crying Indian" that enables the birth of a white
enlightened environmental consciousness. This new consciousness, however, does not entail engaging with current environmental struggles on

Indigenous lands. An example of this tendency can be found in the work of Gayatri Chakravorty Spivak. She describes indigenous peoples as providing a space for ecological knowledge but then argues that this knowledge will be lost once Indigenous peoples, whom she describes as racial minorities rather than as colonized peoples, necessarily assimilate into the settler state. "But must that part of their cultural habit that internalizes the techniques of their pre-national ecological sanity be irretrievably lost to planetary justice in the *urgently needed* process of integration, as a minority, into the modern state?"[21] Thus, some strands of postcolonial thought ironically rest on the continued colonization of Indigenous peoples.

As Elizabeth Povinelli's *Empire of Love* describes, queer politics and consciousness often rely on a primitivist notion of the indigenous as the space of free and unfettered sexuality that allows the white queer citizen to remake his or her sexuality. However, once this sexual praxis is engaged, it does not translate into solidarity with Indigenous peoples' land struggles. The subjectless critique thus calls attention to both the importance of Native peoples within scholarly work and their disappearance within this work. At the same time, a subjectless critique may disguise the fact that the queer, postcolonial, or environmentally conscious subject is simultaneously a settler subject.

This primitivist discourse that relies on the disappearance of the Native is found, ironically, also within ethnic studies and queer of color critique. For instance, within racial justice activism as well as ethnic studies analysis, it is the primitive Native that enables a mature mestizaje consciousness. Gloria Anzaldúa's *Borderlands,* the foundational text on borderlands theory, situates Indians and Europeans in a dichotomy that can be healed through mestizaje. Anzaldúa positions Indian culture as having "no tolerance for deviance," a problem that can be healed by the "tolerance for ambiguity" that those of mixed race "necessarily possess." Thus, a rigid, unambiguous Indian becomes juxtaposed unfavorably with the mestiza who "can't hold concepts or ideas in rigid boundaries."[22] As many scholars have noted, Native identity is relegated to a primitive past, a premodern precursor to the more modern, sophisticated mestizo identity.[23] In queer of color critique in particular, mestizaje and queerness often intersect to disappear indigeneity through the figure of the diasporic or hybrid queer subject. The consequence is that queer of color critique, while making critical interventions into both critical race and queer studies, generally lacks an analysis of settler colonialism and genocide. Within queer of color critique, many scholars engage subjectless critique while fully interrogating its limits. As such, this work can benefit the development of Native studies. At the same time, however, a critical limit often not explored by queer of color critique is the limits of set-tler colonialism. As such, indigeneity frequently disappears within these projects. Once again, a subjectless critique within Native studies assists in interrogating projects based on a queer of color critique that does not directly incorporate an analysis of Native peoples. At the same time, however, queer of color critique's version of subjectless critique can also veil the queer of color subject's investment in settler colonialism.

As an example, Gayatri Gopinath critiques Madonna for cultural theft but then very uncritically celebrates British Punjabi artist Apache Indian's obvious appropriation of Apache culture. Gopinath lauds this move for its "referencing of multiple diasporic locations including the Caribbean, India, the UK, and the United States," neglecting to list the Apache Nation as a national location.[24] She seems to implicitly subscribe to the colonialist notion that Apache nationhood can be subsumed under the settler colonial logic of the United States. Furthermore, this appropriation is celebrated in the service of a "de-essentialized notion of 'Indian' identity."[25] Just as mestizo identity appropriates an essentialized Indigenous identity, this time a mestizo "Indian" identity is dependent on the erasure of Indigenous Apache identity. Quoting George Lipsitz, Gopinath likens Apache Indian's project to the appropriation of Native identity by African Americans during Mardi Gras celebrations as a "poli-tics emanating from Indian imagery to affirm Black nationalism [which] lead[s] logically to a pan-ethnic anti-racism that moves beyond essen-tialism."[26] But why does appropriation necessarily lead to antiracism? First, this appropriation tends to depend on a very essentialized notion of Native identity that becomes the raw material for the building of a complex postmodern identity. Second, where is the evidence that any of these practices actually contribute to solidarity work with contemporary Indigenous struggles?

As many Native scholars have argued, Native peoples are entrapped in a logic of genocidal appropriation. This logic holds that Indigenous peoples must disappear. In fact, they must *always* be disappearing, in order to allow non-Indigenous people's rightful claim over this land. Through this logic of genocide, non-Native people then become the rightful inheritors of all that was Indigenous—land, resources, Indige-nous spirituality, or culture. Rayna Green demonstrates that the cultural appropriation of indigeneity is based on a logic of genocide: non-Native peoples imagine themselves as the rightful inheritors of all that previously belonged to "vanished" Indians, thus entitling them to ownership of this land. "The living performance of 'playing Indian' by non-Indian peoples depends upon the physical and psychological removal, even the death, of real Indians. In that sense, the performance, purportedly often done out of a stated and implicit love for Indians, is really the obverse of another well-known cultural phenomenon, 'Indian hating,' as most often expressed in another, deadly performance genre called 'genocide.'"[27] After all, why would non-Native peoples need to play Indian if they thought Indians were still alive and perfectly capable of being Indian themselves? Thus, the appropriation of Native identity by even people of color or Third World subjects cannot be easily distinguished from a logic of genocide, or a logic of biopower whereby Natives must die so that postmodern subjects can live.

Gopinath's uncritical support for appropriating indigeneity also contributes to her problematic juxtaposition of a simple national identity with a complex diasporic identity. Her work centers the diasporic subject as what troubles national identity. She "embraces diaspora as a concept for its potential to foreground notions of impurity and inauthenticity that resoundingly reject the ethnic and religious absolutism at the center of nationalist projects."[28] She then likens diaspora to queerness. "A queer diasporic framework productively exploits the analogous relation between nation and diaspora on the one hand, and between heterosexuality and queerness on the other; in other words, queerness is to heterosexuality as the diaspora is to the nation."[29] This logic follows Anzaldúa's framework of juxtaposing the complicated, queer Mestizo subject with the primitive, simple, Indigenous subject. A subjectless critique within Native studies enables an Indigenous critique of queer of color projects that do not directly engage Native studies, but do depend ideologically on the disappearance of Native peoples. In particular, such a critique leads me to conclude that just as, for instance, the image of the "welfare queen" becomes coded language to signify blackness, images of nationhood as necessarily simplistic and essentialist rest on the shadow of the primitive Indigenous subject who cannot transcend her nationalistic identifications. The Indigenous subject is once again an "infantile citizen," firmly rooted within a nation and a land base, and hence is insufficiently queered without a mixed or diasporic subject. Thus, even though Gopinath actually critiques the notion that the proper queer subject can be denoted by leaving home and community as a free self-determined

citizen, her likening of queerness to diaspora tends to reify the assumption that the (Indigenous) nation cannot be queered on its own. Left to
its own, the (Indigenous) nation is positioned as a heterosexual norm
that requires diaspora to queer it.

Instead, perhaps we can understand Indigenous nationhood as already
queered. Gopinath's work does suggest some ways nationhood could be
queered. She troubles the normative notion of the home as a place "to
be escaped in order to emerge into another more liberatory space," in
favor of "remaking the space of home within."[30] Echoing Silva's analysis, she reads a variety of texts to argue that the narrative of leaving
home to attain personal liberation again rests on the logic of the self-
determining universal subject transcending particularity. "The equation
of liberation with leaving and oppressing with 'staying put' cannot be
upheld. In rejecting this progress narrative of freedom through exile and
the renunciation of home, these texts instead enable a queer reworking
of the very space of home itself."[31] Thus, if home can be remade, perhaps
we could go further than Gopinath and argue that the home is always
already being remade: this remaking is not necessarily dependent on the
diasporic subject.

Renya Ramirez's ethnography of urban Native communities suggests
a way to put together an analysis of diaspora in conversation with indigeneity to further Gopinath's project of remaking home. She critiques prevalent notions of urban Native peoples "living as exiles without a culture,
inhabiting a nether-world between the traditional and modern,"[32] seeing
them instead as people whose travel to and from reservations actually
strengthens their relationship to their land base. Informed by her ethnographic subjects, Ramirez develops the concept of the "hub," which
can be both a geographic space (such as an urban area) and an activity (such as Internet communication) that allows peoples to maintain
relationships and to develop political coalitions. However, the hub does
not privilege the diasporic subject in relation to the nondiasporic who
remains home. Rather, Ramirez's narrative positions them all as having pivotal roles in developing political alliances, challenging oppressive
behaviors within Indigenous nations, and combating settler colonialism.

A subjectless critique centering an Indigenous analysis can also interrogate the queering of oppositional politics within the works of queer of
color critics who do not directly engage Native struggles. For instance,
Muñoz centers his work on the figure of the mestizo, which he equates
with the queer and the hybrid subject. Hybridity and queerness become

a pivot by which he rearticulates oppositional politics. He argues that queer lives demonstrate that "the importance of such public and semi-public enactments of the hybrid self cannot be undervalued in relation to the formation of counterpublics that contest the hegemonic supremacy of the majoritarian public sphere."[33] His model for political engagement is that of disidentification. According to Muñoz, whereas assimilation-ism seems to identify with the dominant society, and whereas coun-teridentification seeks to reject it completely, disidentification "is the third mode of dealing with dominant ideology, one that neither opts to assimilate within such a structure nor strictly opposes it; rather, dis-identification is a strategy that works on and against dominant ideol-ogy."[34] Muñoz explains that disidentification neither fully accepts nor rejects dominant cultural logics but internally subverts them, using the logic against itself. Muñoz clarifies that disidentification is not a middle ground between assimilationist and contestatory politics; rather, it is a strategy that recognizes the shifting terrain of resistances.[35]

This model of disidentification can inform Native studies' empha-sis on decolonization. While there are many variations on how Indig-enous decolonization is articulated, with many Native studies scholars rejecting this framework altogether, decolonization is certainly a preva-lent concept within Native studies. It generally tends to follow the logic identified by Muñoz as counteridentification. Native communities are frequently called on to reject the modern trappings of colonial society to build Indigenous "decolonized societies." In some cases, these calls frequently lead to political silencing; for instance, Native feminists are often accused of selling out to white feminism because decolonized Native subjects should address sovereignty to the exclusion of gender oppression. Calls for political and cultural purity then contribute to a political vanguardism in which the Indigenous cultural elite govern improperly decolonized subjects. To give one example, I work with the Boarding School Healing Project that attempts to build a movement to demand collective reparations to Native peoples in the United States for boarding-school abuses. The BSHP made healing central to the organiz-ing work because, given the level of severe trauma suffered by boarding school survivors, we could not develop an organizing project if we did not address this trauma. In doing so, we also discovered how a group can unwittingly instill spiritual and religious orthodoxies in the name of liberation. Since most boarding schools were Christian-run, much of the healing work in Native communities focuses on healing "from historic trauma" through promoting traditional spiritual practices. However, when we attempted to hold a "decolonized" traditional ceremony at one event, survivors felt they were back in boarding school again, only this time they were being told they had to be "traditional" rather than Christian. We then learned that in doing spiritually grounded work, we could not make assumptions about what, if any, spiritual practices, people might want to engage in. Many Native peoples today *are* Christian, and yet they become positioned as necessarily inauthentic or "assimilated" even if they are also concurrently involved in struggles for sovereignty and liberation. We found that we could not assert a one-size-fits-all healing model; we had to let the models develop organically from people themselves. We learned that decolonization projects can quickly become very colonial in their implementation. A disidentification strategy might have shifted our focus from expecting boarding-school survivors to adopt a particular traditional identity to providing the space by which their politicization could emerge from their actual multiple identifications.

While helpful, however, a strategy of disidentification has its limits when applied to the problematics of settler colonialism. Some of the inadequacies can be found in Muñoz's reliance on "public spheres" and "counterpublics" as his framework for understanding political engagement. The problem with the public sphere/counterpublic model is that it is implicitly based on a "minority" rather than an anticolonial framework that would seek to dismantle the public sphere. To demonstrate, Muñoz describes those opposing the hostile public sphere as "minority subjects."[36] But as Ramirez notes, Native struggle is not necessarily centered on trying simply to carve out a minority space within the settler state; it may try to dismantle the settler state completely.[37] In this regard, a counteridentification, while "utopian" (in Muñoz's words), is not necessarily unimportant. As Waziyatawin demonstrates, these utopian visions can also provide a way to measure the effectiveness of our short-term strategies. Are our attempts to use society against itself actually working? Or are we simply being co-opted into settler colonial logics? A vision of decolonization can provide a helpful guide for constantly reassessing our strategies and not assuming that our strategies are necessarily effective.[38]

Thus, while queer theorists, such as Muñoz, tend to be critical of binaries,[39] I think it is important to not have a binary analysis of binaries. The presumption that binarism is bad and that hybridism is good often works against Indigenous interests. Hence, in the case of queer of color critique, the subjectless critique actually relies on a "mixed" or "hybrid" subject who is positioned against the Native foil. For example, in his reading of Arturo Islas's novel *Migrant Souls,* Muñoz links queerness to migrancy, and hybridity to mestizaje, seeing them as categories that defy "notions of uniform identity or origins."[40] In particular, he celebrates one character, Miguel, "as a border Mexican with citizenship in a queer nation or a border queer national claiming citizenship in Aztlán."[41] What is erased in this analysis are the land claims of Indigenous peoples who come from the land Chicanos may claim as Aztlán. Of course, Muñoz is not unaware of the anti-Indigenous problematics within theoretical configurations of hybridity, but when indigeneity is not foregrounded, it tends to disappear in order to enable the emergence of the hybrid subject.

This valorization of mixedness then impacts Muñoz's analysis of political engagement. He equates disidentification with a Gramscian politics of maneuver in opposition to a war of position. Antonio Gramsci did not disarticulate the two; a war of position and a war of maneuver are mutually interdependent. A war of position is required to develop an ideological base that can enable a war of maneuver to build political power. But at the same time, a war of position is also insufficient in and of itself; oppressed groups must seize state and capitalist apparatuses or recreate alternative models. "The decisive element in every situation is the permanently organized and long-prepared force which can be put into the field when it is judged that a situation is favourable. . . . Therefore the essential task is that of systematically and patiently ensuring that force is formed, developed, and rendered ever more homogeneous, compact, and self aware."[42] Muñoz, by contrast, dismisses the relevance or importance of a war of position, arguing that it has been temporally displaced by a war of maneuver. "Whereas the war of [position] was a necessary modality of resistance at a moment when minoritarian groups were directly subjugated within hegemony, the more multilayered and tactical war of [maneuver] represents better possibilities of resistance today, when discriminatory ideologies are less naked and more intricate."[43] This temporal supercession implies that the time of direct colonization and subjugation has passed, thus erasing the current colonization of Indigenous peoples globally. Since not all peoples are in a postcolonial relationship vis-à-vis the state, a binary analysis of the colonizer and colonized can sometimes be helpful in highlighting the current conditions of settler colonialism that continue to exist today in both the United States and the rest of the world.

Thus, a politics of disidentification can be helpful to the project of decolonization. It provides a theoretical apparatus that can allow colonized peoples to engage in multiple strategies to build a base of support sufficient to dismantle the settler state. Disidentification forces us to admit that we cannot organize from a space of political purity, that we have been inevitably marked by processes of colonization. When we no longer have to carry the burden of political and cultural purity, we can be more flexible and creative in engaging multiple strategies and creating a plethora of alliances that can enable us to use the logics of settler colonialism against itself. At the same time, however, while political organizing is enabled by disidentification, sometimes it is also enabled by counteridentification that clearly identifies the United States as a settler colonial state. Otherwise, a disidentification approach can lapse into a politics that forecloses the issue of Indigenous genocide by presuming the United States should and will always continue to exist.

Queering the Nation-State

The question arises, then, why is settler colonialism so seriously undertheorized in queer studies, even within queer of color critique? One possibility may be that queer studies has not considered the possibility of alternative forms of nationalism that are not structured by nation-states. To be fair, queer theory does offer strong critiques of the heteronormativity of the nation-state as well as the heteronormativity of the citizen, particularly the U.S. citizen. For instance, Jasbir Puar's work joins Gopinath's in demonstrating how the noncitizen, particularly in the figure of the refugee or the immigrant, queers the heteronormativity of the state.[44] Berlant also looks at how queer activist groups within the United States attempt to reconfigure citizenship within the current nation-state and even to question the "censoring imaginary of the state."[45] Muñoz similarly gestures to "beyond" the current political system when he says, "Our charge as spectators and actors is to continue disidentifying with this world until we achieve new ones."[46] Thus, queer theorists seem to exhibit some desire to think beyond the nation-state.

At the same time, queer theory seems to lapse back into presuming the givenness of the nation-state in general, and the United States in particular. For instance, Berlant contends: "It must be emphasized . . . that disidentification with U.S. nationality is not, at this moment, even a theoretical option for queer citizens. . . . We are compelled, then, to read

America's lips. What can we do to force the officially constituted nation to speak a new political tongue?"[47] This statement curiously occludes the struggles of many Indigenous peoples who have articulated themselves as belonging to sovereign nations rather than as being U.S. citizens. The reason for this occlusion can be found in another statement: she contends that Native peoples "have long experienced simultaneously the wish to be full citizens and the violence of their partial citizenship."[48] She collapses Native peoples into the category of racial minority rather than recognize them as colonized peoples struggling against a settler state.

So, the settler state is presumed within queer theory, while (as mentioned previously) Indigenous nationhood is imaged as simply a primitive mirror image of a heteronormative state. However, many Native scholars and activists are offering internal critiques of contemporary Native politics to imagine potentially nonheteronormative forms of Indigenous nationhood. As Taiaiake Alfred, Glen Coulthard, Jennifer Denetdale, and others note, Native sovereignty struggles are themselves often articulated within, rather than in resistance to, the logics of settler colonialism.[49] That is, articulations of Native governance and sovereignty often mimic the logics of the settler state rather than draw on forms of Indigenous governance that call into question many of the logics of nation-state forms of governance. As they argue, Native sovereignty struggles often focus on gaining recognition from the surrounding settler state. To gain this recognition, Native nations model themselves after colonial states, mirroring their similar colonial logics of the state. Coulthard explains that this politics of recognition also entraps colonized peoples in a death dance with their colonizers. The "key problem with the politics of recognition when applied to the colonial context . . . [is that it] rests on the problematic assumption that the flourishing of Indigenous Peoples as distinct and self-determining agents is somehow dependent on their being granted recognition and institutional accommodation from the surrounding settler-state and society. . . . Not only will the terms of recognition tend to remain the property of those in power to grant to their inferiors in ways that they deem appropriate, but also under these conditions, the Indigenous population will often come to see their limited and structurally constrained terms of recognition granted to them as *their own.* In effect, the colonized come to *identify* with 'white liberty and white justice.'"[50] He calls on Indigenous activists to shift their focus from seeking recognition from the settler state to seeking recognition from one another as well as other oppressed communities. Native peoples' ethnographic entrapment within the academy presumes the politics of recognition that Coulthard critiques. That is, Native peoples are compelled to represent themselves properly to gain recognition within the academy—they are not supposed to define the terms of discourse itself.

As I have discussed elsewhere, these alternative models of sovereignty are not based on a narrow definition of nation that entails a closely bounded community and ethnic cleansing. Native activists often articulate Indigenous forms of nationhood organized around a logic of citizenship based less on rights within a nation and more on a system of interrelatedness and mutual responsibility.[51] Because these visions of national liberation do not necessarily entail a nation-state form of governance as their end goal, they do not imagine a social structure based on social domination. As such, they can *potentially* challenge logics of heteronormativity, because heteropatriarchy is a logic that naturalizes social hierarchy. That is, if under the logic of heteropatriarchy, men are supposed to rule women on the basis of biology, this social hierarchy becomes naturalized. As Karen Warren notes, social domination is effective primarily because it seems natural—otherwise, there is no reason why people want to live under conditions of domination.[52] Once we challenge the idea that domination is somehow "human nature," we have the potential to question the naturalization of all its manifestations, including heteropatriarchy.

Certainly, those who support heteropatriarchy recognize this connection, as can be seen in Christian right leader Charles Colson's articulation of the relationship between U.S. empire and heteropatriarchy. Explaining that one cause of terrorism is same-sex marriage, he asserts:

> Marriage is the traditional building block of human society, intended both to unite couples and bring children into the world. . . . there is a natural moral order for the family. . . . The family, led by a married mother and father, is the best available structure for both child-rearing and cultural health. . . . Marriage is not a private institution designed solely for the individual gratification of its participants. If we fail to enact a Federal Marriage Amendment, we can expect, not just more family breakdown, but also more criminals behind bars and more chaos in our streets.[53]

Morse suggests in a different issue of the same magazine that it is like handing "moral weapons of mass destruction to those who would use

America's depravity to recruit more snipers, more hijackers, and more suicide bombers."[54] He argues:

> ... when radical Islamists see American women abusing Muslim men, as they did in the Abu Ghraib prison, and when they see news coverage of same-sex couples being "married" in U.S. towns, we make our kind of freedom abhorrent—the kind they see as a blot on Allah's creation. . . . [We must preserve traditional marriage in order to protect] the United States from those who would use our depravity to destroy us.[55]

Colson is linking the well-being of U.S. empire to the well-being of the heteropatriarchal family. Heteropatriarchy is the logic that makes social hierarchy seem natural. Just as the patriarchs rule the family, the elites of the nation-state rule their citizens. Consequently, when colonists first came to the Americas, they saw the necessity of instilling patriarchy in Native communities because they realized that Indigenous peoples would not accept colonial domination if their own Indigenous societies were not structured on the basis of social hierarchy. Patriarchy in turns rests on a gender-binary system; hence it is not a coincidence that colonizers also targeted Indigenous peoples who did not fit within this binary model. In addition, gender violence is a primary tool of colonialism and white supremacy. Colonizers did not just kill off Indigenous peoples in this land, but Native massacres were always accompanied by sexual mutilation and rape. As I have argued elsewhere, the goal of colonialism is not just to kill colonized peoples, but to destroy their sense of being people.[56] It is through sexual violence that a colonizing group attempts to render a colonized people inherently rapable, their lands inherently invadable, and their resources inherently extractable.

As Denetdale notes, however, because we have internalized these logics, our liberation struggles often reify the structures of social domination they claim to displace. An uncritical politics of futurity and tradition can contribute to the reification of neocolonialism within our struggles for sovereignty. At the 2009 World Social Forum (WSF), which I attended, a consensus that seemed to emerge from the Indigenous peoples' organizations of Latin America was that indigenous liberation depends on global liberation from the nation-state form of governance. These groups explicitly linked the colonial nation-state system with patriarchy and western epistemology, calling on indigenous and non-Indigenous peoples to break with their internalization of social domination logics to imagine a world based on radical participatory democracy.

These visions of sovereignty entail a critique of western notions of land as property. Patricia Monture-Angus contends that Indigenous nationhood is based not on control of territory or land, but on relationship with and responsibility for land.

> Although Aboriginal Peoples maintain a close relationship with the land . . . it is not about control of the land. . . . Earth is mother and she nurtures us all . . . it is the human race that is dependent on the earth and not vice versa. . . .
>
> Sovereignty, when defined as my right to be responsible . . . requires a relationship with territory (and not a relationship based on control of that territory). . . . What must be understood then is that Aboriginal request to have our sovereignty respected is really a request to be responsible. I do not know of anywhere else in history where a group of people have had to fight so hard just to be responsible.[57]

Similarly, the Indigenous peoples groups at the WSF argued that all peoples are welcome on their lands, but they must live in a different relationship with the land. Within the realm of legal recognition, Native peoples are forced to argue for their right to control their own land to be recognized by the settler colonial state. That is, to fight encroachments on their lands, Indigenous peoples are forced to argue in courts that it is "their" land. What Indigenous peoples cannot question within the dominant legal system is the presumed relationship between peoples and land. That is, should land be a commodity to be controlled and owned by peoples? Once land is not seen as property, then nationhood does not have to be based on exclusive control over territory. If sovereignty is more about being responsible for land, then nationhood can engage all those who fulfill responsibilities for land.

In this respect, the articulations of the Indigenous peoples at the WSF, then, are engaging in a radical Indigenous subjectless critique of settler colonialism. That is, while these groups noted that they are facing literal and imminent genocide, they were not primarily engaged in a politics of representation in order to gain recognition from nation-states. Rather, they argued that their goal was not to save themselves but to save the world. They articulated indigeneity as a critical framework for not simply representing the interests of Indigenous peoples, but deconstructing western epistemology and global state and economic structures in the interests of building another world that could sustain all peoples. This vision also challenges the presumed heteronormativity of national belonging, because it demonstrates that the presumption behind a heteronormative nation is a relationship to land as commodity that must then rely on boundaries to include and exclude. These articulations point to alternative modes of national belonging that are not definitionally exclusivist.

Conclusion

Queer studies highlights the importance of developing analyses that go beyond identity and representational politics. For Native studies in particular, queer theory points to the possibility of going beyond representing the voices of Native peoples, a project that can quickly become co-opted into providing Native commodities for consumption in the multicultural academic industrial complex. Rather, we have a task to uncover and analyze the logics of settler colonialism as they affect all areas of life. The subjectless critique of queer theory can assist Native studies in critically interrogating how it can unwittingly recreate colonial hierarchies even within projects of decolonization. This critique also sheds light on how Native peoples function within the colonial imaginary—including the colonial imaginary of scholars and movements that claim to be radical. As Maria Josefina Saldaña-Portillo argues, the revolutionary subject is generally positioned within a logic of development that defines itself against the primitive Native.[58]

At the same time, Native studies can build on queer of color critique's engagement with subjectless critique. In the move to "post-identity," queer theory often reinstantiates a white supremacist settler colonialism by appropriating Indigenous peoples as foils for the emergence of postcolonial, postmodern, diasporic, and queer subjects. Thus, in making these intellectual projects intersect, perhaps we can speak more of an "identity-plus" politics. That is, we may need a politics that marks *all* identities and their relationship to the fields of power in which they are imbricated. As Judith Butler states: "If the notion of the subject, for instance, is no longer given, no longer presumed, that does not mean that it has no meaning for us, that it ought no longer to be uttered. On the contrary, it means only that the term is not simply a building block on which we rely, an uninterrogated premise for political argument.

On the contrary, the term has become an object of theoretical attention, something for which we are compelled to give an account."[59] With respect to Native studies, even queer of color critique does not necessarily mark how identities are shaped by settler colonialism. Thus, as Chris Finley notes, a conversation between Native studies and queer theory is important not just because Native peoples "are sexy" (although that is certainly true), but because the logics of settler colonialism *and* decolonization must be queered in order properly to speak the genocidal present that not only continues to disappear Indigenous peoples but reinforces the structures of white supremacy, settler colonialism, and heteropatriarchy that affect all peoples.

Acknowledgments

Many thanks to Mark Rifkin, Chris Finley, and the folks from the Queer Theory Group at the 2008 School for Critical Theory, especially Ronak Kapadia, Ramzi Fawaz, and Stephanie Clare.

Notes

Author's Note: This chapter was previously published as "Queer Theory and Native Studies: The Heteronormativity of Settler Colonialism," in *GLQ: A Journal of Lesbian and Gay Studies*, vol. 16, no. 1–2, pp. 41–68. Copyright © 2010, Duke University Press. All rights reserved. Reprinted by permission of the publisher.

1. Chris Finley, "Decolonizing the Queer Native Body (and Recovering the Native Bull-Dyke): Bringing 'Sexy Back' and Out of Native Studies' Closet" (this volume).

2. Qwo-Li Driskill, "Doubleweaving Two-Spirit Critiques: Building Alliances between Native and Queer Studies," *GLQ: A Journal of Lesbian and Gay Studies*, 16, no. 1–2 (2010).

3. Michael Warner, "Introduction," in *Fear of a Queer Planet,* ed. Michael Warner (Minneapolis: University of Minnesota Press, 1993), xxvi; Paula Gunn Allen, *The Sacred Hoop* (Boston: Beacon, 1986); Sue-Ellen Jacobs, Wesley Thomas, and Sabine Lang, eds., *Two-Spirit People* (Urbana: University of Illinois Press, 1997); Will Roscoe, *The Zuni Man-Woman* (Albuquerque: University of New Mexico Press, 1991).

4. Denise Ferreira da Silva, *Toward a Global Idea of Race* (Minneapolis: University of Minnesota Press, 2007), 169.

5. Ibid., 27.

6. Elizabeth Cook-Lynn, "American Indian Intellectualism and the New Indian Story," in *Natives and Academics: Researching and Writing about American*

Indians, ed. Devon Mihesuah (Lincoln: University of Nebraska Press, 1998); Sandy Grande, *Red Pedagogy* (Lanham, MD: Rowman and Littlefield, 2004); Linda Tuhiwai Smith, *Decolonizing Methodologies* (London: Zed, 1999).

7. Robert Warrior, *Tribal Secrets* (Minneapolis: University of Minnesota Press, 1994).

8. Elizabeth Cook-Lynn, "Who Stole Native American Studies," *Wicazo Sa Review* 12, no. Spring (1997); Winona Stevenson, "'Ethnic' Assimilates 'Indigenous': A Study in Intellectual Neocolonialism," *Wicazo Sa Review* 13, Spring (1998).

9. Rey Chow, *The Protestant Ethnic and the Spirit of Capitalism* (New York: Columbia University Press, 2002).

10. To do so, Audra Simpson calls on Native studies scholars to engage in acts of "ethnographic refusal." She details how this politics of representation serves as a strategy of containment for Native communities that domesticates a Native politics of decolonization into a strategy for liberal multiculturalism ("On Ethnographic Refusal: Indigeneity, 'Voice' and Colonial Citizenship," *Junctures* 9 [2007]). Elizabeth Povinelli and Rey Chow further demonstrate that liberal multiculturalism often relies on a politics of identity representation that is domesticated by nation-state and capitalist imperatives. See Chow, *Protestant Ethnic*; Elizabeth Povinelli, *The Cunning of Recognition* (Durham, NC: Duke University Press, 2002).

11. Warner, "Introduction," xxvi.

12. Subjectless critique is also developed within Asian American studies (Kandice Chuh, *Imagine Otherwise: On Asian Americanist Critique* [Durham, NC: Duke University Press, 2003]).

13. David L. Eng, Judith Halberstam, José Esteban Muñoz, "Introduction: What's Queer about Queer Studies Now?" in *What's Queer about Queer Studies Now?* ed. D. L. Eng, J. Halberstam, and J. E. Muñoz (Durham, NC: Duke University Press, 2005), 5.

14. Hiram Perez, "You Can Have My Brown Body and Eat It, Too," *Social Text* 23, Fall–Winter (2005); Sarita Echavez See, *The Decolonized Eye: Filipino American Art and Performance* (Minneapolis: University of Minnesota Press, 2009).

15. Warner, "Introduction," xvii.

16. Perez, "You Can Have My Brown Body and Eat It, Too," 187.

17. The section "Queering the Future of Genocide" is omitted here (see original publication).

18. Lauren Berlant, *The Queen of America Goes to Washington City* (Durham, NC: Duke University Press, 1997), 6.

19. David Stannard, *American Holocaust* (Oxford: Oxford University Press, 1992), 166.

20. Kirpatrick Sale, *The Conquest of Paradise* (New York: Plume, 1990), 203.

21. Gayatri Spivak, *A Critique of Postcolonial Reason* (Cambridge: Harvard University Press, 1999), 385. Emphasis added.

22. Gloria Anzaldúa, *Borderlands* (San Francisco: Aunt Lute, 1987), 18, 30, 79.

23. Sheila Marie Contreras, *Bloodlines: Myth, Indigenism, and Chicana/o Literature* (Austin: University of Texas Press, 2008); Maria Josefina Saldana-Portillo, *The Revolutionary Imagination in the Americas and the Age of Development* (Durham, NC: Duke University Press, 2003).

24. Gayatri Gopinath, *Impossible Desires* (Durham, NC: Duke University Press, 2005), 31.

25. Ibid., 34.

26. Ibid., 38.

27. Rayna Green, "The Tribe Called Wannabee," *Folklore* 99, no. 1 (1988): 31.

28. Gopinath, *Impossible Desires,* 7.

29. Ibid., 14.

30. Ibid.

31. Ibid., 92.

32. Renya Ramirez, *Native Hubs: Culture, Community and Belonging in Silicon Valley and Beyond* (Durham, NC: Duke University Press, 2007), 1.

33. José Esteban Muñoz, *Disidentifications: Queers of Color and the Performance of Politics* (Minneapolis: University of Minnesota Press, 1999), 1.

34. Ibid., 11–12.

35. Ibid., 18.

36. Ibid., 5.

37. Ramirez, *Native Hubs,* 14.

38. Waziyatawin Angela Wilson, *Remember This!* (Lincoln: University of Nebraska Press, 2005).

39. Muñoz, *Disidentifications,* 20.

40. Ibid., 31.

41. Ibid., 32.

42. Antonio Gramsci, *Selections from the Prison Notebooks,* trans. Quintin Hoare and Geoffrey Nowell Smith, 12th ed. (New York: International Publishers, 1971), 185.

43. Muñoz, *Disidentifications,* 114. Muñoz confuses "war of position" and "war of maneuver," using one when he means the other. See Gramsci, *Selections from the Prison Notebooks,* 239.

44. Jasbir Puar, *Terrorist Assemblages: Homonationalism in Queer Times* (Durham, NC: Duke University Press, 2007).

45. Berlant, *Queen of America Goes to Washington City,* 172.

46. Muñoz, *Disidentifications,* 200.

47. Berlant, *Queen of America Goes to Washington City,* 150.

48. Ibid., 19.

49. Jennifer Denetdale, "Carving Navajo National Boundaries: Patriotism, Tradition, and the Diné Marriage Act of 2005," *American Quarterly* 60, June (2008): 289–94; Taiaiake Alfred, *Wasáse* (University of Toronto Press, 2005); Glen Coulthard, "Subjects of Empire: Indigenous Peoples and the 'Politics of Recognition' in Canada," *Contemporary Political Theory* 6, no. 4 (2007).

50. Glen Coulthard, "Indigenous Peoples and the 'Politics of Recognition' in Colonial Contexts," paper presented at the Cultural Studies Now Conference, University of East London, London, England, July 22, 2007.

51. Andrea Smith, *Native Americans and the Christian Right: The Gendered Politics of Unlikely Alliances* (Durham, NC: Duke University Press, 2008).

52. Karen Warren, "A Feminist Philosophical Perspective on Ecofeminist Spiritualities," in *Ecofeminism and the Sacred,* ed. Carol Adams (New York: Continuum, 1993).

53. Charles Colson, with Anne Morse, "Societal Suicide," *Christianity Today* 48 (June 2004).

54. Charles Colson, with Anne Morse, "The Moral Home Front," *Christianity Today* 48 (October 2004).

55. Ibid.

56. Smith, *Conquest.*

57. Patricia Monture-Angus, *Journeying Forward* (Halifax: Fernwood, 1999), 36.

58. Saldana-Portillo, *Revolutionary Imagination in the Americas and the Age of Development.*

59. Judith Butler, *Undoing Gender* (New York: Routledge, 2004).

3
A Queer Caste
Mixing Race and Sexuality in Colonial New Zealand

Michelle Erai

By the time England decided, somewhat reluctantly, to colonize *Aotearoa/New Zealand*,[1] their resources were spread thin—the independence of the United States, and centuries of competition with France, Holland, Spain, and Portugal, had taken its toll. At the same time, the rise of humanistic ideologies—European scientific rationalism, the dominance of Anglicanism, and the influence of the Age of Reason—combined with colonial capitalist expansion to facilitate the creation of a new, racially gendered, classed, and sexualized body in the colony: the half-caste.

Archival texts contain rich examples of how landed nationhood and sexuality were deployed to form the ideological construction of the mixed-race offspring of Maori mothers.[2] The liminal bodies of those children, in their physical existence, exhibited the complex renderings of intimacy, violence, desire, and betrayal inherent in the proximity of colonization.

The pre-imagining of Native subjects was achieved in texts such as the letter below;[3] it tells of commercial interests and prospects, fears of violence from the Indigenous population, labor, war, and expected costs in colonizing a land so far removed from the imperial core. But most strikingly, it builds an argument for the location of settlements based on the assumed sexuality and amenability of Indigenous women, identifying, firstly, the danger of the convict women in Australia (New Holland), and in the margins, the potential availability of Maori women on the coasts of New Zealand.

Sent in 1823, from commercial whalers to an English colonel in the Royal Marines, it begins: "Sir, We have great pleasure in answering your Letter and in giving you our opinion of the very great advantages which we think those Ship Owners who send Ships to fish for Whales off the coast of New Zealand will gain by the establishment of Settlements on that Island." They go on to say:

> The Settlements on the Coast of New Holland are at a considerable distance from the Eastern Coast of New Zealand where our Ships

fish. If a Ship meets with damage, or her crew become sickly, to run to New Holland takes up considerable time, with some risk of loss of Ship or Deaths of Crew. The greatest evil we experience, and which we dread from our Ships going to the Settlements in New Holland, is that the Convict Women so demoralize the Crew, as to make them in a short time, from the best of Sailors, become extremely mutinous, and we scarcely know an instance of any of our Ships going there without greatly altering the conduct of the Crew many of whom desert.[4]

Sexual access to certain bodies, and particularly the less-fraught bodies of Native women, is scripted into the commercial and imperial narratives of contact, settlement, and colonization. These narratives demonstrate "cartographies of desire" and "economies of flow" in colonial history making;[5] they are examples of the spatial and temporal organization of national and colonial fantasies across racialized and gendered Indigenous bodies.

A temptation in a historical project is to excavate queer subjects, to sift through the colonial archives to recuperate individual stories or events that might qualify as "queer." There are a number of reasons that this may not be a simple process of identification. The political procedures that determined what was written and lodged within the archives is not the same for Maori as for non-Maori. Certainly relevant are questions of which Maori became literate and when (slaves seeking refuge in missions may have produced as many documents as the women and men of high rank appealing against the appropriation of tribal lands), and of what kinds of literacy were privileged then and which are privileged now.

There is also the question of legibility. Early missionaries, colonial administrators, and settlers were likely to cryptically encode acts or relationships that might, today, be interpreted as "queer" if they were even committed to paper at all. This raises the question of a certain kind of legibility in the archives, so it becomes necessary to read the gaps and the margins for what might have been omitted, of what constitutes a presence by its very absence.

Given these restrictions, how then might mixed-race bodies in colonial Aotearoa/New Zealand have been "queered"; or how, as Alicia Arrizón puts it, was "[t]he racial imperative instituted with the use of mestizaje . . . in 'queering' the practice of the gendered body?"[6] Perhaps the most generative approach to the historical materials is created by discourse analysis and a critical reading strategy in which the "Maori subject" "stands less as a racialized, gendered identity" and more as a "problematic implying particular modes of theoretical and political analysis for addressing racializing, sexualizing, and gendering forms of oppression."[7]

The dis-Orienting of history is a necessary political labor of constructing new stories about shared pasts—a project of writing fictions of real violence, and contradictions of time, people, and place. Although settlers had histories that traveled with them, those colonial and national claims did not necessarily flourish in ways they had expected in the colony, and by refusing to view the present as a fait accompli—the past successfully concluded—it is possible to retain a sense of decisions that were made, of relationships that were created in necessity, and affection, while not losing the concrete and locally specific enactments of violence and coercion. The present of the inhabitants of the nineteenth century can still be full of unrealized futures, and not the undeniable outcome of contemporary Pacific present/s.

In the Pacific, as elsewhere, geography can express spaces of negotiation, transgression, and transformation. These spaces—the border,[8] frontier,[9] contact zone,[10] or beaches,[11]—are a powerful rendering of the layered, uneven, multidirectional and sometimes brutal encounters between those who are about to become "colonizers" and those about to become "the colonized."

Historically, the lands of the Pacific have been rendered invisible through a globalizing discourse that describes it as a "negative blue space," a place that is constructed as a "nowhere" between "somewheres."[12] This nullification of the Pacific has been achieved both through a historical literature that conceives of the Pacific as "vast and empty," and through a global imagining that concentrates on the Pacific's rim, relegating the ocean and its inhabitants to the gap between America and Japan or Hong Kong. If these dynamics operate simultaneously, then it is possible to see how the twentieth- and twenty-first-century Pacific came to be viewed as a site for the testing of nuclear weaponry, and, at the same time, a source of romantic travel–fantasy. By placing a rationalizing emphasis on its proximity to, but difference from, the global powers of the United States and Japan, the Pacific has been conceived as a convenient, uncontested space that is so large it can "safely" absorb the radiation and pollution of global technologies and remain a healthy, exotic adventure destination.

The Pacific is also a gendered space, imagined through a conceptualization of safe spaces as inherently feminized, as the home of the "Polynesian" body, and as the product of a sexual economy in the greater

Asia-Pacific; the *wahine* is the icon around which desires of sensuality,[13] simplicity, and a "naturalized allure" revolve and are managed.[14] In addition, the potential threat of the Asia-Pacific is contained through a dominant heteronormative fantasy of sexual relations that make a groom of the United States and transform Japan into his bride.[15]

Eighteenth- and nineteenth-century journeys to New Zealand were arduous, and its isolation (1,400 miles from the nearest neighbor, Australia) meant that most voyagers arriving at the port of Kororareka (known as the "Hell Hole of the South Pacific")[16] had been at sea for at least four months, and for whalers the journey might have taken a year. Prepared by a knowledge of their home ports, of women from within their own social class, of peoples from other islands in the Pacific, and artists' images circulating throughout the empire, the sailors could, with some confidence, hope to be greeted by "dusky maidens" with whom sexual access would be just a matter of time.

Men such as Captain James Cook frequently inscribed their encounters with the Pacific and its inhabitants through ships' logs and letters to sponsors and family; in provisioning the ship the *Endeavour*, Cook recorded that "a number of Medals [were] to be struck; the one side representing his Majesty, and the other the . . . Ships. These Medals were to be given to the Natives of New discover'd Countrys and left there, as testimonies of our being the first discoverers."[17] Members of his crew, however, had other ideas about how their movements would be recognized; one sailor wrote of Tahiti, "The Women were far from being Coy. For when A Man Found a Girl to his Mind, which he Might Easily Do Amongst so many, their was Not much Cermony on Either Side, and I Belive Whoever Comes hereafter will find Evident Proofs that they are not the first Discoverys,"[18] such proof presumably being either mixed-race children or venereal diseases, or both.

Cook was a captain very concerned about the health of his crew. He had ideas about preventing scurvy that he was eager to experiment with; he was also cognizant of the potential effects of venereal diseases. Throughout his voyages Cook attempted to strictly control the spread of venereal disease to Pacific inhabitants by both (usually unsuccessfully) confining infected crew on board ship and prohibiting women from going onto the vessels while in port. The ship's surgeon had "sworn on his honor" that none of the crew suffered from venereal diseases; however, after their departures from Hawaii, New Zealand, Tahiti, and Tonga, women with whom the English sailors had sexual intercourse were found to have contracted lymphogranuloma venereum and perhaps gonorrhea.[19]

Early colonial records suggest that the sailors' hopes for sexual encounters were not disappointed in New Zealand, and that Maori, perhaps because of a relatively widespread Polynesian principle of hospitality that included sexual liaison, were sometimes willing participants in such intimate arrangements. However, there are also accounts of women and young girls being forced into sexual service:

> As far as the . . . Maori was concerned, the Watkins soon realized they had come 10 years too late. The licentious whalers had undermined the morals and health of the Maori so badly, that as early as 1841, Watkin wrote they were doomed to extinction. Mrs. Watkin was horrified to find girls not more than children being sold to the whalers, and by 1844 it was safe to estimate two-thirds of the Maori women were living with white men. Yet they seemed happy enough with their lot. . . . They soon became good housewives, and often had a strong influence for good over their wild unscrupulous men.[20]

From the early beginnings in Kororareka there emerged two influential ways of thinking about Maori women; one was as promiscuous, the source of "The New Zealand Fever,"[21] and the second was as protection through marriage for European men wanting to move safely through, and negotiate the acquisition of, Maori tribal territory. In early contact narratives it is possible to trace some of the various means by which Maori women were employed as absorptive agents. For example, Edward Markham, in 1834, spent nine months in New Zealand, during which period he cohabitated "successively with the daughters of chiefs to guarantee his own protection and the women's services as translators and sexual and domestic partners."[22] Maori women, when employed by European men as interpreters, health-care providers, and sometime concubines, acted as catalysts for normalizing or naturalizing the presence of white men:

> Mr. Tapsell's second wife whom he had married at the Bay of Islands, was . . . the sister of Wharepoaka, an influential chief of the Ngapuhis and proved great service to him as an interpreter in his negotiations with the natives, having acquired a very good knowledge of the English language during her stay with the missionaries. Personally, she was of very light complexion and so fair, that at Maketu she acquired the name of "the white woman."[23]

Wars between and against Maori tribes brought soldiers from New South Wales, and later local militia and English soldiers and marines moved throughout the islands. The movements and encampments of soldiers affected local communities, both Maori and settler; an impact of soldiers on the desired morality of Maori women was bemoaned by the Rev. Alfred Nesbit Brown, when he wrote:

> The soldiers, to our great joy, left, but I fear the abominable example that they have set to the Natives of drunkenness and fornication will long continue its pestilential influence. While Major Bunbury was in command, the camp presented a scene of order and regularity. From the period of his departure in January the camp has been a disgrace. Captain Best, who was received into our houses with hospitality, repaid our kindness by having two Native women, one of whom resided with Mrs Kissling & the other with Mrs Brown, to live with him at the camp in open sin.[24]

Militaries have long histories of managing intimacy with Native women, but missionaries also had to prepare for the risks that being near the gendered and sexualized Native subject might involve, providing the climate, absence of society, and Maori women's lack of Christian and civilized morals as alibis for masculine missionary desires.

> When Missionaries change their climate it should be remembered, they do not change their natures as men. To be under the Eye of a Guardian or Parent will sometimes operate as a powerful motive to stimulate us to the greatest Circumspection in our moral conduct. Motives foreign to religion, while being in a civilized Society where we are known and respected, are often sufficient of themselves to induce us to preserve our Moral Character unimpeached. Place a Young man in a foreign Climate amongst Licentious Savages—remove from his mind every other restraint, but that of Religion and even then we can but form a faint idea of how much he will be exposed to the Snares of the devil, and the temptations held out to him by the natives. A Young Man will have daily to contend in these Islands with a Hot climate, the Vigour of Youth and the Most Alluring temptations.[25]

As well as being the location for exotic seductions, the land—and its climate—was perceived as having health-giving properties, a site (not unlike Maori women's bodies) of both temptation and consolation. Mrs. Coote wrote, "I could not feel depressed in the midst of the very beautiful scenery that surrounded me in this most lovely harbour, in fact I was quite enraptured by it;"[26] in her diary, Sarah Mathew, wife of the land surveyor Felton Mathew, noted, "I was very desirous to return to Auckland, . . . principally I was anxious to get back, because I thought my husband's health would be benefited by the more genial climate; he had suffered so much from the cold in England."[27] In a letter to his sister in 1853, Edward Wakefield writes evocatively of how miraculous the climate was:

> Perhaps it is from having been so long ill, that I value so much the constant feeling of health which this climate produces. . . .
>
>   But fine health is general in old and young. In dozens at Canterbury I was astonished at the change from their state at home. It was very marked in some ladies who appeared ten years younger than when I parted from them in London. All the Creole children are plump and ruddy when not suffering from some particular complaint.[28]

The health-giving properties of the colony were reserved for its new immigrants. Reverend Morgan was very concerned about "scrofula and other diseases," amongst Maori,[29] and James Stack believed "the natives may be fairly considered a diseased people."[30] For Maori, the land was to be the site of their eventual extinction. The Reverend Williams predicted, "The Decreasing state of the Natives is truly distressing and appears to threaten their total extinction within a given period of years as the Deaths far exceed the births. The fact is too evident to admit doubt."[31] The following report from Samuel Ford (in what he describes as his "peculiar capacity" as medical missionary) stated: "The prospect of mortality is so rapid that unless there be some signal interposition of the hand of Providence in arresting its course, it amounts almost to a certainty that before many years can have expired they will be expunged from the scale of nations and will be merely regarded as a matter of history as the original inhabitants of New Zealand."[32]

  The immigration of European inhabitants to New Zealand was characterized by uneasy, sometimes violent periodic confrontations occurring simultaneously with the establishment of intimate relations (sexual, platonic, and familial) with Maori. What the missionaries and settlers may not have expected are the ways in which they would be altered by that encounter.[33] The distinctions between missionary, entrepreneur, and settler were often blurred; some of the arguments in support of colonization conflated establishing a colony with empire building. In 1848 James Fitzgerald wrote to W. E. Gladstone, "I hope you will see the directions are equally Imperial as Colonial."[34] Missionaries, sometimes with ambivalence and contrary to the policies of their parent organizations, were acquiring large tracts of land, ostensibly to protect the futures of their children.[35] They were acutely aware of a relationship between their missionary work and that of the colonists; George Selwyn (the first Anglican bishop of New Zealand) wrote in 1854 that "the cause of our country, is the cause of God, and we must be ready, each in his own calling, to spend and to be spent."[36]

While missionaries were trying to advance the civilization of Maori through Christian salvation, they also struggled with the acts of less spiritually minded expatriates who were introducing alcohol and card playing, and establishing public liaisons with Maori. For example, Edward Wakefield noted:

> The New Zealanders are not savages properly speaking, but a people capable of civilization. A main object will be to do all that can be done for inducing them to embrace the language, customs, religion, and social ties of the superior race. The missionaries have already done something towards this object—more than could have been expected considering that they have always been thwarted by English Settlers and visitors not under the restraint of any authority.[37]

Throughout settlement, the industries of colonial life—evangelical conversion of Natives, war, disciplining of land, domestication of labor, and the making and feeding of families—brought Maori and colonial subjects together. As part of this process, many of the missionaries and their family members became fluent in the Maori language; it was considered, by Protestant Christians, necessary for teaching the Bible, and some wrote texts in, and about, the language. There are also, in the archival materials, small uses of Maori, particularly by women settlers, that might reflect how life in the colony was changing them. Caroline Abraham wrote in a letter that "it was only when I got home and found the house empty that I had time for a *tangi* [to cry]";[38] Anne Wilson spoke of how she felt very *pouri* [sad], and how her child said, "Papa, *haere mai* [come here]."[39]

The blurring of racial lines might be seen not only in language usage and actual relationships but also in imagined ones. Take, for example, the suggestion from the captive stories of white women that "far from reinforc[ing] the idea that white women should fear Maori males, the attention given to these accounts in their own day suggests the fascination of European female readers, was not just with life on the frontier but with life within the *whare* [Maori house] and the question 'Would I not make a good Maori wife?' "[40] As Lady Eliza Grey once wrote in a letter to England from on board the *Elphinstone*, "Tell Jane I will not forget John Heke as a husband for her."[41]

Cumulatively, these narratives—the preferential access to Native rather than (convict) white women, fear of contamination from native women, native woman as mediator for white men, the blurring of rigid racializing systems, including language—demonstrate that unions between Native subjects and white immigrants were more than interpersonal interactions; they were public performances of race, gender, and sexuality that marked out the boundaries not only of difference but also of the channels within which certain normative practices might operate.

Early New Zealand culture was saturated with masculine and feminine distinctions in the construction and transmission of appropriate social behaviors.[42] Victorian Puritanism and nineteenth-century British industrialism provided the models for breaking in the new land and socializing a "new people."[43] The models were necessarily of an emergent middle class, allowing immigrant women the role of helpmate and indoor counterpart to the masculine pioneer. Through the export of a "domestic England," European women became fashioned as the guardians of (white, bourgeois) morality.[44] Similar to the situation in the Dutch Indies, white women's roles as "otherwise supporting players on the colonial stage [receded, they were] . . . charged with reshaping the face of colonial society, imposing their racial will on . . . a colonial world."[45] Early settler Anne Wilson writes of her frustration in this role in a New Zealand mission: "13 November 1835: Much confused this week with the native girls who have been uncommonly idle and saucy. The Lord give me that patience of which I have so much need to bear and forbear with them. Also prudence and judgment to guide them aright."[46]

The inculcation of Maori women into roles as domestic help was promulgated through the mission schools, and schools established specifically for half-castes.[47] Not only were schools the site in which young Maori and half-caste girls were taught English, and to read and write, it was where they were trained to become servants.[48] These intentions are exemplified by the reflections of Miss Freda Lily Sharp, a teacher at Rakaumanga Native School, Huntly:

> [T]he status of the Maori girl becomes increasingly important. She is the wife and mother of the future generation; she is going to be responsible for the perpetuation of the Maori people as a race; on her influence will be molded the characters and habits of men and women who will be future citizens of our state. Above all, the girls must be equipped with a sound set of morals, a distinct notion of what is right and what is wrong, habits of cleanliness which will become part of their make-up, and a good basic knowledge of cooking and how to run a house economically, intelligently and hygienically.[49]

This kind of domestic training, or what Ann Stoler refers to as a "habit of the heart," is a means by which children of mixed-race unions were also to be cultivated into a particular kind of morality through labor. The need to do so was based on a theory of race in which there is an assumed superiority of one over others, a theory that certainly appeared in New Zealand's archives: "It was however evident, for past experience had proved it, that the Anglo Maori children could not occupy a medium state between the European and Maoris; they must either sink to the Maori level, or rise to that of Europeans. Our first duty and object therefore was to endeavour to raise them to the European Standard."[50]

In early colonial New Zealand perceptions of mixed-race relationships, and miscegenation in general, appeared relatively benign (in theory, if not always in practice).[51] Examples from archival sources include:

> Mr Nicholas and his wife a most lovely and interesting creature with six interesting children half castes visits the Govr and brings a peace offering of Bread, Butter, Milk, Eggs.[52]

> The half-caste children are a fine intelligent and promising race.[53]

> 7th Jan. 1852 Performed a marriage between an English man and a half-caste girl in the service of Mrs. McKain.[54]

In 1859 the Rev. John Morgan cautioned:

> The education of the Anglo/Maori race is most important. They are generally speaking Grandchildren of leading chiefs and if their education is now neglected and they are suffered to grow up in ignorance amongst the Maori population, they may prove injurious to the

Aborigines, and troublesome to the Government and the Colony, but if on the contrary they are now educated watched over and trained in the habit of religion and honest industry, they will generally speaking marry amongst themselves, or with respectable English squatters and settle down on land given to them by their Maori relatives, and prove we may reasonably open a great blessing to the Colony, and a band of union between the European and Maori population.[55]

Through war, intermarriage, formal education in the missions and schools, and domestic and intimate labor, the bodies of Maori women literally became contact zones. As Rosa Linda Fregoso argues, "we are ultimately left with the deep realization that "contact zones"—zones of crossings and mixings—are not simply linguistic, cultural, and social, but sexual as well."[56] The half-caste product of encounters in those contact zones is invented not only as a savage but as a queer savage.[57] Because of Maori women's textual and physical existence in the liminal spaces of domestic worker, linguist, mother of mixed-race children, wife to European men, object of sexual colonial fantasy, and reproducer of the nation, she embodied a queered threshold, and the source of racially queered offspring.

The mixed-race child embodied evidence both of the unruly practice of imperial order on the colonial ground and of the possibilities on the edges of a previously unquestioned natural order. They bore in their flesh the double bind of a taint that also guaranteed access to resources. They were living proof of a sexual imaginary that could accommodate race through class. As such they represented a possibility for reconciliation that, at the same time, obscured the violence of acquisition. This new caste, the half-caste, was a necessary contradiction in the colony, demonstrating both the need for racial purity and an inherent degeneration in a system of superior races. The degeneration might be excused by distance from the metropole, the environment, individual weakness of faith, and immorality of Indigenous women, but it also proved, in its very disappearance, the necessity for the preservation of a racialized class not contaminated by the inconvenient bodies that inhabited the new colonial outpost.

This chapter is more a proposition than a conclusion. It is a geographically and historically specific examination of the problematic of the "half-caste" in colonial New Zealand. Queer and/or Indigenous perspectives facilitate an interrogation of archival texts illustrating the racializing, sexualizing, and gendering of particular bodies symbolically—as a potential 'band of union' between two races—and literally—as the point of transfer for resources such as land and labor. This is not to claim that all mixed-race subjects were, or are, inherently queer, but to suggest that, by their very existence, those subjects demonstrated an excess of desire that could not be contained within the (hetero)normative category of race.

Notes

1. Translated into English, *Aotearoa* literally means "land of the long white cloud"; it is the Maori name for New Zealand.

2. A pan-tribal term for the Indigenous inhabitants of New Zealand.

3. A process Edward Said describes when he states, "Something patently foreign and distant acquires . . . a status more rather than less familiar . . . allow[ing] one to see new things, things seen for the first time, as versions of a previously known thing," in *Orientalism* (London: Routledge and Kegan Paul, 1978), 58.

4. Samuel Enderby & Son et al., letter to Col. Nicolls, Royal Marines, 16 September, 1823, relating to whale fishery, *The Huskisson Papers: Correspondence, January–September 1823*, vol. 112, Add. 38744, f314, British Library.

5. Piya Chatterjee, *A Time for Tea: Women, Labor, and Post/Colonial Politics on an Indian Plantation* (Durham, NC: Duke University Press, 2001), 4 and 189.

6. Alicia Arrizón, *Queering Mestizaje: Transculturation and Performance* (Ann Arbor: University of Michigan Press, 2006), 14.

7. Angela Y. Davis and Neferti X. M. Tadiar, eds., *Beyond the Frame: Women of Color and Visual Representation* (New York: Palgrave Macmillan, 2005), 5.

8. Gloria Anzaldúa, *Borderlands/La Frontera: The New Mestiza* (San Francisco: Aunt Lute Press, 1987).

9. Trevor Bentley, *Captured by Maori: White Female Captives, Sex and Racism on the Nineteenth-Century New Zealand Frontier* (Auckland: Penguin Books, 2004).

10. Mary Louise Pratt *Imperial Eyes: Travel Writing and Transculturation* (London: Routledge, 1992), 6.

11. Greg Dening, *Islands and Beaches: Discourse on a Silent Land: Marquesas 1774–1880* (Chicago: Dorsey Press, 1980).

12. Jolisa Gracewood, "Sometimes a Great Ocean: Thinking the Pacific from Nowhere to Now & Here," *Hitting Critical Mass: A Journal of Asian American Cultural Criticism* 5, no. 1 (1998): 1.

13. *Wahine* is the word for "woman" in a number of Polynesian languages, including Maori.

14. Teresia Teaiwa, "Reading Paul Gauguin's *Noa Noa* with Epeli Hau'ofa's *Kisses in the Nederends*: Militourism, Feminism and the "Polynesian" Body," in

Inside Out: Literature, Cultural Politics, and Identity in the New Pacific, ed. Vilsoni Hereniko and Rob Wilson (Lanham, MD: Rowman and Littlefield, 1999), 254.

15. Neferti Tadiar, "Manila's New Metropolitan Form," *difference: A Journal of Feminist Cultural Studies* 5, no. 3 (1993): 186, 198.

16. James Belich, *Making Peoples: A History of New Zealanders* (Wellington: Allen Lane/ Penguin Press, 1996), 186.

17. Captain James Cook, *Account of New Zealand from Cook's First Voyage, 1769*, Add. 27889 20, British Library.

18. Anne Salmond, *The Trial of the Cannibal Dog: Captain Cook in the Southern Seas* (Auckland: Penguin Books, 2003), 49.

19. Ibid.

20. Dorothy Black, *Early New Zealand Women of Note 1950*, fl 1947–1959?, qMS-0235, 3, Alexander Turnbull Library.

21. The name whalers gave to venereal disease (James Belich, *Making Peoples: A History of New Zealanders* [Wellington: Allen Lane/Penguin Press, 1996], 175).

22. Bentley, *Captured by Maori*, 93.

23. Philip Tapsell, *Reminiscences, Reminiscences 1779–1869*, 1777?–1873, qMS-1980, 91, Alexander Turnbull Library.

24. Alfred Nesbit Brown, *Transcript of the Rev. A. N. Brown's Journal; 1835–1846*, qMS-0277, 35, Alexander Turnbull Library.

25. Samuel Marsden "Parramatta, 30 January, 1801," *Incoming Correspondence*, CWM: Australia, Box 1, Folder 1, Jacket C, 6, Church Missionary Society Archives.

26. Mrs. Henry Coote (née Rhoda Carleton Holmes), *Extract from Diary of Mrs. Coote, 1853*, Papers 1853–1867, MS-Papers-1248/2, 10, Alexander Turnbull Library.

27. Sarah Louisa Mathew, *Extracts from Diary (Autobiography) of Mrs. Felton Mathew*, qMS-1350, 26, Alexander Turnbull Library.

28. E. G. Wakefield, *New Zealand: Correspondence Mainly Relating to 1815–1853*, Add. 35261, 27, British Library.

29. Rev. John Morgan, "Present State of the Natives and Plans for Their Future Improvement etc., Otawhao, 1849," *CMS Papers* C N/O O 65/1–121/109–113/113, 9, Church Missionary Society Archives.

30. James Stack, letter to Rev. W. Jowett, Church Missionary Society, London, February 16, 1841, *CMS Papers* C N/O O 78/1–27/1–17/10, 2, Church Missionary Society Archives.

31. Rev. Henry Williams, correspondence and notes regarding Maori allies, Paihia, May 1, 1847, *CMS Papers*, C N/O/93/1–231/140, 5, Church Missionary Society Archives.

32. Samuel Hayward Ford, "Report by Samuel Hayward Ford to the Committee from the Time of His Arrival Aug 22/37 to February 1838," *CMS Papers*, C N/O O 41/1–12/10, 1, Church Missionary Society Archives.

33. Matthew Wright suggests, ". . . to some extent the Maori converted the missionaries sent to New Zealand, rather than the other way around. Both [Thomas] Kendall and William Yate found sexual partners among Maori, and Kendall was apparently tempted by Maori beliefs almost to the point of abandoning Christianity," in *Illustrated History of New Zealand* (Auckland: Reed, 2004), 36.

34. James Edward Fitzgerald, letter to W. E. Gladstone, Sept. 13, 1864, *The Gladstone Papers*, vol. 318, Add. 44403, f250, 253, British Library.

35. Rev. Richard Davis, letter to Captain Hobson, Governor, Waimate, Feb. 1, 1842, *CMS Papers* C N/O O 36/1–40/26, 1, Church Missionary Society Archives; Rev. W. Jowett, "Church Missionary Society, London, February 16th, 1841," *CMS Papers*, C N/O O 78/1–27/1–17/10, 1, Church Missionary Society Archives; and Edward Wakefield, letter, March 7, 1845, *The Peel Papers: General Correspondence*, vol. 382, Add. 40562, ff 72–77b, 74, British Library.

36. George Augustus Selwyn, letter to Mrs. W. E. Gladstone, *Mary Gladstone Papers*, vol. 9, Add. 46227, 83, British Library.

37. E. G. Wakefield, *New Zealand: Correspondence Mainly Relating to 1815–1853*, Add. 35261, 9, British Library.

38. Caroline Harriet Abraham (née Palmer), *Correspondence, 1850–1870*, MS-Papers-2305 (Inward Letters) Two, 8.

39. M. G. Armstrong, *My Hand Will Write What My Heart Dictates: The Letters and Journal of Anne Catherine Wilson (1802–1838), Missionary Wife in New Zealand*, MS Papers, 3943–2, 64 and 65, Alexander Turnbull Library.

40. Bentley, *Captured by Maori*, 19.

41. Lady Eliza Lucy Grey, *Letters, 1845–1850*, MS-Papers-0860, 1, Alexander Turnbull Library. John (Hone) Heke was a notorious leader of Maori resistance struggles in the north of the North Island.

42. Beverly James and Kay Saville-Smith, *Gender, Culture and Power* (Auckland: Oxford University Press, 1989).

43. Jacqui True, "Fit Citizens for the British Empire? Classifying Racial and Gendered Subjects in 'Godzone' New Zealand," in *Women out of Place: The Gender of Agency and the Race of Nationality*, ed. Brackette F. Williams (New York: Routledge, 1996), 105.

44. David Morley, *Home Territories: Media, Mobility and Identity* (New York: Routledge, 2000), 55.

45. Ann Laura Stoler, *Carnal Knowledge and Imperial Power: Race and the Intimate in Colonial Rule* (Berkeley: University of California Press, 2002).

46. Max G. Armstrong, *Letters and Journal of Anne Catherine Wilson/collected, ed. and transcribed by M G Armstrong, 1832–1838*, 1984, fl 1984–1996, MS-Papers-3943–1, 7, Alexander Turnbull Library.

47. Rev. John Morgan, letter to Messrs. Martin, Sinclair & Ligar, Government Inspectors of Schools—Auckland, Otawhao, Oct. 20, 1859, *CMS Papers* C N/O O 65/1–121/1–95/56, Church Missionary Society Archives.

48. For example, "We now employ much of the time of the elder girls in washing, and all of them do needlework which brings in some support for the School. . . ." (Mrs. Margaret Kissling, letter to Mr. Venn, C.M.S., May 23, 1850, *CMS Papers,* C N/O 56/1–103/37, 1, Church Missionary Society Archives).

49. Freda Lily Sharp, *Report on personal observations and impressions regarding Education of Maori Girls in the Native Services of New Zealand* 1938, qMS-1795, 2, Alexander Turnbull Library.

50. Rev. John Morgan, letter to Messrs. Martin, Sinclair & Ligar, Government Inspectors of Schools—Auckland, Otawhao, Oct. 20, 1859, *CMS Papers,* C N/O O 65/1–121/1–95/56, Church Missionary Society Archives.

51. Ann Stoler, *Race and the Education of Desire* (Durham, NC: Duke University Press, 1995), 27.

52. Cuthbert Clarke, *Sketches of New Zealand and Diary: 1849–1850* Presented by Sir George Grey, 1854, Add. 19955, 5, British Library.

53. Rev. John Morgan, letter to Messrs. Martin, Sinclair & Ligar, Government Inspectors of Schools—Auckland, Otawhao, Oct. 20, 1859, *CMS Papers,* C N/O O 65/1–121/1–95/56, Church Missionary Society Archives.

54. Muriel Mavis Aitcheson, *We in Our Corner: A Brief History of the Lewis-McKain-Torr Family,* MS-Papers-1353, 39, Alexander Turnbull Library.

55. Rev. John Morgan, letter to Messrs. Martin, Sinclair & Ligar, Government Inspectors of Schools—Auckland, Otawhao, Oct. 20, 1859, *CMS Papers,* C N/O O 65/1–121/1–95/56, 132, Church Missionary Society Archives.

56. Rosa Linda Fregoso, *meXicana Encounters: The Making of Social Identities on the Borderlands* (Berkeley: University of California Press, 2003), 62.

57. I'm thinking here of Luana Ross's important work on the social construction of Native American criminality, in *Inventing the Savage* (Austin: University of Texas Press, 1998).

4
Fa'afafine Notes
On Tagaloa, Jesus, and Nafanua
Dan Taulapapa McMullin

1. I am a mixed-blood Samoan painter and poet and *fa'afafine*. These notes are from wandering memory, and I send them to the dead, to Fa'asapa and Fa'amanu, with my love, my *alofa. Tulou, tulou, tulou lava . . .*

2. The procedure being a separation of the prefix *fa'a*, meaning to cause or to be alike, and *fafine*, meaning woman. The overall being the position fafine and the action fa'a, and the position fa'a and the action fafine.

3. When I was a small boy in the Samoa Islands, my great-grandmother Fa'asapa showed me how to print and paint *siapo* cloth, which was women's work. I walked on her strong thin legs to massage them while she told me of this and that. There is an anthropology tale that I often see told as though it were a matter of fact or research, that Samoan families without daughters choose one of their boy children to become fa'afafine for the expected duties. I have sisters and I wasn't aware of being chosen to fulfill a role. I wanted to hang out with my great-grandmother and make siapo paintings, and iron clothes smooth with the flat iron from its small brazier of coals, and after stories sleep under her mosquito net in its halo of light from the kerosene lamp. That was my desire and choice, and she and my family in Samoa supported my will to be. The naming of *fa'afafine* accompanies the event of the person.

4. "*O loto ma agaga ma finagalo ma masalo ina o ane, ia fa'atasi i totonu o le Tagata; ona fa'atasi ane ai lea, o le mea lea ua atamai ai tagata. Na fa'atasi ane ma le 'Ele-'ele ua igoa ai ia Fatu-ma-le-'Ele-'ele, o le uluga aiga, o Fatu le tane, o 'Ele-'ele le fafine.*" In this *tala* chiefly narrative of the creation, from the chiefs of 'Upolu, we see the human being *Tagata* (pronounced tah-NGAH-tah), blessed by the deity Tagaloa with *loto/* heart, *agaga/*spirit, *finagalo/*will, and *masalo/*thought. The combination leading to *atamai/*wisdom. Atamai, the ability to receive and cast all *ata*,

all shadows, reflections, images of this world, with understanding and ability. This gives the Tagata life itself. Tagata is joined in two, *Fatu-ma-le-'Ele'ele*, Fatu the tane, and 'Ele'ele the fafine. It is their relationship as a couple forming a family, an *uluga aiga*, that determines who they are. Without relationship there is no identity. Thus begins almost every Samoan narrative, relationships determining names. Similarly, in many fagogo (fah-NGOH-ngoh) village stories, all the siblings of a family will have the same name, until a turning point leads to individual naming.

5. *Missionary News*, October 1, 1867: "Asking parishioners of all means to pray for the perishing souls of the heathen, and holding, as did a church in Edinburgh in 1844, 'great missionary' meetings in which three thousand children gathered in a hall decked with idols suspended from the roof."[1] So that's where the goddesses and gods went. Or where they cast their ata. Into the fire of Europe. While their souls fled where?

6. When we moved from the U.S. Territory of American Samoa (Eastern Samoa) to the United States of America, my U.S. Army drill sergeant father made my mother sit with me in the backseat of our family station wagon telling me to act like a boy because we were not in Samoa anymore. I had trouble knowing how she meant; I wasn't sure how I was not acting like a boy. I think she thought she was protecting me. I know many fa'afafine in the United States, in fact the majority of fa'afafine immigrants here, who as children lived like girls in Samoa, as adults live like men in America. We forget our Samoan; language is memory and we forget ourselves a little.

7. The London Missionary Society brought Christianity to the Samoa Islands. There may be a mistaken belief that Christianity came to the islands through a process of guilt and sin, rather than by force and power. In a Suva, Fiji, newspaper article fifty years after the advent of white Christian missionaries in the South Pacific, "South Sea Spiritism," April 10, 1882 (as reprinted in the *New York Times*): "It is not in independent nature, whether savage or civilized, to endure this process of leveling and delimitation, and were it not for English war ships and occasional displays of naval force, few missionaries or traders in these archipelagoes would lay them down at night with untroubled minds. The gunboats of Great Britain are constantly engaged in police service throughout these

seas, prowling from place to place, appearing unexpectedly here and there, and often being called upon to make a demonstration of force in order to keep the natives on their good behavior. Fiji, the Navigators [Samoa], and other groups have for a long time been reasonably quiet, or at least—as about Apia—have indulged only in tribal conflicts and family feuds; but the leaven of barbarism still remains everywhere, and if British guns were withdrawn both mission stations and trade factories would no long survive." Gunboats, leveling, and delimitation indeed. Here we see the violence that followed the peaceful introduction of Christianity by European and American missionaries among the Pacific Islanders. The guns of Europe and America supported them against "the leaven of barbarism." For as it is written in First Corinthians 5:7, "Purge out therefore the old leaven, that ye may be a new lump . . ."

8. One evening, at the end of a jaunt around the island of Savai'i with some fa'afafine friends, recuperating while having dinner at a beach rental, our landlady, who was a *lo'omatua*, an old woman, waggling her long forefinger under my nose, said to me, "You're loose like an old woman." Me, a *lo'omatua*.

9. From *Efeso*/Ephesians 4:11: "*O isi fo'i e fai ma leoleo atoa.*" *Leoleo* in the Samoan translation of the Bible, in the English translation *pastor*. Leoleo means also *police,* as in the similarity between pastoral shepherds and police. "On behalf of himself and the other missionaries living in the islands, Mr. [Rev. Ebenezer] Cooper [of the London Missionary Society] says he wishes to express his joy at the new order of things, and to express his tribute to the good work that the United States has done and is doing in civilizing the islanders and helping the missionaries to more productive labors by establishing a just, firm and stable government where none such had existed before" ("Commander Tilley Praised," *New York Times* August 3, 1900).

10. When I was a young man and started going back to Samoa for vacations, I met my cousin Sheree, again. When we were kids she was Jerry. As an adult she is Sheree. At church, she dresses all in white: long white dress, billowy white blouse, large and shady white hat with white lace, white heels, and a white woven fan. There was a recent movement among fundamentalists in Samoa, influenced by televangelism, to force fa'afafine to dress as men in church. But today fa'afafine still dress as

women at church services, and at the workplace, and in the classroom, and in the home with the family, and at important social functions.

11. There was a series of articles recently in the *Samoa News* out of Apia, following a group of born-again Christian Samoans from Hawaii who went through the islands of Samoa casting out demons (staff reporter, "God vs Tagaloa: Who Is the Real God?" Sunday, March 8, 2009: "Miloali'i Si'ilata is the Coordinator of the All Pacific Prayer Assembly (APPA). He led a delegation of Christians to Manu'a last year to try and rid those small islands of evil spirits.[2] He is the leader of a group called the Pacific Team of Prayer Warriors, "for the glory of God from the Pacific into the USA . . . the Lord told us to go up through American Samoa and claim it since it is a Territory of the USA. We returned home via American [Eastern] Samoa, where I was told that the Head of State for [Western] Samoa, Tui Atua Tupua Tamasese Efi was in American Samoa during the 10th Pacific Arts Festival, promoting his book, which claims that the old gods of Samoa are different manifestations of the God of the Bible. Like most Christians in Samoa, I was very disappointed about this. Tagaloa [pronounced tah-ngah-LOH-ah, the god of the sun, the sky, the sea] is NOT the God of the Bible! Tagaloa was the main Principality and fallen angel in charge of the Polynesian race and people. Tagaloa is still being worshipped in Polynesia today by a few who call themselves Tagaloanians. . . . Since the launching of the new season of Celestial Wars in the Pacific in 2000, Tagaloa was definitely leading all the armies of Satan against the angelic armies of God. . . . Celesex between fallen angels and human beings is not new. The practice is one of the forbidden sexual practices in the Bible including homosexuality, bestiality, adultery, fornication and incest. . . . The Penis as an instrument to infiltrate the Adamic Race. . . . Tagaloa was normally worshipped through his incarnate royal prodigies and through carvings with phallic objects . . ."

12. And again in another article in the quite long series, the diary continues: "Cutting the Root of Tagaloa from Manu'a," Monday 4–Tuesday 5 August 2008: "I had the privilege to lead a team of 7 for this Manu'a mission. . . . I then stuck a '*fue*' (fly whisk [a symbol of chiefly authority, as with the Africans and ancient Greeks]) in the ground to represent the phallic penis, root and authority of Tagaloa in Polynesia. Then with a knife I cut the fue in the Name of Jesus the Captain of the Armies of the

Living God. To cleanse the land, I dug a hole and poured in red wine representing the blood of Jesus. . . . We then danced and praised the Lord on the beach facing east until sunrise at 6:30 a.m. We concluded our mission with the old Samoan hymns. . . . I have said all that I have been commanded to say . . ." And so the work of the missionaries continues in us and through us.

13. Once, having moved to a village far from any of my relations, I met my first male lover in Samoa, F. I was renting an apartment from a friend who had a store next door. The first night I saw my lover, he walked in the store wearing just an 'ie lavalava cinched tight at his narrow waist, his body shiny with coconut oil scenting his broad shoulders and his curly hair. For a week after work in his mechanic overalls, he came every day to the store to talk in Samoan to my friend while ignoring me. I was done with him. Sunday afternoon I heard him drumming his fingers along the wall to my door. I opened to see. There he stood while the village slept. "The store is closed," I reminded him. "Do you have a secret place?" he asked. Oh, so he did speak English. "No," I said. He repeated himself as though I misheard him, with, "I said, do you have a cigarette?" Secret place, cigarette, oh gawd. "No," I pouted. He stared, didn't say another word. I stared back. Then turned around and walked to my bed leaving the door open. Having grown up in an Americanized Samoan family, I was quiet to the village knowing. My friend next door had a first-year birthday party for her son, and the women of the village were there. I couldn't have been more nervous being now the lover of a young man from their village. As I entered the party an old woman did a little dance waving a banana slowly in my face, the other women laughed in good humor, and I was put at ease. The homophobia of my Americanized family faded into distance.

14. In Samoa, a fafine is a woman, a *tane* is a man or husband, and a fa'afafine is a man who lives as a woman. In the English Bible, Leviticus 18:22, it is written, "Thou shalt not lie down with mankind, as with womankind; it is an abomination." In the Samoan *Tusi Pa'ia, Levitiko* 18:22, it is written, "*Aua lua te momoe ma se tane, e pei ona momoe ma se fafine; o le mea e inosia lava lea.*" Thus it is written that a tane cannot sleep with a tane, but it is not written that a tane cannot sleep with a fa'afafine. Elsewhere, where the English Bible law references effeminate men, the Samoan Tusi Pa'ia references, oddly, not fa'afafine

but *tauatane* or homosexuality among tane, again. Then it references *fa'asotoma*, sodomites, a multicultural multilingual conundrum. In reference to the prohibition in Deuteronomy/*Teuteronome* against cross-dressing, the law again pertains to fafine and tane, but not to *fa'afatama* (FTM) or fa'afafine. Samoan-Japanese fa'afafine artist Shigeyuki Kihara tells me that the name fa'afafine originated in the nineteenth century. Were fa'afafine simply known as fafine before then?

15. I remember going to the beach in a small bus with a group of fa'afafine friends around Christmastime, the drunken hired driver careening down the narrow sandy road hitting the branches of the rain forest, as everyone laughing sang Samoan hymns changing words by improvisation, using puns for the body and its functions. . . . I was talking with a Tongan scholar, who told me about a conversation he had with Samoan writer Albert Wendt: that before Christianity came to the South Pacific islands, curses were always directed at the other's family. After Christianity curses were directed at the other's body. In other words, words like *fuck, shit, dick, cunt, bitch, whore*, etc., the normalized or naturalized curse words of our present-day cursing vocabulary, have to do with the parts, functions and actions of one's individual body. Before Christianity, in our old Polynesian polytheism, curse words had to do with the family, the collective body. The exception would be the body that can be cannibalized, the body as food object, although this may be post-Christian too. It would have been absurd in the old days to curse the other's sexual and gendered body.

16. I was in Apia, Samoa, about to visit the village of Ta'u in Manu'a. A friend suggested I stay with his mother Fa'amanu in Ta'u, which I did. Fa'amanu in the evening liked to sit with her small granddaughter in her family meeting house, a lovely round building without walls, just white pillars. Fa'amanu was the local expert in the weaving of 'ie toga, or Samoan fine mats. Her practice involved walking around the village helping and encouraging younger women in their weaving. Fa'amanu's inner forearms were scarred with diagonal lines from the sharp pandanus leaves used in weaving. Every evening during my stay, Fa'amanu and her little granddaughter and I took a stroll round the village of Ta'u, talking with the neighbors. Some of the women neighbors had a very friendly relationship with her, some pointedly ignored her, and some

of the men seemed to have intimate friendships with her too. When I returned to Apia, a friend asked me who I stayed with in Ta'u, and I said, "Our friend's mother, Fa'amanu." At which she remarked, "His mother? His parents died when he was young; he was brought up by a fa'afafine." Fa'amanu wanted me to learn how to make fine mats, and I said I would come back. She said, "Don't wait too long, our time is short." A couple years later she was gone. I hadn't returned in time to visit this fa'afafine elder or learn her craft.

17. There are many notable fa'afafine with traditional *suafa* or chiefly titles, like the choreographer Seiuli Ailani Alo (A *Seiuli* title was given to him by the late head of state of Samoa, His Highness Malietoa Tanumafili II). American anthropologist Jeannette Mageo (married to a Samoan) writes, "In Samoa important titles are normally given to brothers, but sisters may hold titles, and this is no disgrace. Homosexuals may also hold titles. Fa'afafine, however, are seen as jesters, and families will not invest their status and dignity to them. To become a transvestite is, therefore, seriously to compromise one's opportunities for status."[3] In addition to being simply wrong on the issue of fa'afafine and suafa/titles, Mageo uses *homosexual* and *transvestite* as though these English words were cognate in the *fa'asamoa*, Samoan language and culture; and she seems to conflate fa'afafine and *faleaitu*, the Samoan theatrical form in which male jesters will imitate fa'afafine and anyone else at hand. Mageo's writings are filled with such fa'afafinephobic conjectures, although as an anthropologist she is considered the western expert on fa'afafine and Samoan gender.

18. "... and, as we have seen, her later devotion to the missionary stations in Samoa demonstrate, Stevenson's mother tirelessly supported the foreign and domestic missions of the Church of Scotland as well as the efforts of other denominations."[4] Robert Louis Stevenson, the Scots author of *Treasure Island* and other favorites, dying and in ill health, spent his last years in Samoa, which he loved, building a home at Vailima on the hill above Apia. There is a mysterious romantic passage in his travel book *South Seas* where a young islander man follows him into the forest, and he is given a magic box, inside of which is a smaller copy of the magic box, its source of power. At tea in Apia once, *M* told me that at Vailima, where she herself grew up, Stevenson kept a house in back where he would meet boys.

19. A New Zealand critical thinker on fa'afafine and Pacific Islands gender, Lee Wallace of Auckland University, writes: "In contradistinction to the impulse to see sin and homosexuality everywhere, the gender-inversion understanding of fa'afafine that the documentary [*Queens of Samoa*] elaborates preserves the heterosexuality of desire: only opposites attract, as if difference were the engine of desire. The documentary, which seems to be a relaxed or liberal account of how anything goes genderwise, mobilizes an inversion model of sexual identity ("a woman's soul in a man's body") in what Judith Butler, writing of drag, calls 'the service of both the denaturalization and reidealization of hyperbolic gender norms.'"[5] Wallace seems to assume a viewpoint among fa'afafine that the European Australian filmmakers held and avoids Samoan sexuality, using English-language terms of gender like *homosexual, transgender,* and *transsexual,* while ignoring English terms of sexuality like *top, bottom, active,* and *passive,* while assuming that heteronormativity can explain fa'afafine positionality in relation to tane and fafine. She goes on to warn that if fa'afafine don't take on western gender and sexuality terminology, we will be more susceptible to AIDS. This reminds one of nineteenth-century European/American missionaries who told Pacific Islanders that the cure for western diseases was western religion.

20. Midnight Mass, Christmas Eve, the Catholic cathedral in Tafuna, Tutuila Island, American Samoa. Invited by my Aunt *L* and her daughters, my cousins with white lace covering their hair. Outside the church, a group of ancient white Catholic bishops paraded in procession, bent bodies in elaborate robes. They were preceded and followed by about forty Samoan boys in scant *'ie lavalava* wrapped around their waists, and nothing else—barefoot, bodies covered in coconut oil, carrying tall candles. It was a Roman scene like the engravings of Aubrey Beardsley. During the service the white archbishop of the South Pacific spoke in Samoan with an aesthete voice; sounding and looking much like Peter Cook imitating the archbishop of Canterbury, he sermoned in a voice that was powdered and wrinkled.

21. "It followed, by London Missionary Society logic, that people who had undeveloped minds must also be undisciplined in their emotions. On two counts, then, it was feared that many Samoans might be incapable of cultivating the means of grace, being deficient in the powers of reason and self-control essential to a state of piety and morality. That is

not to say that the missionaries all responded by simplifying their theological discourses, but they did shift the emphasis of their role from that of teacher towards that of father or policeman, concerning themselves less with what the masses understood of Christianity and more with overt conduct."[6] For the church it was a question of development, but for the Samoans it was a realization that Christianity was greatly concerned with questions of the body. The peculiarities of Christian sexuality were new to Samoa.

22. Missionary text: "The greatest favourite was the Po-ula (night of play or pleasure). This was an obscene night dance, and a constant source of enjoyment, especially when any visitors were present to take part in it. As the evening set in, the spectators as well as dancers began to assemble, after much care had been bestowed upon their dresses and general make-up. The only covering of the males consisted of the *titi*, or girdle of leaves, often not more than seven or eight inches in width, and about the same in depth, whilst that of the females consisted of a white or red shaggy mat around the loins, the upper part of the body being uncovered. Both sexes paid great attention to their hair, that of the males being long and allowed to hang loosely over the shoulders, whilst the females, who wore their hair short, stiffened it with *pulu*, breadfruit pitch, or else dressed it with a pomade of a certain kind of light-coloured clay, which was afterwards washed off with lime water, thus dyeing the hair to a much-coveted brown colour. . . . The last dance . . . when this skilled dance concluded, the males who had danced exchanged girdles, and commenced a variety of antics and buffoonery which formed a prelude to the closing saturnalia, of which a description is inadmissible here, but which was always received with shouts of laughter and approval from the onlookers. Regrets are often expressed at the manner in which these obscene dances have been discouraged by the missionaries; but such sentiments can be uttered only in ignorance or oblivion of the true character of the dances and their tendency. Even as late as 1839, Commodore Wilkes spoke in terms of strong condemnation of these dances, as witnessed by some of the officers of the expedition; but what they saw would convey no correct idea of the dance as conducted by the Samoans during the times so aptly describes as 'the days of darkness.'"[7] It's recorded that as one went throughout the villages of Samoa, one instantly recognized the remaining Polynesian polytheistic villages, where the men had long hair and the women had short hair, and the

newly Christian monotheistic villages, where the women had long hair and the men had short hair. The image of the long-haired dusky maiden of the Pacific Islands is a Christian image.

23. I had a boyfriend, *M*, in Apia who would come home after work, throw off his clothes, and put on just a lavalava; he was beautiful. Then he'd cook dinner, fish soup with coconut milk. After dinner we'd sit on low rattan chairs across from each other at the low teak table, candles on the table lighting the room. He'd turn on Radio 2AP, the traditional Samoan music station, and dance a *siva nofo*, sitting dance, to me. He'd teach me the movements of the *taupou*, girl chief. He'd make the movements of the *manaia*, boy chief. His hand movements would end up caressing his erection. Pull me in and push me away with his gestures. Push pull, push pull. Back and forth. And I'd respond in my dance. But we didn't touch each other all evening. Then at some undetermined point, we'd break the tension and rush to the next room to our bed under a mosquito net. One day my neighbor told me she and her girl-friend would sit at the far end of her orchid garden in the dark, smoke a number, sip their wine, and watch my beautiful boyfriend, through my lanai screens, dance in the night. And I discovered he knew they were watching. This was our village *poula*.

24. The poula was a vaudeville, a bacchanalia, a dance party. *Po* means "night," where the poula activities utilized the open-air *fale* house lit by a *sulusulu* candlenut flame, and the landscape lit by the moon and *'Aniva* the Milky Way, brighter in Samoa mid-sea than anywhere I know. The poula is a night dance; *ula* is an old word referring to dance throughout Polynesia, as in the *hura* of the Cook Islands and the *hula* of the Hawaiian Islands. In Samoa it has the sense of laughter or joy, echoed in *'ula*, or lei garland, and *'ula*, or crimson, golden, and joyous. But for the monotheists night was heathen, the time of the *pou-liuli*, po/night, uli/black, the darkest times before Eurocentric monotheism. Here, I supplant "western" with "Eurocentric," because for us the West is sacred, the place of Havaiki, of Pulotu, of the blessed; and Europe/America is east of the Pacific. And I supplant "Christianity" with "monotheism," because it is overdetermined and seeks to elide polytheism by the sheer weight of the monolith of its centrality, a cen-trality that is located in its singleness of deity, but whose deity is as variable as anything. The representation of this deity, the missionary,

points upward to heaven and downward to hell, like a royal figure on a playing card, and disappears in either direction. If only among the trees at night, the night of our poula, our pouliuli, our polytheistic day. Like Stevenson and like Mead.

25. Margaret Mead, when she first came to Samoa, stayed as a lodger with my aunt Helen in Leone on my father's side. Mead and Aunty Helen didn't like each other. My aunt didn't like Mead asking her children so many questions and complaining about the rent. Aunty Helen's daughter, my aunt Tutasi, remembers collecting shells at a penny each for Mead, who threw them behind her dresser, making a stink. Later Mead went to Manu'a, where my mother's family was, and there Margaret Mead did her studies of young Samoan girls for her book *Coming of Age in Samoa*, in the village of Ta'u, but this time she questioned them on the porch of the navy dispensary. The first time I stayed in Ta'u, I took an early-morning walk on the beach when I arrived. There was a guy fishing. When he saw me getting near, he signaled and a young man and woman tangled in the beach vines stood and walked casually in opposite directions, the young woman pulling leaves out of her hair, yanking up her blouse. I thought of Mead. Her text is in a way a Christian account from another kind of missionary supported by gunboats, with a nerdy love for the poula of life in Samoa.

26. The leader of the anti–homosexual marriage movement in Hawai'i is a Samoan politician named Mike Gabbard, whose sister and son and niece are gay, so they rumor. "Domestic partnership is just another name for same-sex marriage," said Gabbard, who founded Stop Promoting Homosexuality International. Gabbard opposed the state law that prohibits discrimination of gays in employment. "Special rights should not be given on the basis of sexual orientation and behavior," he said. In 1997, as the president of Alliance for Traditional Marriage, he organized a day-long seminar titled "Hope for the Homosexual," with speakers from the Exodus Foundation, a ministry that claims to cure homosexuality.

27. When I last lived in Apia, my fa'afafine friends called me Miss America, because of my American accent. One day someone saw me coming out of the only McDonald's in Samoa, where none of my friends would eat (terrible food, high prices, tourist crowd), so they began calling

me Cookie Monster. I suppose it's better than being called an ex-homo-sexual. A rose by any other name is a rose is a rose is a rose.

28. The Samoan leader of the antigay movement in New Zealand, Taito Phillip Field was interviewed about gay marriage there: "*INVES-TIGATE:* So your opposition to Labour's whipping on the Marriage Bill, was that the first inkling of trouble? *FIELD:* No, there was always tension in regard to my opposition to homosexual rights, in terms of the civil union proposal. Because again in caucus, I insisted it should be a con-science vote. The argument from some in caucus was that it should not be a conscience vote because it was Labour Party policy in terms of sex-ual orientation. I didn't feel that that was right and I spoke out against it. Some of the older members indicated it was wiser to give members the right to a conscience vote, but clearly the tensions were there. So there were tensions well before all this broke. *INVESTIGATE:* It wasn't just you in the Labour caucus opposed to some of these issues. Paint me a picture about what life was like for you inside. *FIELD:* Oh, clearly there were a number of us that had Christian values, and therefore we fell in opposition to some of the views and agendas that certain people in caucus had, particularly in regard to moral issues. There's no question about that." Field was subsequently voted out of office and replaced by a Samoan Labour candidate, and recently Field was convicted of brib-ery and corruption charges based on actions in office, his moral values intact, I guess.

29. Whereas the older churches in Samoa have reconciled Samoan traditions with Eurocentric monotheism, the new fundamentalists are seeking to reinstate Eurocentrism in Samoa, and elsewhere, by attack-ing traditional Indigenous queer cultures. "Fa'afafine mere existence and morality has been challenged by a strong force in Samoa, the new Churches in Samoa. The message that homosexuality and gays in par-ticular are evil is the message being spread particularly through the new American evangelist churches that have sprung up in Samoa over the last 15 years."[8]

30. Televangelism from American cable television is now a part of Samoan culture. The Samoan television service Radio Graceland is "teaching the people of Samoa Christianity through the Graceland broad-casting network." They have been sponsored by Trinity Broadcasting

(Channel 40 from Santa Ana, California) in Samoa since 1997. After the establishment of Christian TV in Savai'i Island in Samoa, there was a case of two young women on the island who were lovers. The family of one of them, on discovering the relationship, beat their daughter badly and she ended up hanging herself. The other young woman, on learning of her lover's suicide, committed suicide herself by swallowing the poison Paraquat. After a brief mention in the newspaper, the issue was buried with the girls.

31. Nafanua was the greatest warrior of Samoan history. When she went to war, she disguised her gender by covering her chest. One day in battle her covering was torn off, and her sex was discovered. When she retired from fighting, she became an advocate of peaceful discourse and influenced the ways Samoans conduct politics in the *fono* communal meeting house for the *fa'amatai* system of decentralized governance and communal land ownership. After her death she was deified, made a goddess. As the goddess Nafanua she spoke to Samoa through talking chiefs on the island of Savai'i. Through these talking chiefs she predicted the coming of Christianity to Samoa, so the converts say.

32. A few years ago I was invited to go with Team Papua New Guinea, Team Fiji, Team Tonga, and Team Samoa to the Gay Games in Sydney. I went as a poet to the games' Indigenous arts festival that the Aboriginal Australians sponsored, while most of our fa'afafine Team Samoa were netball players and swimmers in their early twenties. They arrived in Sydney with empty bags, and in a week there were limousines pulling up to the building, where we were hosted by our Maori landlords, and men in tuxedos started escorting the young fa'afafine around town. At the Opening Ceremonies at Sydney Stadium, all the other queer teams marched in formation wearing regulation uniforms for their countries. Team Samoa was the only team at the Gay Games in drag. The Aboriginal, Maori, and Pacific Islander communities gave us spontaneous *haka* tributes from the stands. The young fa'afafine had dressed me up like a *lo'omatua*, with a fine mat around my chest and some feathers knocking against my forehead. When I walked onto the field, there was a Samoan cameraman waving at me, I waved back. On the giant screen amid the cheering crowds, an older fa'afafine in close-up was nodding quaintly. Oh gawd, I thought, she's me. Fuck it, I said, and did a catwalk stroll in a big loop across the great field. One by one, the younger fa'afafine

followed in heels, beautifully. Tall, dark drag queens in silver bikinis with high *tuiga* headdresses of orange feathers, like Las Vegas showgirls, smiling and waving at Australia.

Notes

1. Ann C. Colley, *Robert Louis Stevenson and the Colonial Imagination* (Aldershot, UK: Ashgate, 2004), 182.

2. Manu'a is a group of three islands holding spiritual and political significance to Samoa and Polynesia. For more on this please refer to my essay "The Passive Resistance of Samoans to U.S. and Other Colonialisms," in *Sovereignty Matters: Locations of Contestation and Possibility in Indigenous Struggles for Self-Determination*, ed. Joanne Barker (Lincoln: University of Nebraska Press, 2005), 109–22.

3. Jeannette Marie Mageo, *Theorizing Self in Samoa: Emotions, Genders, and Sexualities* (Ann Arbor: University of Michigan Press, 1998), 209.

4. Colley, *Robert Louis Stevenson*, 182.

5. Lee Wallace, *Sexual Encounters: Pacific Texts, Modern Sexualities* (Ithaca: Cornell University Press, 2003).

6. R. P. Gilson, *Samoa 1830 to 1900: The Politics of a Multi-Cultural Community* (Melbourne: Oxford University Press, 1970), 104.

7. Rev. John B. Stair, *Old Samoa, or Flotsam and Jetsam from the Pacific Ocean* (London: 1897), 132–34.

8. Phineas Matautia-Hartson, *Community Legal Research Paper: Fa'afafine in Australia* (Sydney: 2005), 33.

Section II
Situating Two-Spirit and Queer Indigenous Movements

5
ᎠᏝ ᎠᏎᎩ (Asegi Ayetl)
Cherokee Two-Spirit People Reimagining Nation
Qwo-Li Driskill

In Cherokee, the word for "nation" is **ᎠᏎᎩ** (*ayetl*). **ᎠᏎᎩ** literally means *center,* the seventh direction in Cherokee cosmology. Unlike dominant European views of the world, which understand only four fixed flat directions, Cherokee traditions understand the world as multifaceted and in motion. "Center" is neither stable nor singular as a direction—the center is dependent upon one's perspective.

The same-sex marriage controversy and homophobia from both the mainstream and Cherokee communities have spurred Two-Spirit Cherokees to question where **ᎠᏎᎩ** is and what it means. Two-Spirit Cherokees are critiquing Indigenous nationalist projects modeled after colonizing powers and offering alternative notions of Cherokee nationhood. The concept of **ᎠᏎᎩ** enables us to theorize nationhoods that are numerous, multiple, and complex.

The original homelands of the Cherokees include present-day Tennessee, Kentucky, the western Carolinas, northern Georgia and Alabama, and the western part of the Virginias. A series of wars with both Europeans and Americans and subsequent treaties gradually whittled the Cherokee Nation down to what is now northern Georgia, northwestern Alabama, western North Carolina, and eastern Tennessee. In 1830, the U.S. government, under Andrew Jackson, passed the Indian Removal Act, which forcibly removed Cherokees and other Native nations east of the Mississippi to Indian Territory, present-day Oklahoma. One-quarter of the Cherokee Nation perished on the death march. The descendants of the survivors of the Trail of Tears make up the citizenry of the Cherokee Nation and the United Keetoowah Band of Cherokee Indians, both in Oklahoma. A small group of Cherokees escaped removal by hiding in the mountains of western North Carolina; they are today known as the Eastern Band of Cherokee Indians.

The Cherokee Nation has the second-largest citizenry of any federally recognized Native nation, second only to the Navajo Nation. According to the 2000 U.S. census—which allowed people to self-identify and did

not determine Native identity based on citizenship in a federally recognized tribe—Cherokees were by far the largest Native group in the
United States, with a population of over 700,000.

As a way to theorize Two-Spirit identities within Cherokee communities, it is useful to look to a term that is being used by some Cherokees to talk about these identities: **D4Ꭹ** (*asegi*) or **D4Ꭹ ᎤᏓᏅᏙᎥ** (*asegi
udanto*). There are numerous ways and terms to talk about these identities within Cherokee, and **D4Ꭹ** (*asegi*) and **D4Ꭹ ᎤᏓᏅᏙᎥ** (*asegi udanto*)
are two of many.[1] **D4Ꭹ** (*asegi*) translates as "strange" or "odd." Durbin
Feeling translates the word as "peculiar" (49).[2] David Cornsilk translates
this term as "extraordinary."[3]

The word **ᎤᏓᏅᏙᎥ** (*udanto*) does not translate well into English taxonomies. It means "heart/mind/spirit." In their work on Cherokee love
incantations, Jack and Anna Kilpatrick explain: "The Cherokee terms
(there are several) that we have consistently translated as 'soul,' in many
instances might just as fittingly have been rendered 'mind' or 'heart.' All
derive from the verb stem—*da:n(v)dh*- ('to think purposefully') (22).[4]
D4Ꭹ ᎤᏓᏅᏙᎥ (*asegi udanto*), then, refers specifically to a different way of
thinking, feeling, and being that is outside of men's and women's traditional roles. **GᏚ**, a Cherokee traditionalist, posted this comment about
Cherokee gender traditions in a MySpace discussion forum:

> At our Ceremonial Ground and most others, we have three gender
> roles for participation, they aren't enforced, but suggested. Male,
> female and other. A woman could live as a male and vice versa, but
> a third option exists, those that are neither or both. Some folks in
> other Tribes call it two-spirited, we don't. We call it asegi udanto
> or "other heart"; these people are trained in esoteric arts and Tra-
> ditional Medicine. Among non-Traditional Cherokees they are now
> both respected and feared; at one time they were just respected, but
> with Judeo-Christian influence, they have become feared; almost like
> witches among some of our own people ["gay people"].[5]

I want to hold both of these concepts—**DᏰC** (*ayetl*, "nation/center,"
the seventh and movable direction) and **D4Ꭹ** (*asegi*, "other")—to think
about how contemporary Cherokee Two-Spirit people are telling stories
that reimagine and re-story notions of nationhood and disrupt contemporary queer/transphobia within and outside of Cherokee communities.
Listening to these other stories—these **D4Ꭹ** (*asegi*) stories—helps us

think about how they perform Two-Spirit critiques that potentially shift and recreate **DℬC** (ayetl).

D4Ᏹ (asegi) stories, within what Emma Pérez calls a decolonial *third space* between the colonial and the postcolonial, perform Two-Spirit critiques that question reductive and autocolonial notions of "nation."[6] These critiques look at the ways that Native nationalisms are not exempt from falling into the same modes of conduct as other nationalisms. **D4Ᏹ** (asegi) stories are a rhetorical maneuver to intervene in heterosexist imaginings of Cherokee culture and histories. **D4Ᏹ** (asegi) stories place Two-Spirit identities into a *repertoire* of cultural memories, employing Two-Spirit critiques in struggles for decolonization.[7] Andrea Smith writes that "heteropatriarchy is the building block of empire. . . . Heteropatriarchy is the logic that makes social hierarchy seem natural. Just as the patriarchs rule the family, the elites of the nation-state rule their citizens."[8] Through our stories, Cherokee Two-Spirit people are challenging heteropatriarchy within Cherokee nation building, exposing the ways oppression is replicated by narrow notions of "nation." I would like to look to the **D4Ᏹ** (asegi) stories told to me by four participants in On the Wings of Wadaduga—Robin Farris, Daniel Heath Justice, Chad Taber, and Corey Taber—to see how they perform Two-Spirit critiques and re-story **DℬC** (ayetl).[9]

During the interviews, I asked participants what terms they use for themselves to describe their gender-sexualities, and not surprisingly, the answers point to the complexity and slipperiness of identity labels. While *Two-Spirit* is certainly used often as an umbrella term in contemporary Native Two-Spirit/GLBTQ communities, participants in this research have complex and conflicting relationships with the term. Daniel wasn't comfortable using the term *Two-Spirit* for himself, because he felt the term was unnecessarily normalizing:

> I actually don't use *Two-Spirit* very often. *Queer* works really well for me. I like its ambiguity, and I like that it kind of shakes things up a bit. For myself, I think *Two-Spirit* is a bit . . . I understand the reasons for connecting it to a spiritual tradition, and I think that's important, but I think in some ways it normalizes in ways that I don't know if necessarily we need to be normalized. I like the idea that whatever roles we may have had in the past are roles today, that we could be really important in shaking up complacency and conservatism and

reactionary convention, and reminding people that being Cherokee is about a lot more than blood and it's a lot more than breeding. There's a lot to being Cherokee that is really exciting and powerful and disruptive and beautifully quirky and weird and anomalous. So, I'm very happy with *queer*. I probably identify myself much more as *queer* than *gay*.... *Queer* feels very much in keeping with being Cherokee to me. And *gay* is weighted by a lot of representational burdens. Cherokees as a rule have always been . . . weird. For our neighbors. So, in the Southeast we were the only Iroquoian-speaking people. We were the people who lived in the mountains. Socially we were similar to the Muskogeean peoples in a lot of ways, but we were also anomalous in a lot of ways. And anomalies are such a big part of our tradition. I mean, you have *Uktena,* you have Wild Boy, you have . . . even Thunder in some ways is anomalous.[10] These are figures who cross between worlds and represent a lot of different realities. That's been a Cherokee experience. Our history of intermarriage, our history of adaptation . . . we adapted pretty readily. Even traditionalists who didn't speak English adapted to changing circumstances. Not necessarily *gladly* all the time, but pretty practically, so we've always been able to adapt and shift and . . . move ourselves as necessary, and I think *queer* is a term that really gives us that as well.

Chad, Corey, and Robin all used *Two-Spirit* in specifically Native contexts, but also found it a difficult term to use outside of Native communities. Robin said that she uses the word *gay* as more of a "universal" term and also identifies as a lesbian. On her use of the term *Two-Spirit* she says:

> *Two-Spirit* depends on where I'm at, 'cause so many people don't know what that is.... Obviously if I'm with Natives I would [use the term], if I thought they'd understand it. . . . I don't like the word *homosexual,* that's for sure. . . . it sounds like a Christian sermon word to me. It's derogatory, it's meant to separate and define who's doing something they're not supposed to. I like what they said today, about the fact that *Two-Spirit* embraces more that just sexuality, that it embraces the whole spirit part of who we are as a person, honoring and being genuine to who we're born as.[11]

Chad and Corey—twin mixedblood Cherokee/Creek/Osage brothers who are organizers in Oklahoma Two-Spirit communities—also spoke about their situational use of the term *Two-Spirit* and some of the challenges of using it outside of Native contexts:

CHAD: It depends probably I guess to whom I'm speaking. Usually I identify as gay, but also because mainly where I live, it's very urban, there's not many opportunities for me to use the term *Two-Spirit* and be understood. So usually I just use the term *gay*, and I identify as gay and Native American. (*To Corey*). How do you identify?

COREY: You know, I think that people that are not Native American have no idea what the word *Two-Spirit* means in almost every instance, and so I think it's kind of . . . it's a useless term in some scenarios . . .

CHAD: Sometimes . . .

COREY: . . . unfortunately. And I don't mean to take away from it, like to say it's not worth having around, but just that in certain situations it's not applicable as . . . it's lost in translation, almost, you could say.

CHAD: Sometimes I use that as an opportunity to tell people a little bit about our history.

COREY: To educate.

CHAD: Mmhmm. Especially in my day-to-day life, because I come in contact with a lot of people. I work as a stylist, and so I see a lot of people on a daily basis, and a lot of them . . . just because of the nature of the work, I develop a pretty close relationship with most of my clients, and so and a lot of them will ask me. And also, when I return from ceremony like Green Corn Ceremony, where I have scratches on my body and people see that. Or my tattoos they see on my wrists and wonder what that's from or what it symbolizes.[12] And so that kind of gives me an opportunity to explain a little bit more about myself and maybe even identify with the term *Two-Spirit*.

Cherokee people, then, have a complicated and nuanced relationship with the term *Two-Spirit*. While Chad, Corey, and Robin all used the term for themselves, it was not the only term they used as an identity label. Daniel simultaneously questioned the rhetorical work of *Two-Spirit*, while also seeing its value in relationship to spiritual traditions. All four participants, then, are able to *disidentify* with the term as a tactic in constructing **DᏞᎩ** (asegi) and **DᏰᏟ** (ayetl).[13]

Many Cherokee Two-Spirit people who are not fluent in Cherokee— including myself—struggle or have struggled with the absence and trauma caused by language loss in relationship to our identities as Two-Spirit people. One of the first questions I had about my identity as a Two-Spirit Cherokee was, "What word or words exist in Cherokee to talk about who we are?" Just as there is no singular answer to this in English, there is no singular answer to this in Cherokee. The fact that most Cherokees are not fluent in Cherokee adds additional complexities to searching for these terms, as we often have to rely on other people—who may or may not be Two-Spirit and may have various relationships to and opinions about GLBTQ issues—to relay very specific cultural information. The conflation of sexuality and gender expression under umbrella terms like *Two-Spirit* and *queer* may further complicate this process. Asking a language speaker or elder whether there is a word for "gay" in Cherokee, for instance, may cause the elder or speaker to say "no." However, asking elders or speakers if there are words for people who live as a gender other than that assigned at birth may bring different answers. Because the historical identities, roles, and expressions we are calling Two-Spirit are primarily about gender role and gender expression—*not* about what genders a person can fall in love with or are sexually involved with—there is no singular or simple answer to questions about Cherokee terms for our identities.

Cherokee Two-Spirit people are looking to language—or lack thereof—to make sense of our places in history, build our practices in the present, and transform the future through our stories. Because of the importance of language for contemporary Cherokee Two-Spirits, I asked participants if they knew terms in Cherokee for our identities. In answering a question about terms for Two-Spirit people in Cherokee, Robin responded:

> Well, I liked finding out from another Cherokee . . . that there had been a word, because . . . I started out finding that among Native people—'cause I was finding out who I was as a gay person at the same time I was trying to learn more about my culture as a Cherokee—and then I heard through a Cherokee that here amongst Native people, it's a non-issue. That we've always had them in our society, and I thought, "Oh, this is incredible." You know, I'd found this community that will accept me as a gay person. And then, as I started investigating it, I found out—not the case. We've been so assimilated as a culture that a lot of them don't even know their history and don't even remember. And so, I was angry and disappointed and very sad. Then I found out from another Cherokee, of the Eastern Band, that yes indeed, we were accepted and that there was a name for us, it was

Two Heart. And I don't know how to pronounce that in Cherokee. He wrote it down, but I don't remember how to pronounce it.

In response to a similar question, Corey said he hadn't heard a specific positive term for Two-Spirit people in Cherokee contexts:

I would say that a lot of the words that you'll hear, they probably have some sort of negative connotation. Because I haven't ever experienced or haven't ever been informed of any position of reverence, we don't have a pretty word for it—you know what I mean?—like some tribes do. There just wasn't that. Not that I know of anyway. And a lot of the younger people now—well, younger people anyway are the ones who cause a lot of the issues or go out of their way to make people feel uncomfortable and that sort of thing, or harass all of the Two-Spirited people, that sort of thing. It's usually the younger people that do that. The older people have a quieter way. And so, younger people nowadays, a lot of them don't speak our language. And so for that reason *they* don't even know the words to use other than English words. So I've never really had any experiences or anything like that with being called negative or even positive words in the Cherokee language that reference GLBT status or anything like that.

Robin and Corey's responses here lead to a core concept that all participants had about Cherokee Two-Spirit histories and present lives: that the gender role and/or sexuality of a Cherokee person is less relevant to their place in Cherokee communities than the practices of being in reciprocal and balanced relationship with—Ꮪꭶ Ꭰ Ꮓ (*duyuk'ta*)—and productive cooperation with—ᏍᏏ Ꮻ (*gadugi*)—those communities. Questions about the traditional place of Two-Spirit people within Cherokee lifeways and worldviews opened up discussions about larger obligations to community. When asked what he thought our traditional place was in Cherokee communities, Daniel said:

I've asked a couple of elders this, both of whom said they don't think we had a special place necessarily, or a culturally defined place, but they both said that was because it just didn't matter, that it wasn't so different as to require a distinctive role. Which surprised me . . . that wasn't the answer I was expecting. And I wonder about that, I think it's a real possibility that as long as you were still contributing to the community, whether you lived as a man or a woman or whatever, who you had sex with didn't matter. Are you having kids? Are you adding to the safety and security of the town? Are you fulfilling your obligations to your family? That mattered. On the whole, not everybody had to have children. Are you contributing to the welfare of the community? I think that's what mattered. That could very well have been it.

Corey had a very similar answer to this question:

I haven't experienced a great difference between Cherokee and Creek communities, and what I've learned from my experiences with all of those people is that there wasn't necessarily a place of reverence for Two-Spirited people—*necessarily*. And there could have been, you know, I mean all of our people teach different things, but it was told to us that that's not how you're characterized. What's important is how you help out your family and how you take care of your people, whether it be your community, your family, your tribe—whatever circumstance. How you treat the people around you and what you do to give back. That essentially defines you as a person, and not who you choose for a partner.

Chad likewise emphasized the importance of community participation ᏍᏚ (gadugi)—to Cherokee identity, rather than contemporary concepts of sexuality, gender, race, and blood quantum: "Traditionally we're told that you were Cherokee based on your participation in the community and what you do for the community."

When I asked Robin what she thought our traditional place was within Cherokee communities, she replied:

I have no idea. Like [Co-cké] was talking about—and that's what I found in my research—because it's an eastern tribe, so much of it was assimilated before people started getting it down on paper, that unless we do old manuscripts, that the people who wrote down certain things or know because it's been passed down orally or something like that . . . I have no idea. I've heard that you were defined by your work role, so it could be that. I mean, I know there were warrior women. Whether that meant they were considered Two-Spirit or not, I don't know. I know there were Cherokee warrior women, because I've read about them. Like Nancy Ward was considered sort of a warrior woman—Beloved Women—I know there's that, but Beloved Women are not the same thing as warrior women or Two-Spirit. I guess you could be both, but not necessarily, so I don't know. I'm still learning.

While Robin wasn't sure what place Two-Spirit people had within Cherokee communities in the past, she was sure that Two-Spirit people were "a part of the circle," a part of the larger whole of Cherokee community and lifeways: "Now I think we're struggling to get back in the circle. And then I think we were part of the circle, and it was accepted and it was just a different way of being, and unique to each individual, but all part of the whole community. I like what they say about, we didn't throw away people, we put them in their place.[14] I don't think that's true now. But I think we can get back there. I'm optimistic."

GS's posts on MySpace about **ᎠᏎᎩ ᎤᏓᏅᏝ** (asegi udanto) add another layer to a discussion of traditional roles:

It was out in the open, they often had specific ceremonial positions set aside for them. Same for women. It was more about gender roles than sexuality. You took a man's role, a woman's role, or the "other" role. There is historical documentation, that I don't care to quote verbatim . . . that found two men married, one living as a woman, the other a man, and it was considered normal. Gender roles seemed to be more important than sexual identity.[15]

Elsewhere, **GS** further argues

In our culture we had three gender roles. Men anisgaya, women anigehya and other asegi tsundando (different spirit). . . . In my culture men that were born with female or ambiguous genitalia could still live their life as men. Women, or those born with male or ambiguous genitalia could live their lives as other women. The asegi tsundando born with either male or female (or ambiguous genitalia) lived as people that did not engage in the traditional activities of those with a different gender role. There might have been more to it than this, but this is what I have been taught. Women owned the crops, the kids and the houses. Some say the responsibility of taking care of the land was passed down from mother to daughter. The women were in charge of the families, or matrilineal clans. The men hunted, traded and went to war, they also helped clear the fields for planting and helped harvest by women's request. The asegi tsundando did neither and both. Primarily they were spiritual people with spiritual training. They could have lived as men or women, but that is not who they were. They took care of the families, and protected the village. All were sacred ulsgedi degadayelusesdi.[16]

Not surprisingly, participants in On the Wings of Wadaduga both subtly and explicitly critiqued the Cherokee nation's reaction to same-sex marriage, seeing the CN's actions as a detriment to "the circle." Participants countered these politics with **D4Ᏽ** (asegi) stories, unsettling and *disidentifying* with notions of Cherokee **ᎠᏰᏟ** (ayetl) that are reductive and exclusive. Robin spoke fairly extensively about the same-sex marriage case and her own email exchanges with members of the tribal council. Robin challenges the CN's arguments and reasoning regarding same-sex marriage:

> Our history as a people is evolving, just like all people's history, so that was my big argument to the Nation council was (and is) that, I don't argue with your right to say that you've decided at this point in time that—given how you view the world or morality or whatever—that gays shouldn't get married, but I do argue with your denial of the fact the Two-Spirit were a part and accepted as a valuable part of our people and our history. I mean, go ahead and say that it used to be okay in the past but that you no longer find that being gay acceptable or whatever, but don't pretend we didn't exist.

Daniel likewise found moves toward exclusion and normalcy contrary to Cherokee lifeways, experiences, and traditions:

> I'd be a little hesitant to say that to be Cherokee is to be queer, but I think that we are in an anomalous position in a lot of ways in broader Native America. I mean, we're hated in Indian Country 'cause we're supposedly not Indian enough, but it's been our transformative Indian-ness that has made us survive. And I find it really troubling that there are so many people in the nation who would want to take away that transformability out of some sort of weird misguided fear about cultural purity, when we've always been inclusive, we've always been adaptive. Not always *happily*. I think that's an important point, too, but that would be queer. That's also about being queer. That's survival. And not just surviving, but *thriving*.

Corey made explicit and confrontational reference to the erasure of Two-Spirit people by the Cherokee Nation's tribal council during the same-sex marriage case when I asked him what he would want to say to future generations of Cherokee Two-Spirit people.

> There's a lot, a lot, a lot of gay Cherokees and a lot of gay Creeks. And there always have been, and there always will be. And anybody on the

tribal council that tells you different is full of fuckin' shit. (*Laughter*). And I want you to *believe* that. I want you to *know* that from us. . . . Just in case you didn't hear it anywhere else, you heard it here. I mean that from the bottom of my heart, because that's what our medicine people have taught us. You guys aren't something new, you aren't some kind of spectacle we never seen. They treat us as if it's a non-issue, they treat us like it's nothing out of the ordinary. Because it isn't to us. And I wanna make sure that *that* gets in there. Aaayyeee . . .

Participants' re-storying Two-Spirit history is nested within larger work to remember **ᎠᏎᎩ** (asegi) stories that have been marginalized by some aspects of contemporary Cherokee nationalism. Daniel looks to history to disrupt moves to essentialize and simplify Cherokee "tradition" and "history." Part of Daniel's current scholarship, for instance, offers an **ᎠᏎᎩ** (asegi) narrative to the history of Little Carpenter:

Yeah, Little Carpenter is a really interesting figure to me. We have a lot of information on him, but he's . . . he's kinda quirky. He's honored, but it's clear that even in his own community of Chota he holds a somewhat ambivalent or ambiguous position. He's the father of Dragging Canoe, the great Chickamauga war chief. He's the uncle of Nancy Ward, Nan'yehi, the great Beloved Woman. He's a Beloved Man who is an advocate for peace. He was known as a very strong warrior before. But he disappeared for a long time, he was a captive of the Odawas, possibly. There's also some question that he might have been Odawa. He might have been of another nation who was adopted into the Cherokee Nation. He was renowned for his rhetorical skills, but he was also known to be very, very strategic. He was an amazing politician who worked very much for the benefit of Chota, but not necessarily for other Cherokee communities. He was very town-centered. He was one of the first Cherokee delegates that went to London, so he saw this force that was coming across the ocean, and he had a really unique perspective that a lot of other Cherokees at this time did not.

The pictures we have of him, and the descriptions we have of him, always that he was small, slight, and he's effeminized in a lot of these representations, even if it's just kind of by an aside. He had a *very* intimate relationship with a British military officer, I want to say John Stuart, but I don't remember exactly what his name was. Somewhere in memory they did the "brotherhood ceremony," which seems to me to be kind of a nice way of, or a very heteronormative way of, dismissing that intimacy. I guess when Little Carpenter died, Stuart or whoever this man was, was inconsolable with grief, which could be a brother situation, but just a lot of things lead me to wonder. No evidence, I have no evidence that he got it on with men. But just so many little things point to him being an anomalous figure and a figure who—yeah, he had a son, we know nothing, or very little, about his relationship with his wife. We do know he was estranged from his son, which would have made some sense, because the father would not have been any authority. But in their particular relationship, they were both Wolf Clan—not sure how that happened. They would have had a stronger relationship. And Little Carpenter's relationship with Nan'yehi—he was the uncle of Nan'yehi—he would have had a significant influence over her. And she had a very strong and contested relationship with Dragging Canoe. I also wonder—because we don't know a lot about the women's roles in the council, there's scattered bits and pieces. We know that there probably was a women's council. But we know in other Iroquoian and some Muskogeean traditions, but particularly Iroquoian, the women's council has a male representative to men's council. And his relationship with the women seems to be very strong. So I wonder if there was something maybe similar to that. And who better than a queer boy to bridge that gap between the women and the men?

And his nickname: Leaning Wood. It's really hard for me not to see that as a pun. I need to talk to a language speaker to have a sense of whether that would be the case, but things just point over and over to me that he was family. And so, he fathered a child. Yeah, and? That would not in any way preclude him from being queer. He's a Beloved Man at a younger age than a lot of other Beloved Men, if memory serves. So what does that mean? And just because he was a Beloved Man doesn't mean he wasn't also a warrior. But he supported the British. I would love to know what was going on in England when those Cherokee boys were over there. Did they visit a molly house? Not likely, but they certainly stayed in the area of London where same-sex activities were notorious. I don't know. I have a lot of research to do on this, but . . . you know?

Just as Daniel brings an **ᎠᏎᎩ** (asegi) interpretation to this part of Cherokee history, he also challenges Cherokees to remember the role of the erotic in Cherokee traditions, histories, and lifeways. Further, he argues that a denial of the erotic disrupts Cherokee community:

> Cherokees were *incredibly* sexual people, though not nasty about it. At the Peabody Museum there's a pipe bowl from a Cherokee town-site, with a man and a woman having sex, in explicit detail, with their genitalia pointed right at the smoker. So, somebody's getting a little thrill looking at that. Early European accounts were horrified about how sexually free Cherokees were, that young Cherokee women had sex, out of wedlock, sometimes extra-wedlock. And young men. And no mentions are—I haven't seen any mentions at all or hints at all of same-sex intimacies. But people were very much sexual people. And frankly a lot of the fine upstanding folks who don't want to admit it . . . I'm sorry, but you can either deny your sexual desires and get in weird circumstances, or you can just admit the fact that we love sex, we're very sexual people, and that doesn't mean that we're crass about it. I think Cherokees would not have been crass, and I think that even very sexual Cherokees today have personal modesty, but it doesn't neces-sarily transfer always over to sexual prudery. But it's depending on the context. It's depending on who's around, and I think that's okay. I think that's fair. I mean, walking around flashing your dick at every-body is not a nice thing to do. Not *everybody* wants to see that. So, I think part of it is also just a basic consideration for one another.

Robin, Daniel, Corey, and Chad are pointing to an **ᎠᏰᎵ** (ayetl, nation/center) that asks Cherokee people, now and in the future, to remember other stories, other histories, that are inclusive—and in fact grounded—in counterstories—**ᎠᏎᎩ** (asegi) stories—to versions of Cherokee his-tory, sovereignty, and nationhood that seek heteronormativity.

Robin, Corey, and Chad all emphasized a past in which Two-Spirit people were "a part of the circle." Healing the circle—healing histori-cal trauma—was a central part of the interviews with Corey and Chad. These conversations reflected the decolonial work in which Cherokee people and Two-Spirit people are currently involved. This revitalization work critiques the queer/transphobia internalized by Native communi-ties and simultaneously positions Two-Spirit people as necessary to the well-being of both Native communities and the world.

CHAD: . . . I think that the basis of our work, fundamentally, is restor-ing what was lost. And that's a very general statement, but it means a lot of different things. Restoring what was lost as Two-Spirited people, restoring what was lost as Cherokee Two-Spirited people, meaning traditions and ceremonies . . .

COREY: Healing the part of the Cherokee circle that's been *gone* because these people have *ignored* us and cast us out.

CHAD: Not just that but healing and restoring what is lost in the *world*. And I think our work is going to transition from regaining what we've lost in a smaller perspective to restoring what was lost as a whole.

COREY: It's a part of a bigger healing that has to occur.

Corey's and Chad's words here are reminiscent of other waves of Cherokee resistance that place practices at the center of maintaining **ᏍᎬ ᎠᎢ** (duyuk'ta) and the continuance of the world. Like the Cherokee Ghost Dance movement and the Redbird Smith movement that insisted on reclaiming particular dances and practices in order to maintain the world, Cherokee Two-Spirit people are looking to both *archive* and *repertoire* to "restore what was lost" as well as to imagine and create a present and future.

Because the goal of On the Wings of Wadaduga is to both revise the *archive* and the *repertoire* and to explicitly bring our stories in the present to Cherokee Two-Spirit people in the future and to use our stories to imagine what we want our futures to look like, I asked participants about our future as Two-Spirit Cherokees. When asked what she would want our future to be, Robin replied: "That we'll get back into that place where we're accepted, protected, and allowed to add our spirit and gifts into the circle of our people and our community just like any other member of the tribe. I'd like to see all of us, in all tribes, model to the rest of the world that Native Americans see being Two-Spirit . . . as no big deal. It's just a different way of being, like having blond hair or blue eyes, being tall or short."

Daniel replied to a similar question by also speaking of having a place within what Robin, Chad, and Corey call "the circle":

I want us to have a place on the grounds, with our partners, where we don't have to worry or feel like our partners aren't gonna be welcomed. I'm not a Baptist, but I don't imagine that one's partner would be welcome in the Baptist Church. There are some grounds where we're welcome, though not many. I want us to be healthy and happy and to not be seen as compromising our Cherokeeness by living honestly and loving honestly. I want that love and living to be seen as contributing to Cherokee nationhood, not drawing away from it.

While there are many ways that Cherokee GLBTQ2 people are regaining our places within "the circle," one way we are doing this work is through reimagining and reclaiming our cultural memories in order to uncover **D4Ⴑ** (*asegi*) stories that have been forgotten or ignored. Through this work, Cherokee GLBT and **D4Ⴑ Ⴍ'ᏝᎾᏙ** (*asegi udanto*) people are "regaining what we've lost."

Notes

1. During a language immersion with the Eastern band, I asked my language instructor, Bo Taylor, if there were words to describe GLBTQ people in Cherokee. Taylor told me that people sometimes use the terms **DᏑᏩᏋᎯ Ꮎ'ᏝᎯᏙ** (*ageyusd' udanti*) and **DᏪᏍᎴᎣᏋᎯ Ꮎ'ᏝᎯᏙ** (*asgayusd' udanti*) to speak of particular identities. These can be translated as "s/he feels like a woman" and "s/he feels like a man," respectively. I have also been told in informal conversations that there are two other terms that can be translated "not just a man" and "not just a woman." And, as Robin Farris mentions later in this chapter, I have been told of another term that can be translated as "s/he has two hearts."

2. Durbin Feeling, *Cherokee–English Dictionary* (Dallas: Southern Methodist University, 1975), 49.

3. Paula Sophia, "Women Marry in the Cherokee Nation," *Gayly Oklahoman* (Tulsa, OK), March 16, 2005.

4. Jack F. Kilpatrick and Anna G Kilpatrick, *Walk in Your Soul: Love Incantations of the Oklahoma Cherokees* (Dallas: Southern Methodist University, 1965), 22.

5. **GS**, comment on "So What Religions Allow Gay People?" February 1, 2008, MySpace Forums, http://forums.myspace.com/t/3746727.aspx?fuseaction=forums.viewthread&PageIndex=3&SortOrder=0. Some original spelling has been modified.

6. Emma Pérez, *The Decolonial Imaginary: Writing Chicanas into History* (Bloomington: Indiana University Press, 1999), 55.

7. Diana Taylor theorizes that the "rift . . . does not lie between the written and spoken word, but between the *archive* of supposedly enduring materials (i.e., texts, documents, buildings, bones) and the so-called ephemeral *repertoire* of embodied practice/knowledge (i.e., spoken language, dance, sports, ritual)." I will use Taylor's framework of the *archive* and the *repertoire* throughout this essay. Diana Taylor, *The Archive and the Repertoire: Performing Cultural Memory in the Americas* (Durham: Duke University, 2003), 19.

8. Andrea Smith, "Heteropatriarchy: A Building Block of Empire," *Solidarity*, http://www.solidarity-us.org/node/736.

9. On the Wings of Wadaduga is an ongoing project that aims to bring both historical research and interviews with GLBTQ Cherokees to the public through writing and performance. While all participants' identities are kept confidential as a matter of course, they also have the option of waiving their confidentiality. The four participants included in this essay all wanted their real names to be used in this project.

10. ᎤᏍᏗ (Uktena) is a giant, winged, horned serpent that lives in mountains and waterways. Wild Boy, the son of ᏎᎷ (Selu, Corn) and ᎧᎾᏘ (Kanati, the Hunter), was unknowingly brought into existence when ᏎᎷ washed off blood in a river. Thunder is an important deity in traditional Cherokee cosmology, and is considered a protector of Cherokee people.

11. Robin is referring to a presentation and discussion led by John Hawk Co-cké, an Osage Two-Spirit activist, at the 2008 Tulsa Two-Spirit Gathering.

12. Chad has tattoos of scratches on his wrists, symbolizing ceremonial scratches from Green Corn.

13. José Esteban Muñoz theorizes, "Disidentification is meant to be descriptive of the survival strategies the minority subject practices in order to negotiate a phobic majoritarian public sphere that continuously elides or punishes the existence of subjects who do not conform to the phantasm of normative citizenship" (*Disidentifications: Queers of Color and the Performance of Politics* [Minneapolis: University of Minnesota, 1999], 4).

14. A reference to Co-cké's presentation at the Two-Spirit Gathering.

15. GS, comment on "Matriarchy," MySpace Forums, February 6, 2008, http://forums.myspace.com/p/3756663/37792002.aspx?fuseaction=forums. viewpost. Some original spelling has been modified.

16. GS, comment on "Homosexuality in the Eyes of the Native American," MySpace Forums, February 24, 2008, http://forums.myspace.com/p/3791488/38734608.aspx?fuseaction=forums.viewpost#38734608. Some original spelling has been modified.

6

Exploring Takatapui Identity within the Maori Community

Implications for Health and Well-Being

Clive Aspin

Despite hundreds of years of colonization and marginalization, Indigenous peoples around the world have managed to preserve many of the diverse elements from their historical past that contribute today to their sense of identity and belonging. Nowhere is this more important than in the area of sexuality and sexual expression.[1] Despite thousands of years of societal influence and pressure that have underpinned efforts to regulate the most intimate parts of people's lives, it is abundantly clear that human sexuality is diverse, with multiple forms of sexual expression being vital components of sexuality in contemporary times.[2]

Today, our understandings of sexuality and sexual expression are undergoing significant changes and developments. As we peel off the veneer of prejudice and narrow-mindedness that has been associated with sexual difference for hundreds of years, it has become clear that sexuality is far more diverse than people have been conditioned to think and that in actual fact, it is an important component of people's lives that needs to be celebrated rather than vilified and condemned.

Historically, Maori society, as with other Indigenous populations, was characterized by its acceptance and celebration of sexual diversity.[3] It is only within contemporary Maori society that efforts have been made to constrain and restrict diverse and multiple expressions of sexuality. Colonial influences such as religion and governmental regulation that derived from a Victorian Judeo-Christian way of describing the world have contributed significantly to a narrow interpretation of human sexuality, which has in turn served to undermine traditional concepts of Maori sexuality. This was further complicated by the presumption that heterosexuality was the norm and that all other forms of sexuality were perverse. Such an attitude has become so entrenched in our society today that some commentators have compared heterosexuality with whiteness, a powerful component of western society that can be both invisible and presumed to be natural, and which serves to marginalize those who are perceived to be different.[4] Whereas whiteness serves to render power and superiority to white people and thus shores up racism within our society, heterosexuality performs a similar function of ensuring that privilege remains with men and women who are perceived as engaging in heterosexual relationships. This sense of privilege has traditionally been most loudly articulated by voices that emanate from religion, the medical arena, and psychology, and other apparent voices of "officialdom," with no consideration being given to the cultural nuances of history and society.[5] It is disturbing to hear influential voices within the Maori community making proclamations about sexuality based on views espoused by the colonizer rather than the stories of our ancestors, which talk of diversity of sexuality where various forms of sexual expression were celebrated as vital and integral components of society. In 2004, national prominence was given to the homophobic views of the newly appointed Maori head of the Anglican Church in New Zealand, who stated that he looked forward to the day when there would be a "world without gays."[6]

It is no wonder, then, that the arrival of Christian missionaries in Aotearoa/New Zealand led to the imposition of a code of behavior that was based on Victorian concepts of morality. This saw the promotion of the belief within New Zealand and consequently within Maori society that sexual behavior should take place only within the confines of marriage between a man and a woman and that it should be for the purposes of procreation. Similar efforts are known to have occurred among Indigenous communities in other parts of the world, so that only vestiges of the true nature of the sexual diversity of our ancestors remain today.[7] Any form of sexual behavior outside those parameters was viewed as perverse and overlooked the fact that human sexuality carried with it particular nuances that differed from one culture to another.[8] Such a narrow view of sexuality posed significant problems for the colonized as well as the colonizer, many of whom viewed the new world into which they had entered as a haven for satisfying sexual urges that were denied them in their countries of origin. Principal among these were missionaries themselves, some of whom were known to enjoy sexual relations with Natives that fell outside the very norms that they attempted to impose on Indigenous populations. The most-cited case of this was an ordained minister named Mr. Yate who was sent by the Church Missionary Society in England to the north of New Zealand to carry out missionary work among the Maori population.[9] The case of Yate has been well described, thanks to the existence of abundant archival material in the Mitchell

Library, Sydney. The material relates to a trial conducted against Yate for homosexual behavior with Maori men. Evidence presented at the trial showed that Yate engaged in homosexual activity with Maori men in the community where he lived in New Zealand. For two years, Yate cohabited with a Maori man in a local Maori community, and it can be assumed that this relationship would have been known to the local Maori community, and that it would have been condoned and accepted. The response of Yate's fellow missionaries, however, was vastly different. On their discovery of this abhorrent relationship, Yate was banished from New Zealand and sent back to England. To expunge all memory of Yate from the local community, his horse, a precious commodity in early colonial New Zealand, was shot.

These two opposing views of sexuality at the interface of colonization illustrate clearly the tensions that confront agents who attempt to regulate this most intimate part of human behavior, a legacy that informs our understanding of sexuality today. In particular, this historical example demonstrates some of the tensions that exist for Indigenous peoples when we consider sexuality in all its diversity, and it raises some important questions. To what extent is our sexuality today influenced by the colonial past? How important are traditional concepts of sexuality when we describe contemporary expressions of sexuality? Should we ignore traditional concepts of sexuality in favor of colonial concepts and beliefs? And most importantly, how do these questions relate to the health and well-being of Indigenous peoples today?

Historical Understandings of Maori Sexuality

As well as colonial archival material, a number of other sources also testify to the sexual diversity of pre-European Maori society. These include oral accounts, depictions of sexual diversity within artworks, and the fact that other Indigenous cultures celebrated sexual diversity in precolonial times.

For Maori, oral accounts have always been an important means of transmitting knowledge from generation to generation. The arrival of Europeans led to the disruption of a vital channel of communication that had been refined over thousands of generations, and contributed to the suppression and obliteration of important ancestral knowledge. In the case of sexuality, this disruption was led by agents who attempted to reshape Maori society in the image of the colonial forces. Aided with religious texts, early settlers imposed narrow prescriptive forms of sexuality on the perverse Natives with whom they came in contact. As a consequence, sexual expression within the confines of marriage was elevated above all other forms of sexuality. Other forms of sexuality were seen as perverse, and strenuous efforts were made to obliterate them from the pantheon of sexual expression and diversity.

In recent times, research efforts have provided confirmation that sexual expression within traditional Maori society was indeed far more diverse than some commentators would have us believe. In the 1970s, one forthright and influential commentator went so far as to claim that homosexuality did not exist in pre-European Maori society and that in actual fact, this form of sexual behavior was introduced to the Maori by the European settler.[10] Comments such as this need to be considered within the context of the time in which homosexuality was considered to a be serious mental illness, a position that did not change until 1973, when homosexuality was removed from the *Diagnostic and Statistical Manual of Mental Disorders* by the board of directors of the American Psychiatric Association. More than twenty years later, concerns were still being expressed about the homophobic treatment that gay men and lesbians were still receiving at the hands of health-care workers, a legacy that continues to the present day in many parts of the world.[11] While a more enlightened attitude toward nonheterosexual people might contribute to greater acceptance and inclusion of diverse sexualities, there is still a long way to go before all forms of discrimination and stigma based on hatred of homosexuality are removed from contemporary society.

A number of recent research projects have shed some light on important issues related to Maori sexuality. The Maori Sexuality Project provides an up-to-date understanding of Maori sexuality and how it is expressed today. As well, the project has uncovered important information about historical concepts of Maori sexuality as it was expressed by our ancestors. To arrive at accurate contemporary and historical understandings of Maori sexuality, comprehensive data were gathered from interviews conducted with over ninety individuals, either separately or as part of a focus group. This national research program represents the largest project of its kind and marks an important milestone in the development of our awareness of the importance of sexuality to the lives of individuals and communities. Most importantly, the rich source of data confirms that sexual diversity has been an essential component of Maori society in the past and that this diversity continues into Maori society today.[12] This contemporary source of information serves a double purpose of refuting information disseminated by colonial sources and assuring people from sexual minorities today that their sexuality and sexual expression are not vastly different from those of our ancestors and, as such, are parts of our lives of which we should be proud, rather than ashamed. Findings from the Maori Sexuality Project further demonstrate the importance of accepting people from diverse sexual backgrounds as integral members of *whanau* (family), *hapu* (subtribe), and *iwi* (tribe) who have the right to be accepted within these familial networks, rather than being rejected for their perceived difference.

It is worth considering the findings of the Maori Sexuality Project in light of declarations made by the New Zealand Ministry of Health (2001) in their "Sexual Health Strategy."[13] This government document describes sexuality and sexual behavior as fundamental components of people's lives and states that these have a significant impact on both individuals and society as a whole. Further, the strategy identifies two factors that place sexual and reproductive health firmly at the top of health priorities in New Zealand—increasing rates of sexually transmitted infections (STIs), especially chlamydia, gonorrhea, and HIV, and the high level of unintended or unwanted pregnancies—and points out that Maori are disproportionately affected by these concerns. Moreover, the burden of disease that results from STIs needs to be considered within an international context. Throughout the world, STIs are increasingly prevalent, yet they receive little attention from national governments despite the fact that they affect individuals, sexual networks, and the general population.[14] Studies show that improvements to treatment services can result in significant decreases in the incidence of STIs, with this having a beneficial impact on individual and population health and well-being.[15] As well, there are rising rates of STIs, and these are placing individuals and communities at increased risk of disability and death, with mainly women and young people being most adversely affected.[16] With sexuality being so implicated in positive sexual health and well-being, it is clear that there needs to be greater understanding and awareness of the role that this plays in people's daily lives as well as within society as a collective.

This imperative becomes even more urgent when we consider the tragic consequences of the AIDS epidemic, a worldwide health, social, and cultural disaster that has now entered its third decade and shows no sign of let-up. Indeed, there are signs that rates of HIV infection are increasing in many parts of the world, with more and more women bearing the brunt of the epidemic.[17] Increasingly, HIV is affecting traditionally marginalized people within our communities, with women, drug users, sex workers, and men who have sex with men being adversely affected by the epidemic. In recent times, we have seen the emergence of worrying evidence that Indigenous people in colonized countries have been adversely affected by HIV. In Canada, for example, Indigenous peoples make up approximately 5 percent of the total population, yet they account for roughly 20 percent of all HIV diagnoses; and this does not include the two most populous provinces, Quebec and Ontario, where ethnicity data are not collected. Today, we know that the principal means of transmission of HIV in many parts of the world is the result of sexual behavior. This knowledge makes it imperative that we recognize and acknowledge the diversity of sexual expression within our communities. Moreover, this diversity needs to feature prominently in health promotion programs, especially those that focus on the sexual and reproductive health of our communities.

Takatapui Identity

One key component of Maori sexuality today is that which is known as *takatapui* identity. The term *takatapui* has been adopted by increasing numbers of Maori men and women to describe their sexual identity. Indeed, the term *takatapui* encapsulates the sexual and cultural components of one's identity and, as such, is preferable to terms that derive from western understandings of sexuality, such as *gay* and *lesbian*.

The term *takatapui* comes from our past and, as noted in Williams's *Dictionary of the Maori Language* (1971), refers to "an intimate companion of the same sex." Today, the term has been reclaimed and is used to describe people who might otherwise describe themselves as gay, lesbian, transgender, bisexual, and intersexual. The term has greater currency within the Maori community than in the broader community, and there is evidence to suggest that many people who claim takatapui identity restrict their use of the term to contexts where there is a majority of Maori people.[18] On other occasions, these same people might use the term *gay* or *lesbian*. However, increasing numbers of Maori see these terms as part of the mechanism by which sexuality around the world is described according to western paradigms and beliefs. Continued usage of these terms is seen as part of the ongoing colonization of Indigenous peoples throughout the world. Many Indigenous peoples, Maori included, are now looking to their ancestral past in efforts to understand and describe sexuality in a contemporary context. In today's world, terms such as *takatapui* hold special significance, because they remind us that sexual relationships among our ancestors were vastly different from those that are sanctioned by modern-day institutions. The process of colonization has meant that much of the truth about historical sexuality has been lost to present generations. The term *takatapui* provides inspiration to uncover the historical diversity of Maori sexuality, while providing a legitimate and culturally appropriate means of describing our sexuality today.

It is clear that many Maori men and women today are seeking alternatives to the western concepts of sexuality that have been applied to many cultural groupings around the world, especially in developed countries. Sexuality has been used to regulate society and behavior in these countries,[19] and in the process, cultural nuances have been overlooked, minimized, and suppressed.

Stigma, Discrimination, and Marginalization

In many parts of the world, people who belong to sexual minority groups experience severe stigma and discrimination. This can range from prejudicial treatment by authorities based on sexual orientation to the imposition of the death penalty for sexual behavior between two consenting men. Apart from demonizing people based on their sexuality, measures such as these give a strong signal to the wider community that it is fair and reasonable to discriminate against people because of their sexuality. The consequences of this inequitable treatment have a negative impact on the people at whom the discrimination is leveled, as well as on the broader communities from which these people come. On a personal level, discrimination and stigma based on sexual difference can have a major negative impact on individual health and well-being. Recent studies have established a strong link between sexual orientation, mental health, and the risk of suicide, with this being a serious health concern in many parts of the world.[20] Based on a sample of almost one thousand participants, Fergusson et al. (2003) demonstrated that people who were attracted to others of the same sex had higher rates of poor mental health and suicidal behaviors than those with an attraction to people of the other sex, with these rates being noticeably higher for men than for women.[21] It should be noted that young Maori men now have one of the highest rates of suicide, and in light of the evidence presented by these research endeavors one must wonder to what extent sexuality is implicated in these excessively high rates.

A recent investigation into Maori men's experiences of unwanted sex has shown that Maori men from sexual minorities are vulnerable to a range of negative health problems as a result of these experiences.[22] Men who had experienced at least one instance of unwanted sex reported health problems that included mental illness, eating disorders, and heart disease. These same men also reported that access to cultural support systems helped to alleviate some of the negative effects of unwanted sex and the resulting health problems. By providing ready and easy access to a culturally based form of identity such as that encapsulated by takatapui identity, men such as these will be provided with knowledge and resources that will build confidence and protection against enforced and unwanted sexual experiences.

Conclusion

Maori men with a same-sex attraction confront a range of challenges to their health and well-being. Increasingly, the term *takatapui* provides men such as these with a means of confronting and overcoming these challenges. Men who identify as takatapui have access to ancestral knowledge that provides protection against the negative effects of discrimination and marginalization. As we reclaim our ancestral knowledge and acknowledge its central role in the promotion of good health and well-being today, it is important to ensure that Maori have unfettered access to culturally appropriate descriptors of sexual identity. By following our ancestors' example and celebrating and affirming sexual diversity as they did, we will help to ensure the good health of people today, as well as that of generations to come.

Notes

1. Clive Aspin and Jessica Hutchings, "Reclaiming the Past to Inform the Future: Contemporary Views of Maori Sexuality," *Culture, Health and Sexuality* 9, no. 4 (2007): 415–27.

2. Jeffrey Weeks, *Sexuality* (New York: Routledge, 1986), and *Against Nature: Essays on History, Sexuality and Identity* (London: Rivers Oram Press, 1991).

3. Ngahuia Te Awekotuku, "Maori: People and Culture," in *Maori Arts and Culture*, ed. Arapata T. Hakiwai, Roger Neich, Mick Pendergrast, and Dorota C. Starzecka (Auckland: David Bateman, 1996).

4. Kim M. Philips and Barry Reay, "Introduction," in *Sexualities in History: A Reader*, ed. Kim M. Philips and Barry Reay (New York: Routledge, 2002).

5. Jeffrey Weeks, "Sexuality and History Revisited," in *Sexualities in History: A Reader*, ed. Kim M. Phillips and Barry Reay (New York: Routledge, 2002).

6. Catherine Masters, "Top Bishop's Vision: A World without Gays," *New Zealand Herald*, June 5, 2004.

7. Martin Cannon, "The Regulation of First Nations Sexuality," *Canadian Journal of Native Studies* 18, no. 1 (1998).

8. Dennis Altman, "Globalization and the International Gay/Lesbian Movement," in *Handbook of Lesbian and Gay Studies*, ed. Diane Richardson and Steven Seidman (London: Sage, 2002); Gilbert Herdt, *Same Sex, Different Cultures: Exploring Gay and Lesbian Lives* (Oxford: Westview Press, 1997).

9. Judith Binney, " 'Whatever Happened to Poor Mr Yate? An Exercise in Voyeurism,' " *New Zealand Journal of History* 9, no. 2 (1975): 111–25.

10. Laurie K. Gluckman, *A Medical History of New Zealand Prior to 1860* (Christchurch: Whitcoulls, 1976).

11. Peter McColl, "Homosexuality and Mental Health Services," *British Medical Journal*, 308, no. 6928 (1994): 550–51.

12. Aspin and Hutchings, "Reclaiming the Past to Inform the Future."

13. Ministry of Health, "Sexual and Reproductive Health Strategy" (Wellington: Ministry of Health, 2001).

14. Nicola Low, Nathalie Broulet, Yaw Adu-Sarkodie, Pelham Barton, M. Hossaihn, and Sarah Hawkes, "Global Control of Sexually Transmitted Infections," *The Lancet Sexual and Reproductive Health* (October 2006): 77–92.

15. Ibid.

16. Anna Glasier, A. Metin Gulmezoglu, George P. Schmid, Claudia G. Moreno, and Paul F. A. Van Look, "Sexual and Reproductive Health: A Matter of Life and Death." *Lancet, Sexual and Reproductive Health* (October 2006): 11–23.

17. UNAIDS, "2006 Report on the Global Aids Epidemic" (New York: UNAIDS, 2006).

18. David A.B. Murray, "Who Is Takatapui? Maori Language, Sexuality and Identity in Aotearoa/New Zealand," *Anthropologica* 45, no. 2 (2003): 233–44.

19. Carole Vance, "Anthropology Rediscovers Sexuality: A Theoretical Comment," in *Culture, Society and Sexuality: A Reader*, ed. Richard R. Parker and P. Aggleton (London: UCL Press, 1999).

20. David M. Fergusson, L. John Horwood, Elizabeth M. Ridder, and Annette L. Beautrais, "Sexual Orientation and Mental Health in a Birth Cohort of Young Adults," *Psychological Medicine* 35, no. 7 (2005): 971–81; Gary Remafedi, Simone French, Mary Story, Michael D. Resnick, and Robert Blum. "The Relationship between Suicide Risk and Sexual Orientation: Results of a Population-Based Study," *American Journal of Public Health* 88, no. 1 (1998): 57–60;

Frits van Griensven, Peter H. Kilmarx, Supaporn Jeeyapant, Chomnad Mano-paiboon, Supaporn Korattana, and Richard A. Jenkins, "The Prevalence of Bisexual and Homosexual Orientation and Related Health Risks among Adolescents in Northern Thailand," *Archives of Sexual Behavior* 33, no. 2 (2004): 137–47; Lars Wichstrom and Kristinn Hegna, "Sexual Orientation and Suicide Attempt: A Longitudinal Study of the General Norwegian Adolescent Population," *Journal of Abnormal Psychology* 112, no. 1 (2003): 144–51; Keren Skegg, Shyamala Nada-Raja, Nigel Dickson, Charlotte Paul, and Sheila Williams, "Sexual Orientation and Self-Harm in Men and Women," *American Journal of Psychiatry* 160 no. 3 (2003): 541–46.

21. Fergusson et al., "Sexual Orientation and Mental Health."

22. Clive Aspin, Paul Reynolds, Keren Lehavot, and Jacob Taiapa, "An Investigation of the Phenomenon of Non-Consensual Sex among Maori Men Who Have Sex with Men," *Culture, Health and Sexuality* 11, no. 1 (2009): 35–49.

7

Two-Spirit Men's Sexual Survivance against the Inequality of Desire

Brian Joseph Gilley

Anthropology and American Indian studies in the late 1980s through the late 1990s saw a flurry of studies of "alternative" cultural constructions of gender. Of particular interest were nonwestern cultural examples of gender fluidity and difference. To critique Euro-American conflations of sex, sexuality, and gender, poststructuralist anthropologists turned to the American Indian "berdache" tradition, the hijras of India, and the *fa'afafine*, or Mahu, of Polynesia. The goal of early studies was to find nonwestern examples of "gender-bending" behavior to combat Euro-American assumptions about compulsory heterosexuality, gender essentialism, and the deviance of same-sex relations.[1] The questioning of sexual dimorphism and biological paradigms precipitated a new approach that deemphasized bodily sex, sexual desire, and sexual object choice for an emphasis on gender construction. This approach surfaced in academic, social, literary, and political writings throughout American Indian studies. By not emphasizing sexual preference the Indigenous gay movement refocused and reoriented conceptions of Native sexuality and gender studies into the feminist third wave. The strategic deemphasis of sexuality obscured our understanding of the ways desire is implicated in heterosexism and homophobia among American Indian societies. Academic writings on the subject, especially those leaning toward the activist, have been more intent on defending and defining the cultural concept of the gender-diverse Native than they have on examining the conditions that necessitated its revitalization over the last twenty years. The resulting depoliticization of homophobia within the Native societies has failed to consider the role that sexuality plays in the coconstruction of Native gay identity by American Indian communities and the Two-Spirit person.

I propose that we examine the ways in which Two-Spirit people experience their positionality as it is based in dominant perceptions and actions of aversion toward their sexuality and gender. To do this we need an examination of desire as something more than felt by subjects, but also as a conception through which subject relations of inequality are acted out. Inequalities of desire are generated through the ways groups of people endorse specific forms and possibilities of sexual interaction. Legitimate sexual partnering and practices emerge from a cultural history where power relations act to reinforce precise forms of corporeal desire and pleasure. Differentials in power become expressed in sexual cultures and are implicated in sexual inequality. By endorsing specific forms of heterosexuality as legitimately Indian, or tribally specific, heteronormative sexual ideologies create the impossibility of a socially recognized Two-Spirit role. That is, being an Indian man who has sex with other men represents an impossibility among the endorsed forms of Native sexuality, all of which are heterosexual.[2]

When looked at through inequalities of desire, the subjective experience of being a Two-Spirit man is undeniably about sexual desire. Desires are rated, ranked, classified, and discerned based on their ability to meet the discursive requirements of a particular identity. In contemporary Native society when a man crosses gender lines or mixes gender aesthetics, his community most likely reads that action as being explicitly associated with same-sex preferences, not the historic role for the gender-different within their tribe. It is therefore within this association and its "inequality" that Two-Spirit men engage in recovering sex traditions along with those of gender and culture.

This chapter will examine how sexuality was removed as an aspect of the American Indian gender-diversity conversation, while also arguing for the reincorporation of sexual desire into examinations of contemporary gender-diversity traditions. Sexual survivance among the contemporary Two-Spirit social movement challenges the separation between sexual desire and gender that masks the power relations surrounding sexual practice and the social impact of homophobia. Our discussion begins with a brief ethnographic and intellectual background of American Indian gender diversity. I then critically examine the "gender diversity project" and its role in framing the current thinking on American Indian gender diversity as well as how historic displacement onto the contemporary obscured heterosexism and homophobia among Native peoples. As a straight Cherokee/Chickasaw man conducting fieldwork with two Two-Spirit societies, one in Denver and one in Oklahoma, I am always puzzled by the theoretical and methodological avoidance of the importance GLBTQ2 men place on finding partners and engaging in sexual activity. Anthropology, feminism, queer theory, and GLBTQ studies have spent a great deal of time disrupting heteronormative sexuality only to produce a certain form of asexual criticism placing desire in a nebulous realm missing certain visceral realities and agentive subjective corporeality. I found in my fieldwork on the current experiences of contemporary Two-Spirit men the importance of sexual desire in the social and political struggles faced by gay Indian men. I explore how the reincorporation of sexual desire as a topic of inquiry within the ethnography of Indigenous gender difference will provide openings for a critical analysis of homophobia among societies that have more fluid conceptions of gender and sexuality within their social history. My hope is to reignite the conversation concerned with sexual desire and its role in personal and cultural survivability.

The Gender Diversity Project and the Inequalities of Desire

At the height of anthropology's fascination with nonwestern gender constructions, the humanities and social sciences in general were rethinking western sexual dimorphism and the naturalization of heterosexist conceptions of gender, bodily sex, and sexuality in research and society. The result was for theorists and ethnographers to turn their attention away from sexual practices, and toward a separation of bodily sex, sexuality, and gender identity. This interpretation became popular in the early 1990s and was heavily influenced by the work of "third sex, third gender" scholars. Serena Nanda's work on the hijras of India and a volume edited by Gilbert Herdt were enormously influential in this new critique of sexual dimorphism and heterosexism.[3] Sex and gender diversity relied on several principles in their argument against essentialism, primary of which was that nonwestern forms of gender diversity stand as examples of the volatility of sex/gender dimorphism. Theoretically, these "alternative" genders were subsumed under an analytical category of "third genders." The notion of the third gender facilitated the disentangling of sex, sexuality, and gender essentialism. Ultimately, the focus on historic and contemporary forms of gender diversity came to reflect the intellectual trend of playing down sexual practice and celebrating disjuncture in sex/gender essentialism. As Herdt points out, "I urge . . . that we not confuse desire for the same sex with a third sex per se . . . and that sexual orientation and identity are not the keys to conceptualizing a third sex and gender across time and space."[4] Accordingly, Herdt states, "The dilemma in thinking of these desires resides in a simple Western prejudice: to express a certain sexuality is to preclude all other desires."[5] However, as Gayatri Reddy points out, this shift came at a cost to analysis: "it [Herdt's book *Third Sex, Third Gender*] tends to effectively separate the domain of sexuality from that of political economy and the analysis of other axes of identity, thereby limiting its usefulness as an articulation of the complexity of everyday life."[6] I would add that by playing down sexuality as an aspect of identity for gender-diverse individuals, the study of nonwestern gender became encapsulated in the romantic and exotic ideal of "tolerant" cultures far off geographically and historically. The celebration of difference effectively stalled a discussion of homophobia and its role in shaping the life experiences of the individuals being studied.

Challenging sexuality, sex, and gender essentialism was highly influential in the analysis of historic American Indian gender diversity and the contemporary Two-Spirit (American Indian GLBTQ) movement. Roscoe's award-winning and impeccably researched ethnohistorical ethnography *The Zuni Man-Woman* completely reoriented the study of American Indian gender diversity. Roscoe's goal in *The Zuni Man-Woman* and his second book, *Changing Ones,* was to downplay same-sex relations and bodily sex as the analytical factors in our understanding of Native conceptions of gendered personhood. Instead, he focuses on the ways gender was a fluid construction that could operate independently of an individual's sexual preferences and bodily sex. "Gender in this view is a multidimensional cultural category that presumes sexed personhood but is not limited to sex or sex-specific traits . . . in North America, individual, acquired, and ascribed traits outweighed sex-assignment in determining gender identity."[7] In all of his work, Roscoe relies on the notion that the historic "berdache" was a kind of person among multiple possibilities of personhood within Native societies, a concept that Euro-Americans could understand only if thought of in terms of third or fourth genders (man and woman being one and two respectively). Roscoe's ideas are now a standard part of our understanding, but in the 1990s he presented an entirely new lens through which to conceive of historic constructions of sex and sexuality. Roscoe's deemphasis of sexuality became highly influential in academic and activist reinterpretations of historic sex/gender systems and contemporary gay Indigenous identity.

The term *Two-Spirit* began to emerge among the GLBTQ Native community just as the work of Will Roscoe was reaching popularity in anthropology, American Indian studies, and gay Native social circles. *Two-Spirit* essentially refers to a personal subjectivity consisting of two spirits, one male and one female. The notion of Two-Spirit is a contemporary reference to the availability of mixed-gender roles among most American Indian tribes prior to European contact. The idea of Two-Spirit relied on the conception that historic Native societies placed an individual's role within their social structure before an individual's bodily sex and sexual preference. That is, gender and gender roles were variable based on multiple societal factors such as tribal tradition. An individual's sexual orientation, it was argued, had little influence on their role in the community. Despite scholars and activists chiding Roscoe for his insistence on using the word *berdache,* his ideas about historic gender diversity became embedded in writings about and popular conceptions of Two-Spirit. Two foundational pieces concerning the term *Two-Spirit* and its implications are the article "... And We Are Still Here" and the edited volume *Two-Spirit People.* These two works represented a manifesto of sorts for individuals conducting research on American Indian gender diversity and for GLBTQ Natives. In the introduction to *Two-Spirit People,* the authors set out to advocate replacing the term *berdache* with *Two-Spirit,* to separate the American Indian gay experience from non-Native gays and lesbians, and to create a link between contemporary GLBTQ Natives and the culture history of gender diversity.[8] A primary goal of the work by Jacobs and Thomas on Two-Spirit identity was to argue for a contemporary Native identity that recognized multiple forms of gender identity and sexuality. Embedded within this movement was the desire to fight homophobia among Native peoples and to provide a positive identity for GLBTQ Natives based in cultural heritage, not sexual identity.

Jacobs echoes this point: "in some cultures, 'homosexuality' and 'gender alternatives' are not synonymous, as evidenced by the fact that many Native epistemologies or worldviews mark them as separate."[9] The analytical separation of one's sexuality from one's role within one's society led to a significant reworking of the way the "berdache" past was conceived and bolstered the social cause of contemporary GLBTQ Natives who wanted to emphasize their cultural identity over their sexual preference. Emphasizing their cultural connection with "tradition," specifically ceremonialism and powwow culture, no doubt strengthened American Indian GLBTQ goals. Connecting themselves culturally rather than sexually to historic forms of gender diversity allowed Two-Spirit people to argue that their social and gender practices fit squarely within traditional values. Strategically turning attention away from the sexual orientation aspect of historic gender forms, so as to not associate themselves with popular gay culture, and toward cultural practices, generated an entire genre of writing and analysis wherein same-sex desire was merely a footnote. This approach no doubt generated a more accurate portrait of gender construction in prehistoric and historic Native America but, as I argue, muddied our understanding of the experiences of contemporary gay Native peoples.

Making same-sex desire the subject of analysis is complicated by previous scholars' strategic deemphasis of sexual orientation in identity formation among Native sex and gender systems. In arguing that Two-Spirit identity is less about sexual desire and more about culture, scholars of Native gender diversity (and gender diversity in general) fail to recognize that mainstream dominant Indian society views Two-Spirit people according to broadly American notions about "homosexuality." That is, most of the Two-Spirit men I interviewed, socially participated with, and surveyed recognize that their sexual orientation is the single most important alienating factor for them. They also understood that any nonheteronormative expression of gender was read by their communities as explicitly "gay" and not according to any "historic" notions about gender status. By emphasizing the social construction of gender roles, scholars have yet to address the modern social construction of desire in Native communities.

Inevitably, Two-Spirit relations to the communities in which they seek to participate will be affected by a discernment of qualities the community seeks to emphasize, same-sex relations not being recognized as one of them. Accordingly, what we must understand is that the "problem of desire" also resides in the ways that Two-Spirit people perceive and experience non-gay Indian bias against their sexual preferences. This bias is generated in the ideals that allow non-gay Indians to equate Two-Spirit people with their same-sex desire and not cultural competency. Two-Spirit men's communities frustrate their desire for social belonging by equating their personal identity with their sexual orientation. Therefore, we must problematize the whole of desire; otherwise, we run the risk of conceptualizing same-sex sexuality as something extraordinary to a particular contemporary society. To do this requires an understanding of the whole of desire as not only sexual desire but also individual longing for self-acceptance, acceptance in one's community, and a socially affirmed identity that represents how one sees oneself. Dominant perceptions of sexual desire act to complicate the fulfillment of other desires—mainly the desire to participate as a full member of tribal and ceremonial communities as well as of families—but also provide associative potential for various forms of Two-Spirit sexual survivance.

Sexual Survivance

Contemporary Two-Spirit identity places sexuality at the center of the critical intersection of indigeneity and desire. It also brings about a significant problem for social theorists in conceiving of a Two-Spirit sexuality: the act of claiming ancient rights and historic gender continuity at the same time as engaging in what might appear as explicitly modern sexual circulation. Desire, as felt emotion and descriptor of want, may frame much of what we think about sexuality and its relationship to gender for the Two-Spirit men whose lives I documented; desire within this conception can also act as a means of action to achieve certain ends. As an instrument of physicality it is also embedded in broad and microsociological understandings of resistance, oppression, and pleasure. Two-Spirit men's sexual acts become the referential indices of a desire or "shifters" for the state of queer Indigenous affairs.[10]

I am not arguing for a special demarcated space within white homonationalism for Two-Spirit men's sexuality.[11] Nor am I putting their desire as a one-to-one equivalency with the erotic wants of the non-Native GLBTQ "family." Rather, I am arguing for an understanding of GLBTQ2 men's sexuality originating in the axes of Native and gay and of tribally specific sovereign sexuality, of the historical, original, and contemporary. It seems that we must push back against the fact that "the erotic is not expressed as particular *desires* but, rather, as discrete *identities*." Accordingly, "erotic desires which fall outside the trinary of heterosexuality, homosexuality (either/or) and bisexuality (both/and), or which fail to make sense in terms of their basic logic of binary gender are rendered unintelligible."[12] Thus, it seems that the inequality of desire as it is produces certain forms of knowledge—sexualities, queer identities, bodily effects, social theories, critiques—renders a historically founded and cultural continuous erotic desire unintelligible while other intelligible forms of historic practices coexist in the same sociocultural spaces. Moving beyond desire as identity requires a conception of a specifically Indigenous eroticism emanating from the fundamental principles and experience of tribal and community life that articulates with and recognizes, rather than disrupts, fundamental social principles of Native peoples.

Two-Spirit desire, as a broadly Native project and as a tribally specific one, is an aspect of what Vizenor calls the "simulations of survivance," which challenges the construction of an "inequality of desire" that was adopted by communities as a "manifest manner" of heteropatriarchy.[13] Manifest manners, alluding to manifest destiny, are American Indian customs and ideas that Vizenor claims are derivative of the settlement process. As a manifest manner, Native heteronormativity is an accommodation to colonial heteronormativity—because it adapted traditional sex segregation to colonial sexual logics, in order that colonial projects would seem to be compatible with how Native people lived gender and sexuality. One of the effects of this was a later internalization of colonial naturalizations of sex/gender by Native people. Remember, however, first it was an accommodation, one that did not *necessarily* "take on" the naturalizing narratives of heteronormativity, so much as made Native sex/gender arrangements compatible with demands of colonial culture. Yet, in the case of Two-Spirit men, desire serves as a multifaceted, multitribal, and yet individually autonomous as well as sovereign form of survivance. Survivance, a combination of survival and resistance, is a theoretical challenge to a stable, easily discernible, and victimized American Indian identity.[14] As an extension, sexual survivance is a community-based and theoretical challenge to the epistemological understanding of Two-Spirits as victims of Native-community heteropatriarchy through the loss of roles and private/public forms of erotic pleasure. Rather, it is a corporeal continuity with the pleasures of the past and, in this way, is not the token foundation of "identity" or a "structureless" modality of action, but an experience—felt, lived, corporeal—through which other desires are rendered.[15] Through acts of sexual survivance, Two-Spirit men extend Indian-specific meanings about conquest, race, colonialism, and sovereignty to desire, whereby the Two-Spirit sexual encounter is governed by sexual historicity rendered modern.

Notes

1. Kath Weston, "Lesbian/Gay Studies in the House of Anthropology," *Annual Reviews in Anthropology*, 22: 339–67 (1993).

2. Judith Butler, *Gender Trouble: Feminism and the Subversion of Identity* (New York: Routledge, 1990), 23; Brian Joseph Gilley, *Becoming Two-Spirit:*

Gay Identity and Social Acceptance in Indian Country (Lincoln: University of Nebraska Press, 2006), 19–20; Michel Foucault, *The History of Sexuality,* vol. 2: *The Use of Pleasure.* (Harmondsworth, Middlesex: Penguin 1990), 23–24; Richard G. Parker, Regina M. Barbosa, Peter Aggleton, eds., *Framing the Sexual Subject: The Politics of Gender, Sexuality and Power* (Berkeley: University of California Press, 2000), 7–9.

3. Gilbert Herdt, ed., *Third Sex, Third Gender* (New York: Zone Books, 1993); Serena Nanda, *Neither Man nor Woman: The Hijras of India* (Belmont, CA: Wadsworth, 1990).

4. Gilbert Herdt, "Introduction: Third Sexes and Third Genders," in *Third Sex, Third Gender,* ed. Gilbert Herdt (New York: Zone Books, 1993), 47.

5. Gilbert Herdt, "The Dilemmas of Desire: From 'Berdache' to Two-Spirit," in *Two-Spirit People: Native American Gender Identity, Sexuality and Spirituality,* ed. Sue-Ellen Jacobs, Wesley Thomas, and Sabine Lang (Chicago: University of Illinois Press, 1997), 279.

6. Gayatri Reddy, *With Respect to Sex* (Chicago: University of Chicago Press, 2005), 32.

7. Will Roscoe, *Changing Ones* (New York: St. Martin's Press, 1998), 127.

8. Sue-Ellen Jacobs, Wesley Thomas, and Sabine Lang, "Introduction," in *Two-Spirit People: Native American Gender Identity, Sexuality and Spirituality,* ed. Sue-Ellen Jacobs, Wesley Thomas, and Sabine Lang (Chicago: University of Illinois Press, 1997).

9. Sue-Ellen Jacobs, "Is the North American Berdache Merely a Phantom in the Imagination of Western Social Scientists?" In *Two-Spirit People: Native American Gender Identity, Sexuality and Spirituality,* ed. Sue-Ellen Jacobs, Wesley Thomas, and Sabine Lang (Chicago: University of Illinois Press, 1997), 27.

10. Michael Silverstein, "Shifters, Linguistic Categories, and Cultural Description," in *Meaning in Anthropology,* ed. Keith H. Basso and Henry A. Selby (Albuquerque: School of American Research, University of New Mexico Press, 1976).

11. Scott Lauria Morgensen, "Arrival at Home: Radical Faerie Configurations of Sexuality and Place," *GLQ: A Journal of Lesbian and Gay Studies* 15, no. 1 (2009): 67–96.

12. David Valentine, "I Went to Bed with My Own Kind Once": The Erasure of Desire in the Name of Identity," *Language and Communication* 23 (2002): 123–24.

13. Gerald Vizenor, *Manifest Manners: Narratives on Postindian Survivance* (Lincoln: University of Nebraska Press, 1999), 12.

14. Ibid., 4.

15. Elizabeth A. Povinelli, *The Empire of Love* (Durham, NC: Duke University Press, 2006), 13; Marshall Sahlins, *Islands of History* (Chicago: University of Chicago Press, 1985), xii.

8
Unsettling Queer Politics
What Can Non-Natives Learn from Two-Spirit Organizing?

Scott Lauria Morgensen

As a non-Native and white queer person, I learned how settler colonialism shapes queer politics by attending to the work of Two-Spirit organizers. Native GLBTQ and Two-Spirit people long have explained how settler colonialism, gender, and sexuality interrelate—in one another's lives, for Native people generally, and for non-Natives. But U.S. and Canadian sexual minority and queer politics tend to reinforce non-Native investments in settlement, as I found when I studied their relation to these issues.[1] Most non-Native GLBT and queer people I met were aware of or wished to learn about histories of gender and sexual diversity in Native societies. But most were not engaged with the work of Two-Spirit organizers to critique settler colonialism and decolonize Native communities. Non-Native GLBT and queer people evade Two-Spirit critiques when they sustain mistaken premises about Indigenous culture and colonial history, and fail to investigate their inheritance of a settler colonial society.

This chapter calls non-Native GLBT and queer people to engage Two-Spirit critiques by answering three "lessons" I learned while being accountable to Two-Spirit organizing. During years of research and teaching on the non-Native and settler formation of sexual minority and queer politics, non-Natives often asked me to teach them about gender and sexuality within Indigenous cultural traditions. But I failed to meet their expectations if I taught them that settler colonialism has shaped gender and sexuality for Native *and* non-Native people, and that Two-Spirit organizers promote this knowledge as social criticism. My chapter tells non-Native audiences that if they wish to learn about Two-Spirit people, they can commit first to self-reflexively studying settler colonialism as a condition of their own and Two-Spirit people's lives. I mark my intentions in my title, with the word *unsettling*. This term evokes histories of queer politics that promoted *queer* in its English meanings as all that heterosexual culture marks as strange, or any action (queering, unsettling) that carries this effect. But anticolonial critique shifts the term's meaning for non-Native GLBT and queer people who, while familiar with unsettling the lives of straights, must learn to unsettle their own and all non-Natives' lives by critiquing their formation by settler colonialism. My chapter models one way that non-Native queer politics may be unsettled: by responding to the lessons I learned from the critical theories and practices of Two-Spirit organizers.

While I understand non-Natives to be a key audience of this chapter, I write and present it here first to responsibly address conversations among queer Indigenous people in Two-Spirit organizing and Native studies. Specifically, I respond to four decades of Native GLBTQ and Two-Spirit organizing in the United States and Canada by citing publicly circulating texts, augmented by conversations with historical participants.[2] Among many themes within varied Native GLBTQ projects, I highlight those that invoked belonging to traditional culture, such as Two-Spirit identity. Mindful that many Native GLBTQ people do not identify as Two-Spirit or see their lives reflected in traditional roles, I limit my words to responding to the specific histories of Two-Spirit organizing. In kind, I understand that Native GLBTQ people proposed "Two-Spirit" as a diversely gendered term, which defied masculinism in the colonial term *berdache* by centering Native lesbians, transwomen, and transmen alongside Native gay men. Yet Native GLBTQ people in HIV/AIDS activism also found it necessary to address men who have sex with men, which over time has tended to correlate Two-Spirit identity to gay or bisexual men. Mindful of this history, I use the term to invoke gender diversity and the lives of Native lesbian and bisexual women and trans people alongside gay and bisexual men.[3] Finally, my framing of Two-Spirit organizing acknowledges claims like that of Anguksuar Richard LaFortune (Yup'ik), co-founder of American Indian Gays and Lesbians (Minneapolis), who has "[hesitated] to characterize this organizing as being part of a 'movement'"; as he argues, "what is happening, actually, is that we are remembering who we are and that our identities can no longer be used as a weapon against us."[4] In kind, I use the term *organizing* to indicate the many ways Native GLBTQ people gather to create community and knowledge, which at times also lead to forms of political activism or social movement.

I write these lessons as one response to a shift heralded by this book, as work in Native studies displaces non-Native accounts of Indigenous gender and sexuality in anthropology and queer studies. In Linda Tuhiwai Smith's terms, Two-Spirit and allied Native writers are "decolonizing methodologies" by displacing the colonial authority of non-Natives in scholarship and pursuing self-determined queer work in Native space.[5] As a non-Native queer scholar trained in anthropology, I respond by questioning my inherited authority to appear to tell truths for Native people. Instead, my work has focused on critically examining *non*-Natives, notably their inherited power as settlers, while citing the prior theories by Native people that already model this critique. Thus, my work highlights that far from being the first author on this theme, I am a respondent to a long history of criticism of non-Native queer politics by Native GLBTQ and Two-Spirit organizers. While I do mean to tell accurate stories about Two-Spirit organizing while citing activists' own texts, my translations necessarily tell as much or more about me and the power I retain as they do about Two-Spirit organizing. Yet I *want* my translations to be read in this way, as they will indicate to Native and allied readers what follows— the risk, or opportunity—if non-Native respond to Two-Spirit people with the intention of being allied critics of settler colonialism. My claims might be familiar in Two-Spirit circles, but they still invite radical change among non-Native GLBT and queer people, who have barely begun to respond. If non-Natives were to do so, they would question the colonial origins and uses of sexual minority and queer identities, displace desires for a history or future on stolen land, and challenge the colonial power of settler states and global institutions. In the process they would recognize themselves *as* "non-Natives"—persons defined in relationship to Native peoples by settler colonialism—who respond by holding themselves accountable to alliance with Native struggles for decolonization. Non-Native GLBT and queer people can begin this work by grounding their politics in engaging critical theories and practices that arose historically in Native GLBTQ and Two-Spirit organizing.

Lesson One: Two-Spirit Is Not a Native Sexual Minority

Each lesson I discuss reflects the history and clarity of the first that I learned: the category "Two-Spirit" does not describe a Native sexual minority. I argue, by extension, that Two-Spirit identity calls into question the colonial origin and logic of sexual minority identity for non-Natives. From their earliest organizing, Native GLBTQ people argued that their place within Native societies cannot be explained as that of a sexual minority. They sought to explain Native histories of gender and

sexual diversity by rejecting the colonial term *berdache* and by seeking language to link historical and contemporary Native culture. Their
efforts led to proposing Two-Spirit identity. While this term remained
open to allying with GLBTQ non-Natives, it marked more importantly
a difference in Native identity. Unlike a sexual minority, Two-Spirit
identity was defined by qualities beyond sexuality or gender. It did
not describe a minority group in Native societies defined by sexuality
or gender that existed in oppositional difference to a sexual or gender
majority. Instead, Two-Spirit described an integral location GLBTQ
and other Native people might occupy in the shared culture of a Native
nation, which through kinship, economics, social life, or religion linked
all Native people in relationship. Two-Spirit identity in this way defies
appropriation as a version of any non-Native sexual or gender identity. Furthermore, as a term of Native decolonization, it ensured that
non-Natives would have no basis to evaluate Two-Spirit identities or
organizing before studying how their own identities and organizing are
located as non-Native within histories of settler colonialism.

The call to identify differently than as a sexual minority arose in the
1970s, as Native GLBTQ people migrated to and gathered in U.S. and
Canadian cities supporting urban Native and sexual minority politics.
For instance, the community organization Gay American Indians (GAI)
formed in 1975 in San Francisco under the leadership of Barbara Cameron (Lakota) and Randy Burns (Paiute), overlapping the late-1970s
cultural work of the Vancouver Native Cultural Society and, in 1981,
the Winnipeg social group Nichiwakan. Such groups formed spaces
of respect and support by and for Native GLBTQ people, even as they
sought to educate non-Native and Native communities in Native GLBTQ
people's existence. For instance, GAI members sought a presence in
regional Native communities by collaborating with urban American
Indian activist and service groups, and by doing outreach at events like
rodeos and powwows.[6] GAI also worked to educate non-Natives in sexual minority politics and beyond, by promoting Native inclusion in gay
pride parades, gaining civic recognition from the City of San Francisco,
or raising awareness of Native GLBTQ people in mainstream media.[7]
A major theme in their work was that Native GLBTQ people inherited
Native cultural traditions that should be accepted by Native people
today, as in GAI's anthology *Living the Spirit* and contributions to it
by longtime members Burns, Erna Pahe (Navajo), and Clyde M. Hall
(Shoshone Bannock).[8] GAI members called on non-Natives to respect

Native histories even if they did not share in them, and in this way edu-cated about Native GLBTQ people without seeking their absorption into non-Native sexual minority politics. Organizers sought recognition of a distinction *from* non-Native sexual minorities as one element of gaining respect in Native and non-Native social spaces.

The worth of asserting distinctions from sexual minority politics while working in relation to it was illuminated when Native GLBTQ people allied with non-Native GLBTQ people of color. Such an alli-ance defined the historical growth of Two-Spirit organizing in New York City. In 1989, Leota Lone Dog (Lakota), Curtis Harris (San Car-los Apache), and Kent Lebsock (Lakota) drew from prior organizing with the American Indian Cultural House, and notably its HIV/AIDS program, to form WeWah and BarCheeAmpe as the first NYC group for Native lesbians and gays. The group embraced Two-Spirit identity immediately on its proposition in 1990.[9] This moment coincided with WeWah and BarCheeAmpe members joining a new initiative to found a citywide coalition of GLBTQ people of color, the Cairos Collective.[10] The collective announced its formation by publishing a first issue of its magazine *COLORLife!* even as WeWah and BarCheeAmpe's newsletter *Buffalo Hide* entered circulation. Between 1990 and the 1992 quincenten-nial, WeWah and BarCheeAmpe members in both magazines addressed the distinctions of Two-Spirit identity from non-Native sexual minori-ties, even as they called all GLBTQ people of color to join Two-Spirit people in challenging settler colonialism.[11] In response, the Cairos Col-lective named Two-Spirit identity as a linked yet distinct identity among those it aimed to represent, as it described its mission to serve "LGBTST people of color," a phrase sustained by the collective's successor, the Audre Lorde Project.[12] Yet WeWah and BarCheeAmpe members went a step further, by arguing that Native Two-Spirit people who allied with GLBTQ people of color were members of sovereign peoples with his-tories and cultures that remained distinct from all non-Natives. Their insistence on national difference was not a barrier to coalition, but its condition. Only by affirming Two-Spirit's distinction in Native nations could Natives and non-Natives meet in gender and sexual politics across a sustained difference, rather than through the absorptive logic of mul-ticulturalism. "LGBTST" might seem to read as a set of sexual and gen-der minorities linked by racial multiculturalism. But so long as WeWah and BarCheeAmpe engaged Cairos, "LGBT" identities were known to be potentially shared by all its members, while "TS" was known not to be, regardless of how anticolonial non-Natives might become. Antiracist and anticolonial alliance among Indigenous people and peoples of color formed the first context in which Two-Spirit identity politically aligned with sexual minority identities while remaining distinct. This history shows that effective coalitions across differences can form without suggesting that sexualities or genders universally equate—here, based on the explicit commitments of the organizers as Indigenous people and people of color to fight colonial legacies. The alliance work of the Cairos Collective and WeWah and BarCheeAmpe announced that in a settler society, all sexual politics will be non-Native until they admit a distinction in Two-Spirit identity and mobilize non-Natives under Two-Spirit leadership to fight the ongoing activity of settler colonialism.

Despite the dynamic of such anticolonial alliance politics, Two-Spirit organizing primarily confronted unexamined whiteness in sexual minority and queer politics. In its first years, GAI mobilized by fighting anti-Indian racism in white gay and lesbian bars and community centers, and by challenging discrimination against Native GLBTQ people who sought social services.[13] One of the first mass mobilizations of Two-Spirit groups across the United States and Canada in the 1990s was in critique of appropriations of Native history by the anthropology of *berdache* and in promoting writing by Two-Spirit people about Native culture and politics.[14] This work coincided with Two-Spirit people forming and leading Native AIDS organizations, where they opposed colonial heterosexism as a determinant of health and linked diverse Native people in defending their communities, as in the work of the Indigenous People's Task Force in Minneapolis under director Sharon Day (Ojibwe), 2 Spirits in Toronto under director Art Zoccole (Anishnabe), and NNAAPC's Two-Spirit capacity-building curricula guided by Larry Kairaiuak (Yup'ik).[15] In such work, if Two-Spirit organizers ever appealed to sexual minority politics, they did so to challenge their erasure or appropriation within it to assert a sovereign difference from it. Brian Joseph Gilley explains that Two-Spirit activists at times sought visibility in the cultures and politics of white sexual minority communities in order to seek out Native GLBTQ people and draw them away into Two-Spirit space.[16] Two-Spirit activists thus have participated in sexual minority organizing without asking to be absorbed. In turn, they have asked that non-Natives recognize and honor their distinction while agreeing to challenge colonial legacies.

Two-Spirit organizing histories suggest that GLBTQ politics will remain normatively white and non-Native until both qualities are marked and critiqued. Non-Native GLBTQ people can alter their organizing by neither erasing nor absorbing Native people, but by critiquing settler colonialism, and on that basis meeting Native people in accountable relationship based in anticolonial alliance politics. Doing so will link non-Native and Native GLBTQ people as allies across *national* differences that perpetually condition any ties they might sustain. Under these conditions, Two-Spirit people may claim a closeness to *and* a distinction from non-Native sexual politics by forming relationship with them across a sovereign difference.

Lesson Two: Non-Native Narratives of Two-Spirit Have Reflected Non-Native Desires

Native sexual and gender diversity was popularized in the late twentieth century by an array of non-Native GLBTQ writing, from the anthropology of berdache to sexual minority cultural and activist literatures.[17] These texts are important for both what they say and why they say it. A key theme in them addressed non-Natives in a normatively white register, saying that Two-Spirit histories grant non-Natives self-acceptance in their own bodies, identities, and social lives. This story recognizes that colonialism occurred and even suggests its critique, but it functions to appropriate Native history so non-Natives—here, white people—will feel more at home as settlers on Native land. Appreciation works here as appropriation not just by taking Native culture out of context, but by failing to note that settler colonialism is what makes inspiration by Native culture possible, and *desirable* for non-Natives inheriting life on stolen land. While cultural appropriation is marked as white and colonial in antiracist criticism, non-Native GLBTQ people of color at times also adopted Two-Spirit histories to reimagine cultures displaced by colonization and diaspora, in ways that may or may not have been responsible to Two-Spirit people. Thus, across great differences in the power relations of race and nation, non-Natives have told stories about Two-Spirit to explain their own lives. In this light, and by inspiration of Two-Spirit organizing, we must ask how non-Native narratives of Two-Spirit have reflected non-Native desires. Texts that appear on the surface to be telling truths about Native people may be telling more about the *non*-Native social locations or political investments of their writers and readers. The popularization of these texts *as* Native truth marginalized writing by, for, and to Native GLBTQ audiences, but the latter never ceased to proliferate as a key legacy of Two-Spirit organizing.

Critique of non-Native storytelling in the 1990s notably defined Two-Spirit organizing when Native GLBTQ people demanded change in the anthropology of berdache. This object long had focused claims by U.S. anthropologists that "primitive" societies retain a cultural diversity that can educate "modern" societies in accepting social differences, as when Margaret Mead and Ruth Benedict cited berdache as inspiring change in gender and sexual norms for "Americans" unmarked as normatively white, class privileged, and settler colonial.[18] Yet this progressive intention reinforced anthropologists' colonial authority over Native people, even as their work modeled the open secret that its apparent reference to Native truth in fact addressed settler desires to change *themselves* by taking an excursion through Native life. In contrast, when Two-Spirit organizers critiqued anthropological writing to propose a category defined uniquely by them, they acted in accord with Linda Tuhiwai Smith's intention to displace colonial knowledge by making Native knowledge the methodological ground of research by and for Native peoples.[19] Indeed, Two-Spirit identity's misalignment with categories of anthropological analysis or GLBTQ politics marks its success at confounding non-Native desires to define Native truth. While Two-Spirit critiques sometimes get framed as having "replaced" *berdache* with *Two-Spirit,* they in fact destabilize the entire logic of accounts of *berdache* and indirectly or directly challenge non-Native desires.

The anthropology of berdache had to be targeted by Two-Spirit activism because of its 1980s revival by U.S. gay and lesbian anthropologists. Formed to challenge homophobia in the American Anthropological Association, the organization ARGOH (Anthropological Research Group on Homosexuality, 1978–1987), later renamed SOLGA (Society of Lesbian and Gay Anthropologists, 1987–2010) and AQA (Association for Queer Anthropology, 2010–present), promoted research on same-sex sexual practices worldwide in order to defend sexual minorities in the United States and in anthropology.[20] Scholars in ARGOH/SOLGA revisited old writing on berdache, conducted new historical and ethnographic study of Native GLBTQ people, and popularized this in anthropology and gay and lesbian studies by inviting non-Natives to take inspiration from berdache when defining their sexual identities and politics. Their writing granted professional legitimacy—Walter Williams's *The Spirit and the Flesh* won the first SOLGA Book Prize; Will Roscoe's *The Zuni Man-Woman* won the AAA Margaret Mead

Award—and renewed the non-Native anthropology of Native people in a new generation. Roscoe notably conducted community-based research accountable to Native people by collaborating with GAI and the Zuni Nation and writing a book that would be useful to Native people. But Roscoe's book became one of a variety of texts in which he popularized berdache for non-Native gay men to adopt as a resource for discovering their own Indigenous sexual nature.[21] The very ways such work appeared to serve Native people thus also or first served non-Native desires; and whether in anthropology or in a broader gay and lesbian readership, those desires were normatively white. Such work joins broader histories of non-Native GLBTQ people pursuing their desires to belong to Native culture and land, in the cultures and politics of settlers reconciling to inheriting stolen land and settler citizenship. I argue elsewhere that this quest for indigeneity defines non-Native and settler sexual politics in relationship to Two-Spirit organizing, although separated by colonial desires from Two-Spirit people's commitments to decolonization.[22]

Even as white gay and lesbian writers popularized berdache, GLBTQ people of color studied their relationship to Native gender and sexual diversity. Notably, Gloria Anzaldúa and Cherríe Moraga explored their Indigenous heritage as Chicanas by taking inspiration from Two-Spirit histories.[23] Their writing on indigeneity inspired Chican@ and ethnic studies and women of color feminisms to theorize interdependence in new work on borders and borderlands, mestizaje/mixed heritage, and alliance and coalition. Such themes also shaped Two-Spirit activism, which drew people across nationality, gender, or sexuality into pan-tribal work. But debate did arise in Native and Chican@ studies about Chicana lesbian claims on Native roots. Recognizing Native heritage affirmed a relationality of Chican@ and Native communities and politics, even as it marked their distinct racialization in the United States, and potential conflict between Chican@ nationalism and the sovereignty of Native Nations.

Scholars of Chicana lesbian writing reflect on these ties and tensions by asking how writers sought to shift but often sustained colonial discourses. Debate remains regarding the degree to which Anzaldúa or Moraga practiced cultural appropriation while envisioning Indigenous sexual subjectivities.[24] I engage this debate by making a simpler observation that, I think, agrees with all sides. When Anzaldúa and Moraga crossed differences of language, geography, culture, or time to embrace Two-Spirit histories, they knew they reached across their lived differences from the contemporary identities of Native American Two-Spirit people. At the moment that they affirmed their own indigeneity, Anzaldúa and Moraga did not claim to be identical to Native American Two-Spirit people. Rather, they proposed linking *Chicana lesbian* desires to the histories Two-Spirit people claim. I thus invite reading their work as tracing the borders of Indigenous identities, as they affirmed Chican@ indigeneity while announcing a desire from a location different than that of Native Americans. Scholars of *Borderlands/La Frontera* and Moraga's writing on "Queer Aztlán" agree that the histories they told were imaginative political narratives reflecting Chicana lesbian desires. Such stakes informed theory and politics in women of color feminisms: that *all* stories are driven by desire, and that radical politics will invest subjugated desires in stories from which they are erased.

Noting that all stories are filled with desire usefully frames the history of Two-Spirit organizing. From their earliest activism, Native GLBTQ people targeted stories told about them as sources of oppression, by countering anthropology, sexual minority romanticism, and Native homophobia with tales of Two-Spirit identity's decolonizing renewal of traditional culture. If we reread *The Spirit and the Flesh* or *Borderlands* as an earlier era's accounts of desires for Two-Spirit histories by people located near to or far from Native identity, we also can revisit Native writing about Two-Spirit as thick with desire. Yet, to echo Smith, the process of doing so will center Native knowledge production by and for Two-Spirit people as the context for any conversation about their lives. If earlier texts promoted non-Native desires because they arose at a certain distance from this conversation, future non-Native writing must arise within it, although with no result guaranteed other than their accountability to the self-determining claims of Two-Spirit people.

Lesson Three: Two-Spirit Organizing Challenges Power Relations in Settler Society

While the degree to which Two-Spirit organizing is political remains under discussion by participants, its work directly informs both Native and non-Native politics. Native GLBTQ organizations arose by linking community building to its implications for broader social change. Most writers attest that Two-Spirit groups arose to help Native GLBTQ people find a new sense of identity, community, or ancestral and cultural ties by reclaiming Two-Spirit histories. Some did this by pursuing directly political ends, as when GAI advocated for Native GLBTQ people in city and state government, or when WeWah and BarCheeAmpe led the Cairos Collective in critiquing settler colonialism during the 1992 quincentennial. One key site that linked Two-Spirit community building, personal growth, and social action was Native HIV/AIDS organizing. Native GLBTQ leaders in Native AIDS services argued that protecting Native communities and challenging the colonial conditions of AIDS hinged on ending heterosexism and accepting GLBTQ people.[25] In these ways, Two-Spirit organizing inspired social and political change even as its theme remained revitalizing identity and community among Native GLBTQ people.

Mindful of this history, I argue that for non-Natives, Two-Spirit organizing bears directly political implications. Notably, in calls to end non-Native control over Native knowledge, and to respect Two-Spirit people's distinction from sexual minority and queer politics, Native people have directed non-Natives to comprehend and challenge settler colonialism. This implication arises from Native requests that the identities, roles, and cultures of GLBTQ people be embraced in Native communities. But this implication is lost if colonial discourses let non-Natives depoliticize Native peoples by reading them as a history or culture for their own edification, rather than as sovereign nations that by surviving conquest challenge non-Natives' standing in a settler colonial society.

Erasing the politics of Two-Spirit organizing follows from queer studies naturalizing the political norms of a settler society. Queer studies tends to historicize GLBTQ politics as the work of white middle-class organizations operating within the racial and national bounds of electoral politics. This political model historically led people of color to gather apart in community-based activism where they challenged multiple oppressions. Yet their move also led white activists and scholars to frame them as "cultural" groups concerned with "identity," and to reserve "political" status for groups that arise near and engage the (white, national) political establishment. This misreading extends to Native GLBTQ people by playing on colonial discourses of Native people as authentic cultures far from the time-space of modern politics, rather than as sovereign nations that disrupt political boundaries in a settler society. Even when Two-Spirit organizing emphasizes transforming identity for Native people, its challenge to the colonial legacies of heteropatriarchy invites change in Native and non-Native politics.

Decolonization is the challenge non-Natives face when learning from the histories of Two-Spirit organizing. Non-Natives must consider their colonial inheritance when occupying Native land or investing in belonging to a settler society, where feeling at home is inseparable from the displacement of Native peoples. Defining gender or sexual liberation in civil rights or multicultural inclusion makes the settler state the horizon of freedom and reinforces settler authority on Native land. Two-Spirit organizing differs by engaging settler institutions from the locations of sovereign Native peoples. For instance, Native GLBTQ organizers sought civic recognition from within a web of treaty and trust relationships whose responsibilities to Native peoples in the areas of housing or health care remain inaccessible to many, while keeping all Natives in a unique relation of control by state authority. This location remains unrecognized in non-Native GLBTQ movements and cannot be absorbed by their focus on citizenship in the settler state. In this and so many other ways, Two-Spirit organizing marks the non-Native and settler formation of sexual minority and queer politics. Truly confronting it will challenge non-Natives' sense of belonging to *themselves* as much as to the settler state or stolen land.

If these shifts were to occur among non-Natives, they would be effects of Two-Spirit organizing, but secondary to its core purpose to transform Native politics. Two-Spirit organizing may overlap sexual minority and queer politics, but it did not arise there. Native GLBTQ networks emerged by engaging their constituents' belonging in their communities, including by calling religious institutions and tribal governments to question belief that nonheteronormative gender and sexuality are effects of colonization. A resounding message from GAI to Two-Spirit and Native AIDS organizations today is that *heteropatriarchy* is a colonial legacy, and that Two-Spirit people are working to renew and defend traditional culture. Two-Spirit organizing thus promotes decolonization not for Native GLBTQ people as a separable group, but for Native peoples *as a whole* in which GLBTQ people are integral members. In turn, even while working to shift Native communities and resistance to colonization, Two-Spirit organizers did this work precisely by engaging settler society. Demanding accountability from non-Native GLBTQ people without joining or being absorbed by them asserts a sovereign relation to settler culture that interrupts its power to contain all differences on stolen land.[26] Challenging colonial power without hesitating to continue to engage it, Two-Spirit organizing acted in the legacy of broader activism for Native sovereignty.

One example of Two-Spirit organizing for Native sovereignty appears in the global growth of Indigenous HIV/AIDS organizing. Scholars recognize AIDS activism in the United States and Canada as a key site where Native GLBTQ communities formed and Two-Spirit identity was promoted, even as responding to AIDS shaped decolonizing gender and sexual politics among Pacific Indigenous peoples, as Clive Aspin argues of *takatapui* identity in Maori GLBTQ and AIDS organizing.[27] Indigenous GLBTQ people in AIDS activism critiqued the colonial conditions of health while adapting settler state resources to community-based services defined by Indigenous ownership and knowledge production. Work within states already inspired transnational collaborations, as when federal funds directed the Canadian Aboriginal AIDS Network to engage First Nations, Métis, and Inuit people, or NNAAPC to serve American Indians, Alaska Natives, and Kanaka Maoli. But the pandemic's global management also linked Indigenous activists across greater distances and differences. For instance, Indigenous AIDS organizers at the biennial International AIDS Conference (IAC) in 1996 organized a first International Indigenous People's Summit, while a second summit at the 2006 IAC launched a major policy intervention, The Toronto Charter: Indigenous People's Action Plan on HIV/AIDS 2006.[28] By working internationally to represent Indigenous peoples, not the settler states that occupy them, Indigenous AIDS activists negotiate the power of states and global agencies to argue for Indigenous sovereignty in local, national, and global AIDS programs. Indigenous GLBTQ people play key roles in this work, as they present the decolonization of sexuality and gender and revitalization of tradition as Indigenous methodologies for healing amidst the AIDS crisis. In AIDS activism, Two-Spirit organizers join Indigenous efforts to decolonize gender and sexuality worldwide in broadly challenging the authority of colonial governance over Indigenous peoples.

Two-Spirit activist challenges to settler states and international law hold non-Native GLBTQ people accountable to the politics of Indigenous sovereignty and decolonization. They remind that Two-Spirit organizing does not reduce to the work of a sexual or racial minority, or any form of multicultural diversity, but asserts an Indigenous relationship to ongoing colonization that non-Natives meet across a national difference. Non-Natives must respond by questioning the colonial logics of the institutions in which they have sought representation or rights. Engaging Two-Spirit activists' sovereign relation to those institutions will hold non-Native sexual minority and queer politics accountable to Native politics, within settler states and worldwide.

"Applying What We Learn": How Can Non-Natives Unsettle Queer Politics?

Queer Indigenous critiques call participants in non-Native queer politics to investigate their formation by settler colonialism and respond with new radicalization. I now consider how the lessons I translated from Two-Spirit organizing suggest radical new directions for non-Native queer politics. While I mean my claims to impact non-Natives, I present them first as a contribution to conversations defined by GLBTQ/Two-Spirit and allied Native people, within Native studies and Two-Spirit organizing. I believe useful change will arise in queer politics once non-Natives commit to engaging the conversations on gender, sexuality, and decolonization already being led by GLBTQ/Two-Spirit and allied Native people.

While the claim that Two-Spirit is not a Native sexual minority has a long history, non-Natives have barely begun to engage its anticolonial implications in sexual minority and queer politics. When Two-Spirit people resist colonialism by asserting a national context for gender and sexuality, they also call non-Natives to ask how nation, gender, and sexuality interrelate for them in settler society. At root, Two-Spirit people critiqued sexual minority identities as colonial when applied to them. This questioned any universal definition of "sexual minorities" outside a national or cultural context, such as tends to follow claims on science or human rights. Thus, if non-Natives in a settler society argue universal claims, they participate in a colonial discourse that can erase the specificity of Native culture and leave their non-Native and settler locations unmarked. Two-Spirit people claimed a Native national context for gender and sexuality in response to the colonial conditions of settler society. In response, non-Natives also must name how nation, gender, and sexuality link for them in a settler colonial society. For them, claiming a sexual minority identity apart from recognizing its non-Native formation will be a settler colonial act that remains disengaged from Two-Spirit organizing.

At times, non-Natives hearing this critique of their colonial formation answer it by trying to emulate Two-Spirit people in a quest for their own indigeneity. In a play on colonial discourse, non-Natives extrapolate from Two-Spirit identity a primitivist idea that all original human societies accepted gender and sexual diversity, and that liberation for GLBTQ people hinges on their reclaiming their indigeneity. As I discuss elsewhere, white U.S. Americans have organized by claiming European paganism as a racially and nationally authentic Indigenous root that embraced gender and sexual diversity. Some also sought cultural exchanges with Two-Spirit people as mutually Indigenous defenders of gender and sexual diversity. Over time, some Two-Spirit people responded by supporting their reclaiming of gender and sexual diversity, including by engaging non-Native queers of African or Asian descent or by joining Chican@/Latin@ queers in making Two-Spirit a means to recall ancestral belonging. These quests require complex evaluation.[29] But I call on any reading of them to ask how they engaged Two-Spirit organizers' call to non-Natives to confront their inheritance of settler colonialism. Trying to "indigenize" non-Native gender or sexuality is a response to having inherited settlement. Especially for white settler descendants, doing so does not differ from how non-Natives are normatively supposed to appropriate Indigenous culture as modern settlers' own past. I call non-Native and Native people to note how GLBTQ people evade critiquing their power as non-Native inheritors of settlement by taking the less threatening but more appropriative path of creating communities that try to emulate Indigenous people.

If any non-Native sexual minority identity is potentially colonial—whether it blends non-Natives into settler society or asserts its own indigeneity against it—this may seem to be good for queer politics. Queer politics historically critiqued sexual minority politics by questioning the naturalness of minority *and* majority gender and sexual identities and by historicizing their formation. In their place, queer activists critiqued heteronormativity and the majority/minority model by shattering beliefs that people must "have" or "be" a natural sex, gender, or sexuality. These radical implications of queer politics are tempered once they engage Two-Spirit organizing. Doing so marks that queer radicalism in its historical epicenters of the United States and Canada has been non-Native and settler if it remained unsituated by race or nation or appeared universally applicable. Two-Spirit organizers call on all non-Natives in a settler society to admit their formation by colonialism, including both sexual minority and queer activists. I argue that queer politics holds a particular promise to respond well to Two-Spirit organizing if it is grounded in anticolonialism, antiracism, and antiimperialism. Non-Native queers can critique heteropatriarchy and the nation-state by marking both as specifically colonial projects within the national histories of settler societies. Localizing critique in this way will form distinctly *non-Native* queer politics whose participants will act at once as inheritors and critics of settler colonialism. By rejecting belonging to the settler state *and* desire for indigeneity in its place, non-Native queers can remain in the groundless space of critiquing settlement as their condition of existence. Staying within the tensions of that space can inspire radical critiques of sexuality, gender, and settler colonialism at once.

My second lesson from Two-Spirit organizing, that non-Native narratives reflect non-Native desires, calls writers and teachers to redefine how Two-Spirit people are named and discussed in academia, popular culture, and movements. The book in which this chapter appears has centered Native GLBTQ and Two-Spirit writers in conversation with allied Native and non-Native writers, all of whom engage Native communities under GLBTQ/Two-Spirit leadership. Shifting the terms of discussion in this way calls people to engage conversations that arise from and return to Native communities. In these contexts, early writings by non-Natives about Native gender and sexuality may be read today in the same way Native GLBTQ people first read them: as non-Native accounts that nevertheless presented resources to be adapted to Two-Spirit organizing. But, by corollary, older literature now can be read not as *about* Two-Spirit people so much as about the desires of writers located near or far from Two-Spirit identity, who applied that knowledge to justify or transform their own lives. Teaching texts in this way can support the turn to centering claims spoken in community by Native GLBTQ and Two-Spirit people, as reflected in the contributions to this collection. In response, academic courses in anthropology and gender/sexuality studies that address Two-Spirit can shift radically. This will occur not by replacing old non-Native texts with new Native texts, but by positioning all old and new texts within conversations in Native studies. Older non-Native texts then will offer evidence of how Two-Spirit people became objects of desire for non-Natives. Bringing non-Natives to mark and displace their non-Native locations in this way aligns with the "decolonizing methodologies" called for by Linda Tuhiwai Smith as well as with the decolonizing directions of Two-Spirit organizing. Non-Natives will shift their desires to study Native culture to studying their own and Native people's mutual formation by settler colonialism, while learning to actively critique its effects.

This and all my arguments reinforce my third lesson, that Two-Spirit organizing called non-Native queers to act as critics of settler colonialism. But rather than just questioning a personal relationship to colonial history or settler identity, non-Natives also can form movements to challenge the power of settler states in national and global affairs. Non-Native queers responding to Two-Spirit critiques must shift our work from narrowly defending our own gendered or sexual lives, to challenging colonial heteropatriarchy and our power as settlers as central to any work we do. By locating as non-Native inheritors of settler colonialism, non-Native queer people and movements will act in tension with the settler society and state, whether those seem normatively white or inclusively multiracial. Anything less will reproduce movements that are at best neutral to Two-Spirit people, but that more likely reinforce the politics that Two-Spirit organizing critiques. Non-Native queers can evaluate their own organizing by the degree to which they trouble settler colonialism—including narratives of independence, rights, or freedom in the settler state—and engage struggles for Native decolonization. Challenging settler society and state power is not an all-or-nothing endeavor, as neither is ready to disappear. But Native struggles for sovereignty and decolonization are placing new limits on their power and promise to transform their authority in the future. Non-Natives can engage such work as part of pursuing a way of living on settled land beyond conquest. This can begin by affirming that Two-Spirit people live in a sovereign relationship to non-Native gender and sexual politics, which may be bridged by non-Natives' allied commitments to work for decolonization.

Engaging Two-Spirit organizing inspired my visions of radicalizing non-Native queer politics. But in conclusion, I return all my claims and intimations to the place where they began: accountable relationship to conversations among Native GLBTQ and Two-Spirit organizers and allied Native people. As I joined other non-Natives in these conversations and learned about Native politics and knowledges, I also learned about myself and my inheritance without either being made central. All this taught me to work proactively from a displaced location. I learn from my errors, am encouraged in my successes, and know where I and my work can and cannot go, in conversations with Native people. My chapter indicates that learning what it might mean to be a white and non-Native queer ally to Two-Spirit people shifted my social locations and sense of self. Breaking from the idea that the world already positioned me in a way that is useful to Native organizing, I became repositioned within Native conversations on gender, sexuality, and decolonization that inform the claims I make and return to conversation. Non-Native queer people who wish to study their colonial inheritance can ask if they have ever engaged Two-Spirit people from participation within Native conversations. In a decolonial reading, these conversations are places where non-Natives are invited, not where they already live or can arrive unannounced. Thus, non-Natives can ask what they have done or can begin to do that might make them sufficiently accountable to Native people to be invited into conversation. Yet to be repositioned in this way only begins a challenging project of committing as non-Natives to work for the decolonization of a settler society. Entering accountable conversation under Native leadership will expose non-Natives' mistaken premises, unexamined desires, and collusions with settler power, while inviting transformation. I invited these outcomes by revisiting my own learning from Two-Spirit organizers, which I now return to the work of Native GLBTQ and Two-Spirit people who tell self-determined stories while leading Native studies and Native communities in work for decolonization.

Notes

1. My other writing primarily addressed academics, while this chapter intends to communicate themes from that work to broader Native and non-Native audiences. See in particular Scott Lauria Morgensen, *Spaces between Us: Queer Settler Colonialism, and Indigenous Decolonization* (Minneapolis: University of Minnesota Press, 2011), and "Settler Homonationalism," *GLQ: A Journal of Lesbian and Gay Studies* 16, no. 1–2 (2010): 105–31. In this chapter, the phrase "sexual minority and queer politics" suggests the late-twentieth-century political split between the promotion of minority sexualities and genders and the questioning of heteronormative institutions and identities. At times I summarize these projects as "queer politics" to reflect a usage of "queer" as a catch-all for gender and sexual diversity that still suggests the critical edge of early queer politics. However, this paper's conclusions distinguish the colonial implications of a sexual minority or queer politics that naturalizes settlement, from the anticolonial potential of a queer politics that critiques *colonial* heteronormativity—in explicit alliance with Indigenous queer critiques.

2. The groups I cite include: Gay American Indians (San Francisco), WeWah and BarCheeAmpe (New York City), American Indian Lesbians and Gays (Minneapolis), and the International Two-Spirit Gathering (Canada/United States), representing GLBTQ2 organizing from 1975; and the Indigenous People's Task Force (Minneapolis), National Native American AIDS Prevention Center

(Denver), 2 Spirits (Toronto), and Canadian Aboriginal AIDS Network (Vancouver), representing HIV/AIDS organizing from 1988. Some disbanded while many sustain. I center these because of the focus of my writing on the late twentieth century and on efforts to coordinate Two-Spirit people across the United States and Canada. The specificities of Two-Spirit people's lives and organizing in rural and reservation/reserve contexts are less well described by my focus and require their own account. I contacted or was contacted by historical organizers in these groups, to whom I communicated my intentions and sent my writing for review, and who gave me critical advice. I offer my writing as a contribution to their ongoing work of documenting their own histories and organizing, and I remain accountable to them.

3. On the proposal of Two-Spirit identity at a third International Gathering of American Indian and First Nations Gays and Lesbians (now, International Two-Spirit Gathering), see: Wesley Thomas, Sue-Ellen Jacobs, " '. . . And We Are Still Here': From *Berdache* to Two-Spirit People," *American Indian Culture and Research Journal* 23, no. 2 (1999). Repetition of the term *berdache* after Native organizers called for its demise appears in the work of Will Roscoe: Will Roscoe, *Changing Ones: Third and Fourth Genders in Native North America* (New York: St. Martin's Press, 1998). The need to center Native AIDS services on MSM (men who have sex with men) was noted by organizers in the mid-1990s, amid debate about erasure of Native women: Ron Rowell, "HIV Prevention for Gay/Bisexual/Two-Spirit Native American Men: A Report of the National Leadership Development Workgroup for Gay/Bisexual/Two-Spirit Native American Men" (Oakland: National Native American AIDS Prevention Center, 1996). By the year 2000, use of the term *Two-Spirit* in sole reference to Native gay and bisexual men structured publications by AIDS organizations and their commentators: Larry Kairaiuak, "Addressing Two-Spirits in the American Indian, Alaskan Native and Native Hawaiian Communities" (Oakland, CA: National Native American AIDS Prevention Center, 2002); Irene S. Vernon, *Killing Us Quietly: Native Americans and HIV/AIDS* (Lincoln: University of Nebraska Press, 2001).

4. Richard LaFortune Anguksuar, "A Postcolonial Colonial Perspective on Western [Mis]Conceptions of the Cosmos and the Restoration of Indigenous Taxonomies," in *Two-Spirit People: Native American Gender Identity, Sexuality, and Spirituality,* ed. Sue-Ellen Jacobs, Wesley Thomas, and Sabine Lang (Urbana: University of Illinois Press, 1997), 218, 222.

5. Linda Tuhiwai Smith, *Decolonizing Methodologies: Research and Indigenous Peoples* (New York: Zed Books, 1999).

6. Beatrice Medicine, "Changing Native American Roles in an Urban Context *and* Changing Native American Sex Roles in an Urban Context," in *Two-Spirit People: Native American Gender Identity, Sexuality, and Spirituality,* ed. Sue-Ellen Jacobs, Wesley Thomas, and Sabine Lang (Urbana: University of Illinois Press, 1997); Roscoe, *Changing Ones.*

7. Randy Burns, "Preface," in *Living the Spirit: A Gay American Indian Anthology*, ed. Will Roscoe (New York: St. Martin's Press, 1988); Jonathan Katz, *Gay American History: Lesbians and Gay Men in the USA* (New York: Thomas Y. Crowell, 1976),332–34; Roscoe, *Changing Ones.*

8. Burns, "Preface"; M. Owlfeather (Clyde Hall), "Children of Grandmother Moon," in *Living the Spirit: A Gay American Indian Anthology*, ed. W. Roscoe (New York: St. Martin's Press, 1988); Erna Pahe, "Speaking Up," in *Living the Spirit: A Gay American Indian Anthology*, ed. Will Roscoe (New York: St. Martin's Press, 1988).

9. Thomas and Jacobs, " '. . . And We Are Still Here.' "

10. Cairos Collective, "Founding Matrons & Patrons," *COLORLife!* June 28, 1992.

11. WeWah and BarCheeAmpe, "500 Years of Survival and Resistance," *Buffalo Hide* 2, no. 1 (1992); WeWah and BarCheeAmpe, "New Movement for Two Spirits," *Buffalo Hide*, Early Spring 1991.

12. Audre Lorde Project, "About the Audre Lorde Project," *Missive*, June 1997.

13. Medicine, "Changing Native American Roles."

14. Sue-Ellen Jacobs, Wesley Thomas, Sabine Lang, eds. *Two-Spirit People: Native American Gender Identity, Sexuality, and Spirituality* (Urbana: University of Illinois Press, 1997).

15. Gilbert Deschamps, "We Are Part of a Tradition: A Guide on Two-Spirited People for First Nations Communities" (Toronto: 2-Spirited People of the 1st Nations, 1998); Kairaiuak, "Addressing Two-Spirits"; Andrea Green Rush, "Models of Prevention: Minnesota American Indian AIDS Task Force," *Seasons: Newsletter of the National Native American AIDS Prevention Center* (1989).

16. Brian Joseph Gilley, *Becoming Two-Spirit: Gay Identity and Social Acceptance in Indian Country* (Lincoln: University of Nebraska Press, 2006), 90, 95, 98–100.

17. See, for example: Judy Grahn, *Another Mother Tongue: Gay Words, Gay Worlds* (Boston: Alyson, 1984); Will Roscoe, *The Zuni Man-Woman* (Albuquerque: University of New Mexico Press, 1991); Walter Williams, *The Spirit and the Flesh: Sexual Diversity in American Indian Culture*, 2nd ed. (Boston: Beacon Press, 1986).

18. Ruth Benedict, *Patterns of Culture* (Boston: Houghton Mifflin, 1934); Margaret Mead, *Coming of Age in Samoa: A Psychological Study of Primitive Youth for Western Civilisation* (New York: William Morrow, 1928); Margaret Mead, *Sex and Temperament in Three Primitive Societies* (New York: William Morrow, 1935).

19. Smith, *Decolonizing Methodologies: Research and Indigenous Peoples* (New York: Zed Books, 1999), 15, 125–29.

20. Anthropological Research Group on Homosexuality, "A.R.G.O.H. Charter," *Anthropological Research Group on Homosexuality* 2, no. 1 (1980).

21. See, for instance, Will Roscoe, *Queer Spirits: A Gay Men's Myth Book* (Boston: Beacon Press, 1995).

22. Morgensen, *Queer/Native/Settler*.

23. Gloria Anzaldúa, *Borderlands/La Frontera: The New Mestiza* (San Francisco: Aunt Lute Books, 1987); Cherríe Moraga, *The Last Generation: Prose and Poetry* (Boston: South End Press, 1993).

24. Sheila Marie Contreras, *Bloodlines: Myth, Indigenism, and Chicana/o Literature* (Austin: University of Texas Press, 2008); Emma Perez, "Queering the Borderlands: The Challenges of Excavating the Invisible and Unheard," *Frontiers: A Journal of Women's Studies* 24, no. 2–3 (2003).

25. Scott Morgensen, "Activist Media in Native AIDS Organizing: Theorizing the Colonial Conditions of AIDS," *American Indian Culture and Research Journal* 35, no. 2 (2008); Irene S. Vernon, *Killing Us Quietly*.

26. This resembles Bruyneel's formulation of "the third space of sovereignty," where asserting enduring Native difference troubles the totality of settler rule (Kevin Bruyneel, *The Third Space of Sovereignty: The Postcolonial Politics of U.S.–Indigenous Relations* [Minneapolis: University of Minnesota Press, 2007]).

27. Clive Aspin, "Exploring Takatapui Identity within the Maori Community" (this volume); Vernon, *Killing Us Quietly*.

28. International Indigenous People's Summit, The Toronto Charter: Indigenous People's Action Plan on HIV/AIDS 2006 (Toronto: International Indigenous People's Summit, 2006).

29. See Morgensen, *Queer/Native/Settler*.

Section III
Reading Queer Indigenous Writing

9

Indigenous Fantasies and Sovereign Erotics

Outland Cherokees Write Two-Spirit Nations

Lisa Tatonetti

Though writing about gay, lesbian, transsexual, queer, and/or Two-Spirit (GLBTQ2) people has existed in various forms for over a hundred years, critical studies of GLBTQ2 *literary* criticism is in its infancy. As I write, we head toward the conclusion of the first decade of the twenty-first century, which also marks the first full decade in which academic studies of queer Indigenous literature came into their own in the contemporary scene of literary criticism. There is no doubt that the field is still evolving, as reflected by the ongoing indeterminacy of terms: is it "Queer," "GLBTQ," or "Two-Spirit"? Does "queer" erase the specificity of Indigenous GLBTQ2 concerns or open up possibilities of coalition? Is Two-Spirit a New Age misrepresentation or a marker of activist Native resistance to the legacies and lexicons of settler colonialism? While there are no concrete answers to such questions—the responses are as diverse as are Two-Spirit people themselves—there have been concrete gains in the field in recent years. In this chapter, I first map some of those important gains by offering a brief history of GLBTQ2 literature in North America and then turn to an analysis of the work of two contemporary GLBTQ2 writers—Qwo-Li Driskill and Daniel Heath Justice—to demonstrate how their creative and critical work marks a particular critical intervention in the analysis of GLBTQ2 literature, a queer investment in Indigenous nationalism.

The Beauty behind Us

Based on the work of white anthropologist Will Roscoe, who coedited *Living the Spirit*, the first anthology of gay Native literature, in 1988, we currently trace the publication of the first contemporary queer Native literature to the work of noted Mohawk author Maurice Kenny.[1] Kenny published a poem, "United," and an essay, "Tinselled Bucks: An Historical Study of Indian Homosexuality," in the Winter 1975/76 issue of a San Francisco paper called *Gay Sunshine: A Journal of Gay Liberation.* As part of the rise of gay publishing in San Francisco that followed not long after the 1969 Stonewall Rebellion, *Gay Sunshine,* edited by Winston Leyland, was a counterculture journal that included a mélange of pieces in each issue, ranging from poetry to interviews, art, journal excerpts, and political pieces on contemporary gay politics. Interestingly, Kenny published these early pieces in a special "Latin American" issue that, according to the editorial note, was primarily "devoted to material from (or about) Mexico, Argentina, and Guatemala."[2] Kenny's essay is appended toward the end of the issue as "an historical article on homosexuality among North American Indians during the eighteenth and nineteenth centuries [that] concludes [the] special Third World Section." The fact that *Gay Sunshine's* first piece by an American Indian writer is situated within this array of arguably related, but still fairly disparate pieces speaks to the dearth of published writing by GLBTQ2 people during this period.

As Kenny's landmark publications might suggest, 1970s San Francisco held possibilities for queer American Indian people that were not necessarily mirrored across the nation. San Francisco had been one of the major cities in the U.S. government relocation program in the 1950s, which had resulted in a significant Native presence in the city. At the same time, the growing Castro district was a "premiere destination" in what anthropologist Kath Weston terms "the great gay migration."[3] Unsurprisingly, then, as Walter L. Williams points out, "San Francisco was a city with a large Indian population as well as a highly visible gay community."[4] Even in the "gay mecca" of 1970s San Francisco, however, queer Native people often found themselves set apart from both the dominant gay counterculture, in which "gay" automatically equated to "white," and their tribal communities, in which homophobia was often commonplace. Thus, when activists like Barbara Cameron (Lakota) and Randy Burns (Paiute) came together to form Gay American Indians (GAI) in San Francisco in 1975, they saw "bringing together gay Indians" as their "most important task."[5] But despite Kenny's publications and the rise of the GAI in the mid-1970s, it wasn't until the late 1980s that we saw the rise of anything like a body of queer Native literature.

A number of early authors in the field followed Kenny's lead in the 1980s. One of the most significant of these was Beth Brant (Bay of Quinte Mohawk), who published the work of Native women in *A Gathering of Spirit: Writing and Art by North American Indian Women* (1984), which included work by eleven Native lesbians. Brant followed her landmark anthology with her collection of short stories, essays, and poetry, *Mohawk Trail*, in 1985. Shortly after, Menominee poet Chrystos published *Not Vanishing* (1988), while both Janice Gould (Concow) and Vickie Sears (Cherokee) published their first books in 1990—Gould's poetry collection, *Beneath My Heart,* and Sears's short stories, *Simple Songs.* In terms of full-length fiction, Laguna author Paula Gunn Allen's 1983 *The Woman Who Owned the Shadows* was the first novel to engage a queer Indigenous protagonist until Anishinaabe author Carole LaFavor's detective fiction, *Along the Journey River* (1996) and *Evil Dead Center* (1997). The fifteen-year span between these novels saw the slow but steady rise of a body of GLBTQ2 literature.

In terms of the development of an academic field, studies of GLBTQ2 literature came well after the emergence of an early canon of texts. If Kenny's work marks the inception of contemporary queer Native literature, then Paula Gunn Allen's undoubtedly marks the rise of queer Native literary criticism. And just as Kenny's poems were published well before most other literary work, so Allen's 1981 essay "Beloved Women: Lesbians in American Indian Cultures" and 1986 critical text *The Sacred Hoop: Recovering the Feminine in American Indian Traditions* debuted well before other critical work in the field. In fact, until the mid-1990s very few articles on queer Native literature had been published. When a significant rise in literary criticism did occur in the mid-1990s, that rise was marked by essays on *The Woman Who Owned the Shadows,* which underlines the significance of Allen's work to the emergence of an analytical framework in the field.[6] While—or perhaps I should say because—interpretations of Allen's novel are at the heart of Two-Spirit literary studies, reaction to her creative and critical writing offers a window into the development of the field itself, demonstrating how approaches to Two-Spirit literature shift along with critical understandings of Two-Spirit ideologies. Thus, early critical interpretations of Allen's novel from within Native studies tended to focus on indigeneity and elide considerations of sexuality, while later feminist readings employed dominant feminist ideologies as an interpretive frame. While these early feminist analyses break ground by bringing conversations about queer sexuality into the realm of Native literary studies, they also tend to espouse a somewhat monolithic (read: white) feminist lens. As a result, in early critical work we tend to see *either* a focus on indigeneity *or* a focus on queerness. A more recent approach in Native literary studies, which arose since the late nineties, represents a tribally grounded investigation of sex/gender diversity based on a Two-Spirit ideology, which I define as a nuanced understanding of gender and sexuality that (1) recognizes the historical diversity of gender roles in many Indigenous communities; (2) acknowledges that gender diversity is not necessarily aligned with sexual preference; and (3) allows for the significance of spiritual traditions within understandings of gender and sexuality. Most recently, this Two-Spirit critical framework has circled around how discussions of nationhood and sexuality coalesce.

The Beauty before Us

The body of this essay examines Two-Spirit literary criticism's focus on Indigenous nationhood by offering a case study, an investigation of the intersections of sovereignty and sexuality in the work of two outland Cherokee authors: Qwo-Li Driskill and Daniel Heath Justice.[7] By comparing Driskill's 2005 poetry collection, *Walking with Ghosts*, to Justice's fantasy trilogy, *The Way of Thorn and Thunder* (2005–7), I show how these texts use two very different genres to link sociosexual revitalizations with affiliation to land, clan, and nation. Through close readings of Driskill's poetry, I demonstrate how s/he highlights the direct ties between heterosexist and/or homophobic responses to queer sexualities and oppressive colonial ideologies, thereby constructing what Driskill calls a "sovereign erotic." Similarly, I show how Justice's fantasy fiction resists the same oppressive ideological meldings by mapping a third-gender tradition onto an allegorical retelling of the Cherokee nation's fight to retain sovereignty. Ultimately, my essay argues that despite their differing genres, these Cherokee texts forward complementary arguments about the productive intersections of Two-Spirit sexualities and Indigenous histories and about the need to make such intersections visible. I contend that Driskill's and Justice's nuanced depictions of queer Native identities represent Two-Spirit literary criticism's important contributions to the ongoing dialogue on Indigenous nationhood in the field of American Indian literatures.

Qwo-Li Driskill's Sovereign Erotics

Qwo-Li Driskill's collection consists of forty-one poems that follow a number of distinct but overlapping critical threads: the first focuses on classic considerations of Indigenous literatures, issues of history, memory, and cultural revitalization; the second focuses on the contemporary violence perpetrated on both Native and non-Native queer, transsexual, and transgendered people; and the third thread powerfully invokes the intersections and the indivisibility of sexuality and indigeneity. It is through this last thread that Driskill most effectively elucidates a Two-Spirit aesthetic. I offer a close reading of Driskill's opening poem, to show how Driskill maps a third-gender tradition onto both the history of the Cherokee nation's fight to retain sovereignty and contemporary revitalizations of culture and language.

Driskill opens *Walking with Ghosts* with a poem entitled "Beginning Cherokee," which, in four sections, or "lessons," examines "mourning," "ghosts," "memory," and "birth." In "First Cherokee Lesson: Mourning," Driskill's ungendered narrator considers the impact of language loss, explaining that as a beginning Cherokee speaker, one will "learn to translate the words you miss most:/*dust love poetry*/Learn to say *home*."[8] The speaker's language acquisition is immediately situated as more than a rote memorization of words. In fact, the poem implicitly ties the visible twists and turns of Cherokee syllabary, which the speaker struggles like an infant to articulate, with the twisted bodies of Cherokee people. Thus, in Driskill's opening piece, the very fabric of Cherokee language functions as a metonym for Cherokee removal, for Cherokee survivance, and for both historical and contemporary Cherokee bodies. Using language as a metaphor, Driskill references the ways in which historical bodies were regulated by instances of fear and oppression. So, for example, the nineteenth-century Cherokee are forced to contain their physical and spatial movement: in "First Cherokee Lesson," they evade the colonial gaze by "play[ing] dead" and remain sequestered in the "mountains" to escape that gaze. At the same time, Driskill also addresses the way present-day Cherokee bodies are regulated by the ongoing reverberations of colonial violence—the speaker's tongue must be taught and "train[ed]," must "lie still" like the bodies of the Eastern Cherokee who attempt to evade removal. This regulation of the body implicitly recalls the history of such regulations—the trauma of boarding-school experiences, the forced sterilization of Native women, and the assault on Indigenous peoples' expressions of gender and sexuality by early explorers, settlers, and missionaries, who often ridiculed and sometimes killed Indigenous people who fell outside western gender norms. Driskill's representations of the body reference these fragmenting histories by depicting language acquisition that, rather then being a practice occurring in a communal, tribally relevant setting, is stripped of cultural connection and relegated instead to the sterile, detribalized, and isolated world of "instruction tapes" and "flashcards."[9] The violent aftermath of linguistic and physical removals is underlined in the section's concluding stanza, in which, in response to such removals, "blood roars skin to blisters," "bones splinter/jut through skin/until all of me/is wounded/as this tongue."[10]

This visceral representation of settler colonial violence in the form of contemporary language loss is extended in "Second Cherokee Lesson: Ghosts," through the narrative of the speaker's mother, whose story represents the generational aftermath of boarding-school trauma; she explains: "*I knew some Cherokee /when I was little/My cousins taught me/ . . . When I came home speaking/your grandmother told me/I forbid you to speak that language/in my house/learn something useful.*"[11] Such stories of loss are countered with the concept of embodied memory in which language and story are not erased but, like "seeds" stored within the body, are instead "bur[ied] deep within flesh," waiting to "take root/ in . . . bones" to "split skin," to "blossom."[12] Though settler colonial ideologies have, for more than two hundred years, attempted to eradicate Indigenous languages and the Indigenous cosmologies those languages hold within, Driskill contends that resistance in the form of Indigenous knowledge is a latent power, awaiting the sounds of Cherokee language and the stories of Cherokee people to burst forth anew.

In terms of the movement of the poetic narrative, then, Driskill's "Third Cherokee Lesson: Memory" counters the painful images of forced assimilation and internalized racism invoked by the second stanza's references to the suppression of language with the *ongoing* power of story and history, when the narrator's mother also "remembers/Great Grandmother Nancy Harmon/who heard white women/call her uppity Indian during/a quilting bee/and climbed down their chimney with/a knife between her teeth."[13] As in the earlier representation of introductory language lessons, the speaker again ties this familial history not just to a remote nineteenth-century past but also to the present, situating the reciprocal transmission of history as an exchange of gifts tethered to both language and body. The speaker explains: "she passes stories down to me/I pass words up to her/braid her hair."[14] Such images rest on the ways in which the physical body can serve as a repository of culture, as in the references to hair that accrue throughout the sections. These references function first as an allusion to a material practice of mourning— "find a flint blade/. . ./cut your hair/. . ./cry your throat raw"—and then, like the seeds of language, as both a physical repository of latent knowledge—"stories/caught in my mother's hair"[15]—and a physical practice, storytelling, that reinforces familial and historical connections.

While these metaphors are resonant and powerful, they are also, at this point in Native literary studies, familiar. The distinction of Driskill's text rests in its use of a Two-Spirit cosmology to structure such familiar historical metaphors. Throughout the four sections of the poem, but especially in the last, "Fourth Cherokee Lesson: Birth," the narrator frames these historical and contemporary commentaries on Cherokee culture outside the constraints of traditional western gender binaries. Thus, in three of the four sections of the poem, images of milk and motherhood function as nongendered signifiers of both birth and loss. In the first section, "Mourning," the speaker's "tear ducts fill with milk";[16] here milk, a common symbol of maternal sustenance with its subsequent connotations of bodily ties to family and history, is that which is spilled from the body in sorrow. This image repeats as the speaker's mother "weeps milk" at "what she can't say," invoking again the trope of language loss and all the cultural resonances such loss contains.[17] In the final section of the piece, the multiple references to milk and loss tie instead to birth, when the speaker depicts hirself as a diversely gendered creation figure, who though "born without a womb" painfully delivers first syllables and, ultimately, language into being.[18] As the newborn sounds "shriek with hunger and loss," the speaker explains, "I hold them to my chest and weep milk/My breasts are filled with tears."[19] The concluding stanza of the poem clearly situates this birth as a form of cultural renewal: "We are together at sunrise/from dust we sprout love and poetry/We are home/Greeting our ancestors/with rare and tender tongues."[20] Through such images, while Driskill evokes what are by now in Native literature classic ties between language, family, and history, and classic scenes of familial storytelling, s/he also unmoors a sex/gender binary in which motherhood, birth, and nurturing are inherently tied to biologically defined women.

The move away from a sex/gender binary is part of the project of Two-Spirit literature, which often explicitly invokes the history of gender diversity in many American Indian communities as a means by which to counteract the historical erasures of such Indigenous complexity. In *Walking with Ghosts*, Driskill weds this recovery of alternate sexualities and genders to conversations about Native nations and politics. In hir theoretical work, Driskill has termed such intersections a "Sovereign Erotic," pointing out that "sexual assault, sexism, homophobia, and transphobia are entangled with the history of colonization."[21] Given that sexual violence is a cornerstone of settler colonialism, Driskill contends, "the journeys of . . . First Nations people back to their bodies, necessarily engage historical trauma."[22] Driskill's speaker's recovery from just such historical trauma is an example of the sovereign erotic, as it is bound not only to land, memory, and history, but also specifically to the body, as my analysis of "Beginning Cherokee" demonstrates. Thus, Driskill's multiply gendered narrator becomes the conduit for the healing of psychic wounds and the recovery of language, cultural memory, and gender diversity. By casting gender diversity as one of the central facets of healing, Driskill brings sexuality into the matrix of tradition and national identity and thereby situates not only the body but, importantly, the diversely gendered body as an integral part of Indigenous nationhood. As a result, Driskill's work promotes decolonizing ideologies by explicitly challenging heterosexist depictions of indigeneity that have, for so many years, been the very bedrock of colonial fantasies of Native people. In this way, Driskill's theory and poetry recognizes and confronts the ways in which colonial violence continues to the present day.

Daniel Heath Justice Takes on Tolkien

Like Qwo-Li Driskill's *Walking with Ghosts*, Book One of Cherokee author Daniel Heath Justice's *The Way of Thorn and Thunder* trilogy also opens with a lesson of sorts: "I want to tell a story. This story has many beginnings. . . . I hold to these teachings and I tell these stories, with the hope that they'll stay true to what we fought for, and what so many died for. This isn't my story alone, but this is my knowing of the story, and this is my understanding of its beginnings."[23] The "beginnings" of *The Way of Thorn and Thunder* trilogy have roots in places that, at first glance, seem worlds apart: one emerges from the halls of 1930s Oxford; another is rooted a hundred years earlier, in the Cherokee nation's bitter fight to retain stolen land and maintain tribal traditions in the face of genocidal U.S. government policies; and still another arises when a young Outland Cherokee boy, while lying on his bed in late 1980s Victor, Colorado, began dreaming his own history over the pages of J.R.R. Tolkien's epic fantasy. Together, these beginnings enact change and reinforce tradition and, in this liminality, Daniel Heath Justice changes the face of fantasy fiction.

I turn to Justice's recent fantasy novels to demonstrate how the Cherokee allegory he constructs in *The Way of Thorn and Thunder* intervenes in the genre's colonizing traditions by presenting an alternative narrative tradition that includes Driskill's concept of a sovereign erotic. Ultimately, Justice's work functions as a palimpsest in which the actual history of the Cherokee nation's fight to retain sovereignty overlays the classic tropes of fantasy fiction to decolonize the genre. At a moment in which fantasy is again wildly popular in both print and film, I contend that Justice's text functions as an important corrective: first by making visible the colonizing history of the genre, and second, by interjecting the very real subjects of Native sovereignty and sexuality into the discourse of imagined nationhood that undergirds so much fantasy fiction.

It can be argued that the history of fantasy fiction traces back to the oral tales of time immemorial, and many aspects of modern fantasy fiction have roots in creation myths or oral narratives that include reference to alternate worlds, mythical beings, and seemingly inexplicable events that many would see as fantastical. In terms of print history, contemporary fantasy fiction has ties to the romances of the Middle Ages and Renaissance and the gothic novels, literary fairytales, and ghost stories that gained popularity in the late eighteenth and early nineteenth centuries. While the roots of fantasy fiction run both deep and wide, J.R.R. Tolkien is often called the "father of modern fantasy." The unprecedented popularity of Tolkien's 1937 *The Hobbit* and his *Lord of the Rings* trilogy, which includes *The Fellowship of the Ring* and *The Two Towers,* both published in 1954, and *The Return of the King,* published in 1955, ushered in the contemporary era of fantasy fiction. In fact, according to Jane Yolen, Tolkien's runaway popularity from the 1960s to the present is single-handedly responsible for making "fantasy" a marketing category all its own in the publishing industry.[24] The worldwide blockbuster success of producer/director Peter Jackson's live action *Lord of the Rings* film trilogy, released in 2001, 2002, and 2003 respectively, underscores the enduring appeal of Tolkien's epic.

Given the cultural capital of Tolkien's words and Jackson's images in late-twentieth and early-twenty-first-century culture, it's troubling to recognize the limitations these well-loved narratives have in terms of their representations of indigeneity. For example, land, so central to the very definition of indigeneity, represents danger in the world of Middle Earth. Tolkien's wilderness landscapes, as James Obertino points out, are depicted as "barbarian," "desolate, savage place[s], hard to penetrate, traversed only with danger and difficulty, and not easy to leave with one's skin intact."[25] Tolkien's Moria, in particular, with its "'dark

waters under the mountains,' suggests the horror and peril of the limit-
less and undefined. These dark waters, like the Orcs who live within the
mountains [of Moria], Tolkien associates with the primal abyss, [which
he describes as] 'the deep places of the world.'"[26] Tolkien's characters,
too, fall for the most part into classic dominant hierarchies. Marjorie
Burns explains, "It is not difficult to pick out Tolkien's likes and dislikes,
his values and preferences, and his sense of who belongs where. This
remains so even though there is more complexity to Tolkien than would
first appear evident in a fictional world where social and cultural roles
are firmly specified and where . . . all the usual clues apply to mark the
moral and hierarchical extremes: light and dark, ugly and fair, black and
white, high and low, up and down."[27] And, indeed, despite the nearly
fifty years between the publication of Tolkien's original texts and the
production of Jackson's cinematic trilogy, the darkness and associated
evil of Tolkien's indigenous Orcs and Uruk-hai (with their dreadlocks
and face paint) and the savageness of their landscape are replicated rather
than critiqued by Jackson.[28] But my larger claims don't rest upon the
racial politics of Tolkien's or Jackson's Middle Earth. Instead, my central
work here is to use Tolkien and Jackson as benchmarks that enable us
to better understand the implications Justice's *The Way of Thorn and
Thunder* has for the genre of fantasy fiction.

Like Tolkien, whom he read avidly while growing up, Justice constructs a narrative that, in the vein of *The Lord of the Rings,* can be
characterized as epic or high fantasy. Set in an alternate and most
often highly detailed universe—what Tolkien in "On Fairy-Stories"
famously called a "Secondary World"—high fantasy is serious in tone
and aim: such fiction often centers on an unusual or orphaned hero who
becomes a prime force in a large-scale struggle between good and evil.
Thus, Justice gives us Tarsa'deshae, a young Redthorn warrior whose
fate is inextricably bound to that of the Kyn Nation, which comprises
both the Kyn, the Indigenous inhabitants of Everland, and the spiritual
and physical geography of Everland itself, which has been "home of
the tree-born Kyn since time immemorial."[29] While Justice's narrative
undoubtedly pays tribute to Tolkien's landmark work, his divergence
from the genre's classic hierarchies is just as apparent. A female heroine,
Tarsa packs both a feminist and nationalist punch as she learns to control her power, becoming an Indigenous healer, what her people call a
"Wielder," through slowly coming to understand traditional knowledge,
or "the Way of Deep Green."

If in Tolkien Indigenous beliefs like the Way of Deep Green, and a wilderness like the forests of Everland, represent darkness, savagery, or, at the very least, isolation for the hobbit heroes, in Justice, by contrast, Everland is not a threat to, but the foundation of, the Kyn's physical survival and cultural continuity. Tarsa's identity and power are derived from the land through her ties to a force called the "Wyr," which is the lifeblood for all Kyn, even those who have turned away from their belief in Zhaia, the Tree-Mother, toward the Human religion of the Celestials. The split between the traditional Kyn, and their ties to the Wyr, and the ever-growing contingent of Celestials, who see the Wyr as part of a shameful and primitive tribal past, provides a clear allegory for the influences of assimilation in early-nineteenth-century Cherokee country. In fact, I suggest Justice's description of the Wyr reflects what Dakota theorist Elizabeth Cook-Lynn calls an "indigenous view of the world" in which "the very origins of a people are specifically tribal (nationalistic) and rooted in a specific geography (place)," in which "mythology (soul) and geography (land) are inseparable."[30] The narrative surrounding Tarsa's discovery of her healing power illustrates how fantasy fiction can be employed to validate just this type of culturally specific Indigenous cosmology. To use Cook-Lynn's terms, tribal nationalism, cast here in the form of adherence to the Deep Green, is "rooted in a specific geography" in which mythology, or belief in the Wyr, and land, in this case Everland, are not only "inseparable," but essential. And so Justice sets up a secondary world that relies on key concepts in existing conversations about American Indian nationalisms. But he does so using classic tropes of high fantasy: the wounded hero, the epic journey, the life-and-death struggle between good and evil. If Tolkien's "moral and hierarchical extremes" are "light and dark, ugly and fair, [or] black and white," then Justice's hierarchies are built on levels of affiliation to land, clan, and nation. With this focus, *The Way of Thorn and Thunder* constructs an aesthetics of sovereignty, art that has, as its very foundation, questions of Indigenous nationhood.

The discourse of nationalism and the allegorical tie to Cherokee history become even more apparent in *Wyrwood*, Book Two in *The Way of Thorn and Thunder* trilogy. Book One ends just after a Sevenfold Council is held at the Kyn capital, Sheynadwiin, to decide how the folk will answer the nation of Men's demand that they make "the Oath of Western Sanctuary."[31] The demand brings the Folk of Everland to an impasse disturbingly familiar to those who know American Indian history: they must choose "removal or death."[32] The council votes to reject the oath at the conclusion of Book One. In Book Two, however, the Kyn are betrayed by their own people. Rather than Major Ridge, John Ridge, Elias Boudinot, and Stand Watie, Justice crafts betrayal in the form of Neranda Ak'Shaar, a "she-Kyn leader of the Celestial Shields,"[33] who explains to Vald, the leader of the Human empire:

> Most of the Folk are superstitious and ignorant of the wider world. They are easily influenced, especially by the long discredited conjurors who use fear of ghosts and spirits to separate the People from their good sense. They are not capable of making a wise decision in this matter. It is thus a heavy burden that my compatriots and I must assume. We come to make the difficult choice for all the People, even if it is against their baser wishes. We have come to sign the Oath.[34]

And with Neranda's pen stroke, the Kyn, like the Cherokee to whom the allegory relates, are not only deceived by a contingent of their own leaders but are split in two as a people. The clarity of this allegory is both painful and instructive. In this way, Justice's deployment of the now-traditional forms of epic fantasy provides an effective way to address the years before and after the signing and congressional ratification of the Treaty of New Echota in 1835 and 1836: in Cherokee history of this period, as in epic fantasy, there *are* heroes and orphans, a difficult and dangerous journey, and a life-changing struggle between a multitude of opposing forces. Thus, despite its sometimes problematic history of representation, fantasy fiction offers Justice a particularly appropriate genre within which to imagine this fraught moment in Cherokee history, when the very fabric and definition of nationhood was being pulled from every direction.

Like Driskill, Justice overlays conversations about Indigenous nationalism with representations of gender diversity: most obviously, Justice matter-of-factly ties his heroine Tarsa's path to traditional knowledge to alternate understandings of gender and sexuality. Consequently, Justice's Kyn have three genders: she-Kyn, he-Kyn, and zhe-Kyn. The narrator explains that zhe-Kyn "straddled the male and female worlds in all things, garbed in blouse and skirt, head tattooed and shaven but for a braided topknot, moving between the blood of war and the blood of the moon without fear."[35] A zhe-Kyn figure named Fa'alik is key to the scene of monster-slaying that opens the first text, where this character "[draws] the group together and, singing a song of healing and reconciliation, [drives] the flames into the monster's chest."[36] This same character is also central to Tarsa's initiation into the Redthorn warrior society. Tarsa recalls "every moment of that night—from the body markings, the songs and dances, and the feasts, to the tender-love-making with Fa'alik that followed. . . . every moment had been a reminder of all that was perfect and beautiful and balanced in the world."[37] Thus, as Justice constructs Everland's national identity and traditions in ways that parallel American Indian history, he also deftly integrates into his nationalist imaginary a parallel narrative of sex and gender diversity that has been largely erased from the historical record. In this way Justice employs the genre of fantasy, which is often seen by detractors as a juvenile escape from reality, to return complex Indigenous understandings of gender and sexuality to visibility.

Throughout Justice's text, he clearly intertwines such images of sexual diversity with the threads of Indigenous nationalism. In *Kynship*, for example, Tarsa's discovery of her power as a Wielder, an event the Kyn call her "Awakening," links the story to a tribal nationalist paradigm. Tarsa is cast into a pit by her clan relations, who, because of their assimilation into a Celestial, or human belief system, now view the Way of Deep Green and thus Tarsa's Awakening as "witchery."[38] As a result of their rejection of Greenwalker ways, Tarsa's kin have lost the knowledge to guide her through the physical and emotional changes of the Awakening. Thus, when Tarsa's body produces thorns, vines, and other manifestations of the power of the land in random and uncontrolled succession, she is abandoned to her fate, which the Celestial Kyn assume will be death. But Tarsa is ultimately saved by the arrival of her aunt, Unahi, a Wielder who, twenty-six years before, had been banished from her family and home in Red Cedar Town because she continued to adhere to the Way of Deep Green when the town became Celestial. When Unahi's traditional knowledge and the power of Tarsa's memory of her initiation rites save Tarsa from death, Justice's commentary is clear: traditional knowledge is the means to survival. Moreover, by casting Tarsa's sexual experience with the third-gendered Zhe-Kyn as one of the central facets of her initiation rites, Justice brings sexuality into the matrix of tradition and national identity and, like Driskill, thereby situates the body as an integral part of the geography of Indigenous nationhood.

Dreyd, the final book in Justice's trilogy, extends the importance of the zhe-Kyn to Justice's fictional nation and, in the process, sets up the book's most powerful argument for erotic sovereignty. This claim is best demonstrated in the final, apocalyptic battle scene that is the penulti-mate moment in *Dreyd*. The Kyn, at this point in the text, have been betrayed by their own, driven from their homelands, and are in a final pitched battle for their world and their lives. As Dreyd and his human and inhuman allies near victory, Tarsa is able to gain her strength and freedom through her connection to the Wyr, to the land. She begins to sing "a memory song,"[39] which is taken up by those around her. Though Tarsa, as the book's central protagonist, is key to the song's initiation, Averyn, one of Justice's zhe-Kyn heroines, brings it to fruition, freeing the Kyn from their potential bondage: "The zhe-Kyn, like all the zhe-Folk, was a between-worlder, neither male nor female, something other than them both. The healer inhabited a space between and among the others, and such a position brought with it knowledge and a respon-sibility distinct to the zhe. Of all worlds and none . . . as zhe sang, the world changed."[40] This change is the rebirth of the Kyn's "Eternity Tree," which emerges from the body of the Dreydmaster, Lojar Vald, who like Tolkien's Sauron represents the forces of evil. Averyn's part in defeating Vald's colonial violence is another moment when Justice's secondary world parallels historical Cherokee traditions. In "Stolen from Our Bodies: First Nations Two-Spirits/Queers and the Journey to a Sovereign Erotic," Driskill points out that "many Cherokee stories deal with characters considered outsiders, who live in liminal spaces, help bring about change and aid in the process of creation."[41] The narrator's description of the zhe-Kyn aligns Averyn with such traditions, but rather than depicting a water spider or a dragonfly as a catalyst for change or creation, Justice situates the potential for regenerative transformation in the song, body, and role of the zhe-Kyn, highlighting the function of the third-gendered body in his alternate universe. Driskill argues that "a Sovereign Erotic is a return to and/or continuance of the complex reali-ties of gender and sexuality that are ever-present in both the human and more-than-human world, but erased or hidden by colonial cultures."[42] I contend that through his depictions of the zhe-Kyn, Justice enacts such a return in the world of fantasy.

In the end, *The Way of Thorn and Thunder* does more than merely drop in references to alternate genders; Justice's work promotes decol-onizing ideologies by explicitly challenging racialized and heterosexist depictions of indigeneity common in fantasy fiction. At the same time, his Cherokee allegory expands American Indian studies by bringing epic fantasy into the canon of American Indian literature and employing that fantasy to introduce American Indian history to entirely new audiences. Justice might take up the tropes of Tolkien, but through his use of a sovereign erotic, he employs the well-known conventions of fantasy fiction to craft a very different world order, one in which Indigenous nationhood is privileged and the multiplicity of sex and gender categories is incorporated and maintained.

Together, Justice and Driskill are at the vanguard of the contemporary Two-Spirit tradition in fiction, poetry, and theory. I offer these short, focused analyses of their texts to show how both authors skillfully meld tribally specific commentary on the colonial violence of Cherokee removal with explicit recognition of multiple gender traditions through the deployment of what Driskill calls a Sovereign Erotic. Justice, as I've shown, does so in the realm of fantasy fiction in ways that change the genre, while Driskill's theory and poetry explicitly recognize and challenge the ways in which settler colonial violence continues to resonate in the present day. Ultimately, I argue that despite their differing genres, these texts forward complementary arguments about the productive intersections of Two-Spirit sexualities and Indigenous histories, and about the need to make such intersections visible. In an era in which, as Andrea Smith and J. Kehaulani Kauanui point out, "tribal nations have begun to pass bans on same-sex marriages in the name of 'Indian tradition,'" and "the politics of sovereignty are being built on the backs of women and those who are not gender- or heteronormative,"[43] Driskill's and Justice's nuanced depictions of queer Native identities represent important contributions to the dialogue on indigenous nationhood.

Notes

1. Will Roscoe, ed., *Living the Spirit: A Gay American Indian Anthology* (New York: St. Martin's Press, 1998), 514.

2. Winston Leyland, ed., "Editorial Note," *Gay Sunshine: A Journal of Gay Liberation* 26/27 (1975/76), 1.

3. Kath Weston, *Long, Slow Burn: Sexuality and Social Science* (New York: Routledge, 1998), 32.

4. Walter L. Williams, *The Spirit and the Flesh: Sexual Diversity in American Indian Culture* (Boston: Beacon Press, 1986), 210.

5. Cameron qtd. in ibid.

6. See my essay "The Emergence and Importance of Queer American Indian Literatures, or, 'Help and Stories' in Thirty Years of *SAIL*" (*Studies in American Indian Literature* 19, no. 4 [2007]: 143–70) for more on these patterns.

7. The term "outland Cherokee" is taken from Daniel Heath Justice's *Our Fire Survives the Storm*. Justice employs the term for "those who are raised outside the geopolitical and cultural boundaries of the established Cherokee communities of northeastern Oklahoma, western Arkansas, or western North Carolina" (xvi).

8. Qwo-Li Driskill, *Walking with Ghosts* (Cambridge: Salt, 2005), 1.

9. Ibid., 2.

10. Ibid.

11. Ibid., 3–4.

12. Ibid., 5.

13. Ibid., 6.

14. Ibid.

15. Ibid., 1, 5.

16. Ibid., 2.

17. Ibid., 6.

18. Ibid., 7.

19. Ibid.

20. Ibid., 8.

21. Qwo-Li Driskill, "Stolen from Our Bodies: First Nations Two-Spirits/Queers and the Journey to a Sovereign Erotic," *Studies in American Indian Literature* 16, no. 2, (2004): 51.

22. Ibid.

23. Daniel Heath Justice, *Kynship: The Way of Thorn and Thunder* (Wiarton, ON: Kegedonce Press, 2005), 9.

24. Jane Yolen, "Introduction," in *After the King: Stories in Honor of J.R.R. Tolkien*, ed. Martin H. Greenberg (New York: Tor Books, 1994), viii.

25. James Obertino, "Barbarians and Imperialism in Tacitus and *The Lord of the Rings*," *Tolkien Studies* 3 (2006), 123.

26. Ibid., 122.

27. Marjorie Burns, "J.R.R. Tolkien: The British and the Norse in Tension," *Pacific Coast Philology* 25 (1990): 49.

28. As Brian Rosebury points out, Tolkien's "racial generalizations, however nuanced, have incited charges of racism. . . . In particular, critics point out that all the races enlisted by Sauron (Orcs, Southrons, and Haradrim) are dark-skinned and, not incidentally, 'evil,' while the races arrayed against them are generally light-skinned and, not incidentally, 'good'" (555). However, as is oft pointed out in Tolkien's defense, despite the fact that his textual imagery often aligns with racialized ideologies, Tolkien was clear about his antiracist stance during World War II. (See Anderson Rearick, "Why Is the Only Good Orc a Dead Orc? The Dark Face of Racism Examined in Tolkien's World," *Modern Fiction Studies* 50, no. 4 (2004): 866–67.)

Such racialized patterns are common in fantasy fiction and its sibling, futuristic or speculative fiction. Discussing the limited number of Black writers in fantasy and speculative fiction, Gregory E. Routledge notes that "although the imaginative intent behind the raceless future is benign, it could well give rise to a White future that reinscribes existing racial division" (239). He also points to the ways in which this pattern persists in contemporary media portrayals of sci-fi futures, saying: "One need look no further than standard televised and cinematic representations of futurist-fiction futures . . . to find evidence of the blanching of the future" (239).

29. Justice, *Kynship,* back cover.

30. Elizabeth Cook-Lynn, "The American Indian Fiction Writers: Cosmopolitanism, Nationalism, the Third World and First Nation Sovereignty," in *Why I Can't Read Wallace Stegner and Other Essays: A Tribal Voice* (Madison: University of Wisconsin Press, 1996), 32.

31. Justice, *Kynship,* 202.

32. Ibid., 201.

33. Daniel Heath Justice, *Wyrwood: The Way of Thorn and Thunder, Book 2* (Wiarton, ON: Kegedonce Press, 2006), 72.

34. Ibid., 73.

35. Justice, *Kynship,* 18.

36. Ibid.

37. Ibid., 31.

38. Ibid., 23–29.

39. Daniel Heath Justice, *Dreyd: The Way of Thorn and Thunder, Book 3* (Wiarton, ON: Kegedonce Press, 2007), 217.

40. Ibid., 219.

41. Driskill, "Stolen," 56.

42. Ibid., 57.

43. Andrea Smith and J. Kehaulani Kauanui, "Native Feminisms Engage American Studies," *American Quarterly* 60, no. 2 (2008): 242.

10
The Erotics of Sovereignty

Mark Rifkin

In his special message in 1970 laying out his administration's position on federal Indian policy, Richard Nixon repudiated the logic of termination, beginning with what has come to be known as the *era of self-determination*.[1] Termination had resuscitated many of the ordering aims of allotment policy, seeking to end federal aid to and recognition of Native peoples, dismantle Native governments, and increase settler access to Native land and resources.[2] Nixon's commitment to ending this policy officially inaugurated a new kind of relationship between tribes and the federal government, suggesting the potential for a more substantive engagement between the United States and Native peoples, premised on mutual respect. Although couched in a performance of national shame for previous mistakes,[3] his expression of support for "self-determination" promises *autonomy,* but its meaning seems to inhere primarily in the government no longer actively seeking to destroy the "tribal group" as such. In other words, this rubric seems less to offer a sustained reconceptualization of the jurisdictional presumptions previously undergirding U.S. Indian policy than simply to remove, in his terms, the "threat of eventual termination." If "autonomy" functions as a catachrestic figure for the absence of a direct assault on the existence of Native nations, what are the legal dimensions of peoplehood? Or, perhaps more to the point, what aspects of peoplehood remain unintelligible within U.S. policy frameworks despite the promise to attend to Indigenous formulations of collective "self"-hood? Ailenne Moreton-Robinson's description of contemporary policy in Australia is quite apt: "While it is often argued that self-determination has been the dominant policy framework since the late 1960s, a closer analysis of government processes and practices would reveal that self-management has occupied center stage."[4] How does the experience of indigeneity in the contemporary moment exceed these ways of acknowledging tribal identity?

More specifically, how might individual sensation register aspects of collective memory and belonging occluded by the federal government's apparently affirmative narration of Native "community"? Such a dynamic, in which affective configurations bespeak the presence of unacknowledged political negotiations, historical trajectories, and social formations, can be characterized as a "structure of feeling." In *Marxism and Literature,* Raymond Williams develops this concept to address the ways that "practical consciousness is almost always different from official consciousness," registering "experiences to which the fixed forms do not speak at all, which indeed they do not recognize."[5] He further observes, "all that is present and moving, all that escapes or seems to escape from the fixed and the explicit and the known is grasped and defined as the personal,"[6] and earlier he notes of "modes of domination" that "what they exclude may often be seen as the personal or the private, or as the natural or even the metaphysical."[7] The kinds of *feeling* characterized as "personal" can refer not only to forms of experience that lie at the edge of conscious awareness, but to those associated with entire social configurations that lie outside or challenge the parameters of existing structures of *domination.* In this way, an Indigenous structure of feeling can refer to a sensation of belonging to place and peoplehood excluded from settler governance but that remains present, most viscerally in the affective lives of Native people. Structure of feeling, then, has a dual reference: to the continuing presence of Native sociopolitical formations that are not reducible to, or substantively recognizable within, settler ideologies and administrative networks; and to the effects of living under that regime for Native people and peoples, registered as emotive and physical responses that can be dismissed by narrating them as "private." Although U.S. Indian policy formally circulates the topos of "self-determination," portraying the federal government as engaging with tribes' lived sense of landedness and representations of themselves, it continues to foreclose indigeneity, both as a residual geopolitics predicated on principles other than those of the liberal state and as the collective memory of an ongoing history of violence. The force and consequences of that foreclosure are experienced as *feeling.*

In "Stolen from Our Bodies," Cherokee scholar and poet Qwo-Li Driskill offers the notion of a "Sovereign Erotic" as a way of bridging the apparent gap between individual desire, wounding, and longing and collective histories of dispossession, imposition, and removal. S/he suggests that the project of "healing our sexualities" cannot be separated from "ongoing processes of decolonization,"[8] and from this perspective, a "Sovereign Erotic relates our bodies to our nations, traditions, and histories."[9] Driskill offers this concept as a way of marking and contesting how Native people(s) "have internalized the sexual values of dominant culture,"[10] and in doing so, s/he argues that Native discrimination toward other Native persons on the basis of their eroticism and/or gender expression is a function of that internalization. Decolonization, then, partially entails a changed understanding of the relation between *sexuality* and *sovereignty*, in which the former does not serve as a basis for exiling people from inclusion in the latter. This articulation of indigeneity as an erotics, though, also can be reversed, taking the kinds of physicality, intersubjectivity, and vulnerability categorized and cordoned off as "sexuality" within dominant discourses as a starting point for mapping the ongoing management of Indigenous polities. Such a shift potentially offers an alternative vision of Native politics, and an attendant account of the intimate effects of settler imperialism, by foregrounding embodiment as the entry point for representing Indigenous political ontologies. Affect in this context is not solely psychic but also somatic, indicating an Indigenous philosophy and praxis in which the personal, natural, territorial, metaphysical, and political are not readily contradistinguished. How might *erotics* offer a way of rethinking the meaning of *sovereignty*, a way of addressing modes of peoplehood and placemaking made unintelligible in U.S. legal geographies but still alive as individual and collective sensations?

More than addressing and validating forms of individual sexual and gender subjectivity that could be categorized as queer, Driskill's collection of poetry *Walking with Ghosts* offers a queer critique of the settler state and its persistent efforts to rescript Native histories and identities to fit its geopolitical imperatives.[11] By centering physical sensation and affective relation in depicting indigeneity, s/he refuses the somewhat hollow recognition of Native presence in U.S. policy. The collection registers the primacy of lived connections to land and one's people, in place of a view of self-determination as primarily the administration of a jurisdictional grid (one that follows U.S. principles, just on a smaller scale). In taking up these kinds of experiences and making them the basis for representing both the ongoing "historical trauma" of settlement and the survival of Indigenous "nations, traditions, and histories,"[12] s/he refuses to accept narratives of who Native people and peoples were, are, and should be that measure them against an imperially imposed (set of) norm(s).

In "Love Poems: 1838–1839," Driskill uses embodiment and desire as a way of portraying Cherokee territoriality and the violence of state projects of dispossession and the jurisdictional logics that animate them. Driskill creates a parallel structure in which comments by "Tennessee" and "Indian Territory" are laid out in adjacent columns on the page, creating the effect of an overlapping conversation. The names of the interlocutors and the poem itself make clear that the context for these articulations is the forced removal of the Cherokees from their traditional homelands to what eventually would become the state of Oklahoma, in what has come to be known as the Trail of Tears.[13] The poem explores the kinds of collective subjectivity rendered unintelligible within the terms of U.S. law and the imperatives of Indian policy. Notably, while the lands from and to which the Cherokees were removed are given voice here in parallel columns on opposite sides of the page, the Cherokees themselves are silent, occupying the seeming emptiness between the two. However, this mute absence, and the visual elision of the horrors of the Trail of Tears itself in the apparently neutral blankness of the middle of the page, is brought into stark relief by the story told of lacerating excision and wounded arrival. The text begins by asking, "What was left behind?" From the outset, absence, or lack, is depicted in terms of unfulfilled longing, the residue of a largely unacknowledged and powerfully unresolved history of brutal dislocation, heightened by Indian Territory's first line: "I know you were driven away,/taken from everything that/taught you love." If the address for the initial question is somewhat amorphous, posed to the reader as much as anyone, the introduction of "I" and "you" in the parallel statement by Indian Territory indicates a conversation in which one of the participants—the Cherokee people—is mute, depicting the absence of speech not as implied assent, but as a kind of yearning and terror that defies easy representation, particularly in the language used by those who *drove them away*. The official imperative to conceal the evidence of violation, to articulate a subjectivity ostensibly unmarked by imperial force, is reflected in Indian Territory's caveat, "I don't expect you to forget,/only to love me as well," and Tennessee amplifies this intimation of state-mandated amnesia in asking, "(Did you know they tried to/erase you, forbade me to/speak your name?)" In this way, the poem positions its account as an effort to trace the contours of the collective experience sanitized, and thereby falsified, in dominant narratives of removal.

Personifying place and the Cherokee Nation allows Driskill to use the tactile sensations of embodiment and the emotional vocabulary of intimacy to explore dimensions of peoplehood that do not register in the archive of settler governance. The logic of removal, and of acquiring territory through treaties more broadly, relies on envisioning land as a thing to be exchanged either for an equivalent quantity elsewhere or for its "value" in money and/or goods. There is no intrinsic relation to place; or, put another way, the Cherokee Nation can be conceptualized as separable from any particular place. Within U.S. policy, the collective Indigenous subject that consents to the expropriation of land or to wholesale dislocation is not constituted through an embeddedness in a lived geography that provides the condition of possibility for peoplehood. Rather, the voice of the polity can be treated as distinct from any specific spatiality, enacting a kind of disembodiment that is registered in the literal absence of the Cherokees from the poem. By contrast, Driskill presents the relation between the Cherokees and their land in terms of erotic connection, refusing the homogenizing and commodifying legal narratives of land as fungible.

The initial juxtaposition of the perspectives of Tennessee and Indian Territory index this nexus of affection and desire. As Indian Territory observes that removal denied the Cherokees "everything that/taught you love," Tennessee answers the question "What was left behind?": "Love formulas/written in dark syllables,/whose incantations/undulated/like our tongues." Implicit in this pairing is that "love" is what the Cherokees learned from their traditional homeland, what bound them to that place. This relation is precisely what the new home calls for, imploring the Cherokees "to love me as well" and then repeating this request as a demand in the next line—"Love me." In this context, speech is not the contractually mediated expression of the arm's-length transactor, but "dark syllables" laden with spiritual import that are tied to the "undulat[ion]" of "tongues" as in a kiss. Rather than denoting a (collective) consciousness whose relation to corporeality is incidental, voice is physicalized as a pleasurable entwining with a lover.

Moreover, the phrase "our tongues" indicates that Tennessee also possesses one, representing the land as sensate and desiring. "Love" for the land appears as more than an abstract feeling, a broad appreciation for a given locale; "love" indicates a dynamic mutuality in which they are the land's as much as the land is theirs. Both Tennessee and Indian Territory are depicted as bodies, in ways that fairly explicitly sexualize Cherokee inhabitance:

> My arms, muscled rivers
> you came to
> each morning.

> Love the winding trails to my
> belly,
> the valleys at my sternum,
> the way I slope towards you like
> promise.

Beyond merely indicating residence, these lines suggest a seduction. These images, however, are not similes: the rivers are not *like* arms; the valleys are not *like* a sternum. Driskill here refuses the easy distinction of tenor and vehicle in which embodiment serves as a *metaphor* for territoriality. Instead, s/he draws on the reader's experience of attraction, arousal, and gratification as a means of reframing what Native territoriality *is*. As Daniel Justice suggests in his discussion of the work of Marilou Awiakta, "this is not mere symbol or metaphor; these relationships are real and tangible."[14] To understand peoplehood, the poem suggests, one needs to grasp the physical immediacy and yearning that characterizes the *reciprocity* of place. The land is both desired and desiring, is not a thing that can be priced and traded, is a feeling entity.

Through this erotics, Driskill refigures sovereignty, shifting from the idea of an exertion of juridical control over a dead quantum of space to the emotional interdependence and physical joining of lovers. The Cherokees are not the same as the land, simply an extension of it, but as envisioned here, neither is Native nationhood reducible to administrative processes, jurisdictional claims, and legal personae/speech acts. Driskill presents the Cherokee people as a *somos* whose capacity for erotic, sensuous engagement also makes it vulnerable. In addition to refusing the privatizing ideologies by which "sexuality" is severed from "sovereignty," Driskill's intertwining of the two casts Indigenous relations to land as a kind of perverse, criminalized desire, implicitly expanding the critique of heteronormativity to include the imperial process by which Native collectivity is divorced from place and Native territory is translated into U.S. law as an inert, saleable thing. Within the normalizing parameters of bourgeois domesticity, sensual pleasure and enduring emotional bonds are contained inside the boundaries of the conjugally defined household, defining intimacy through isolation. The expansive attraction and gratification between people and place that Driskill envisions transects this distinction between public and private domains, between the governmental and the familial. In addition to proliferating the spaces and functions of desire, the poem suggests that a collective Cherokee sense of space itself is predicated on a sensuous engagement with the specificity of the land they occupy. Tennessee observes what the Cherokees have left behind:

> Rows of corn
> ears swaying slightly on
>   their stalks;
> pumpkins thick with flesh;
> tomatoes swollen with juice,
>   so acidic
> they could blister your lips.

The "flesh"-iness of the pumpkins and the tomatoes fairly tumescent with "juice" ready to burst on waiting "lips" further concretizes the "love" articulated at the outset, casting agricultural labor as foreplay building toward climax, the land offering itself to the people in joyous abandon. This joining crosses the threshold of domesticity. In this context, Indian Territory's insistence at the end of the poem, "This is home now"; "You are home./You are home" reads as something other than the interiorizing topos of the single-family household. "Home" here marks a collective connection to territory that includes a sense of a polity's relation to its territory usually encompassed by the term *sovereignty*, but without the sense of ownership or the implicit invocation of a nuclear imaginary in which the supposed biological imperative behind this formation of kinship and residency helps naturalize the shape of (settler)statehood.

Landholding itself is infused with desire, suggesting that the seizure of Cherokee space functions as part of a broader effort to insert Native peoples into dominant Euramerican modes of "home"-making. The poem plays with the linkage between these two forms of domestication—to bring under the authority of the U.S. government (as in domestic policy) and to incorporate into (the model of) the bourgeois household.[15] Driskill indicates the relay between these two kinds of regulation in Tennessee's comment "(After they seized you/they told me not to touch/anyone again.)" Through this image of prohibited "touch," the poem depicts removal as not simply a struggle over space, a quantity of land, but over how land tenure will be conceptualized and lived. Portraying the expropriation of territory as part of a management of Indigenous erotics helps highlight the ways the expansion of U.S. jurisdiction relies on other, seemingly nonpolitical discourses to translate Native sociality and spatiality into terms consistent with U.S. governance. More than analogizing settler processes of legalized dispossession to the patholo-gizing discipline exercised on attractions deemed aberrant, making the latter a *metaphor* for the former, Driskill's fusion of the two narrates the Trail of Tears and other state-orchestrated projects of settlement as predicated on a disavowal of Indigenous modes of "love"—Native geog-raphies in which neither the people nor the land can be understood as disembodied juridical abstractions, and in which affect, sensation, and intimacy cannot be insulated/isolated within privatized modular units in ways consistent with liberal political-economy and the logics of the United States.

What emerges, then, is a queer critique of removal in which *the erotic* provides a rhetorical register and experiential template through which to manifest Native placemaking as feeling (in both its senses) in ways pur-posively rendered unintelligible within U.S. administrative discourses. After Indian Territory's assertion that the Cherokees are "home," the poem ends with Tennessee's final response to the repeated question "What was left behind?": "your body's/silhouette/scratched forever into me." Refusing the objectifying implications of "what" (as opposed to *who*), the poem's last lines point to the memory of the body as a trace of that which has been lost through removal. Or put another way, the tactile and emotional dynamics of embodiment provide a resource for trying to capture the violence and violation of collective exile, while they also provide a means for articulating the experience of indigeneity that the U.S. government seeks to foreclose—an experience neither forgotten nor erased, but etched into the body of the land.

If "Love Poems: 1838–1839" seeks to envision sovereignty as a col-lective erotics of place, "Map of the Americas" highlights how Native individuals' sense of their bodies is shaped by histories of settler inva-sion. Linking the most private of moments to the ongoing dynamics of conquest provides a dialectic through which to reconceptualize the meaning of sovereignty, indicating how geopolitical struggle becomes encoded and remembered as feeling, while also using such feeling as a way of leveraging the logics and narratives through which the assault on Native peoples is naturalized, euphemized, erased, and displaced into the past. The opening gestures toward a profound desire that desire itself could be the vehicle for escaping the past. The narrator insists: "I wish when we touch/we could transcend history in/double helixes of dark and light/on wings we build ourselves."[16] The pairing of "touch" and "transcend" connects the tactile to the possibility of a kind of experience that could break the participants free from their immanence in geographies of the everyday, pushing them toward a state more closely approximating the divine (as further suggested by the angelic picture of people with "wings"). Referencing DNA in the image of "double helixes" suggests conception, and the fact that these twining strands are "dark and light" intimates racial difference. The interweaving of this miscegenation imagery with the fantasy of *transcendence* implicitly locates this race/reproduction matrix within the contemporary push toward postracial promise in which the horrors of the past supposedly can be abandoned in an embrace (here, literally) of the ideal of a color-blind society. Notably, the achievement of this goal is correlated with death—becoming angels. A procreative erotics appears here somewhat ironically as a movement toward a future that simultaneously is the end of "history." The intimacy of "touch" erases difference in the creation of an (impossible) sameness, a perfect equivalence that provides the eschatological aim for a liberal sort of national amnesia.

Both identifying with and mocking this notion of romantic couplehood as an avenue to freedom from history, the text quickly shifts away from the internal life—the *wishes*—of the couple themselves to focus on the ground that supports them. Whipping back from the imagined heights achieved on the "wings" of love, Driskill directs the reader to the literal territory beneath their feet: "But this land grows volcanic/with the smoldering hum of bones."[17] The land itself seems to revolt against this intimate union, or at least to respond by bringing forth the remains of those killed in the invasion of Native space. In contrast to the futurity projected by the DNA imagery, the "bones" will not stay buried, making present a past steeped in violence.

All that's left
of men who watched beloveds
torn apart by rifles
Grandmothers singing back
lost families
Children who didn't live
long enough to cradle a lover
arms around waist

> lips gently skimming nape
> legs twined together
> live a river cane basket[18]

The mention of "beloveds," "grandmothers," and "children" refracts the genetic figure at the heart of the first stanza into a generational narrative, one that pushes against the insulated intimacy of the opening. Doing so highlights the ways the desired *transcendence* depends on erasing the process by which a future has been denied to these other "families," the history of the decimation of their intimacies. Moreover, unlike the dream of romance as an angelic flight away from the killing fields of settler occupation, the sensual "twin[ing]" of those lost is portrayed as deeply connected to that place—"like a river cane basket." Such baskets are a densely symbolic figure of Cherokee cultural practices, shifting relations to their environment, skills passed across generations, and the potential for weaving together disparate materials into a coherent whole.[19] Here it signals the enmeshment of erotic life within a sense of shared history, daily practice, community, and deep knowledge of the space of dwelling, as against the vision of intimacy as total separation from everyone and everything else.

Although the poem juxtaposes the ephemerality of the "wish" for escape with the brutal materiality of corpses and a land made molten in their "volcanic" reemergence, Driskill suggests that the awareness of this history, the rending of networks of love and care as well as of bodies that it encompasses, is already woven into the speaker's sense of selfhood. S/he lives this past as part of hir physical and emotional life, engagement with hir lover calling forth what might be called a physical memory: "Sometimes I look at you/and choke back sobs knowing/you are here/ because so many of my people are not."[20] Hir body involuntarily recalls the dead, the "chok[ing]" and spasming making corporeal their continued presence. They do not remain buried, safely sealed into a *then* fully sequestered from *now*. Instead, murdered "families" erupt into the present, as bodily shocks. To be part of the "people" is to have one's personal identity routed through a sensory experience of a collective past that is shot through with horror. A communal "knowing" of that violence is lived as individual trauma, a seizing that breaks the rhythm of breath itself triggered by the ways the legacy of settlement suddenly coalesces around the space occupied by the speaker's lover. The juxtaposition of "here" and "not" suggests less a simple opposition than a palimpsest in which the lover's body signifies simultaneously in two dialectically entwined ways: as a synecdoche for the process of conquest that has made, and continues to make, possible the "you"'s occupation of (once) Indigenous space, and as a metonym for the lives and futures lost in securing settler dwelling. Thus, "touch" cannot "transcend" the past, because the Native narrator's senses root hir in the place of hir people and continue to resonate with the force of their planned erasure, while the lover bears (and, in many ways, *is*) that legacy of displacement.

This embedding of history in the flesh, though, is not simply figurative, a substitution in which bodies stand in for the dynamics of imperialism in ways readily distinguishable from literal relations in the present—the actual lives of Native people and the real politics of Native nations.[21] Such a distinction depends on already knowing the boundaries of persons and polities. Yet such *knowing* is precisely what the poem puts in question, suggesting that the narrator's experience of collective grief for hir people raises questions about the givenness of the categories through which land, personhood, and political community are known. In *The Cultural Politics of Emotion*, Sara Ahmed argues that "emotions create the very effect of the surfaces and boundaries that allow us to distinguish an inside and outside in the first place": "surfaces of bodies 'surface' as an effect of the impressions left by others"; "the surfaces of collective as well as individual bodies take shape through such impressions." She adds, "emotions are not 'in' either the individual or the social, but produce the very surfaces and boundaries that allow the individual and the social to be delineated as if they are objects."[22] Driskill suggests that Indigenous feeling—the mesh of emotive and sensory experience I have described as erotics—can push against the boundaries inscribed by settlement. Or, perhaps more to the point, indigeneity itself can refer to the ways certain bodies in the present bear the impression of histories of collective occupancy (peoplehood) and of the objectifications and dislocations within settler imperialism. Those histories are lived as an affective nexus that helps give shape to Native bodies and consciousness—settler bodies, as well, but in that case emotions largely work to reaffirm institutionalized boundaries in a structure of feeling that helps literalize the shape of liberal governance and state jurisdiction.

Driskill pushes the politics of metaphor even further in having the narrator describe hir body as a way of figuring continents. Integrating the poem's title phrase, s/he declares to hir lover, "Look: my body curled and asleep/becomes a map of the Americas,"[23] and the next page typographically approximates that shape with the speaker comparing parts of hirself to various features of the landscape (such as, "My chest the plains/and hills of this land My spine/the continental divide"[24]). Portraying the narrator's body as a map creates an ambiguous relation between hir physical form and the hemisphere. Does the speaker's flesh function as a kind of screen on which to project the topography of the Americas, providing concretion at a far smaller scale that can allow readers to grasp the contours of the continents in their completeness? Or is the narrator's experience of corporeality, of felt indigeneity, offered as the substance of the postcontact construction of Native spaces in the "New World"? Which term, the body or the Americas, is real and which the figure for describing the other? To make a Native body a map contrasts a located specificity/subjectivity with the ostensibly objective, encompassing perspective from high above that tends to characterize post-Enlightenment cartographic imaginaries (a maneuver that repeats in a different register the move from "wings" to "land" discussed earlier),[25] and this juxtaposition also implicitly puts into relief the kinds of abstraction, homogenization, and totalization that the imagined view from the heavens can enable—an orientation that potentially effaces the sensations, relations, and knowledges that arise from and constitute an embedded connection to place. The issue of how the gaze of the non-Native will be directed and framed explicitly is at stake in this moment in the poem; the imperative "Look" is spoken to the "you." The command suggests that the conjunction of the speaker's body with the Americas "becomes" a way of apprehending both differently, opening possibilities for taking the broad and potentially genericizing icon of "the Americas" and endowing it with a new set of meanings by filtering it through the erotics of memory.

Driskill refigures the existing relay between Indian bodies and lands in settler ideologies, using it to stage an alternative way of *looking* at both. Having already traced the ways the speaker's sense of hirself in the present is shaped by persistent feelings of collective belonging (including trauma), and the ways the lover's body occupies the space of those murdered and displaced to secure its presence, the text positions the intimate event of their "touch" as an example of a broader pattern, making the speaker's "knowing" a prism for refracting the act of mapping and its role in imperial governance. The body of the "I" emerges out of, and bears the impressions of, the history of Indigenous occupancy and dispossession, and this feeling of *peoplehood* frames the text's jump to a hemispheric scale, such that instead of approaching Indigenous person-hood through a settler imaginary (as a point on the map—a localized embodiment of its objectifying logic of jurisdiction), it takes an Indigenous experience of subjectivity as the basis for extrapolation. Rather than merely contrasting the account of Native embodiment the text has offered thus far with the perspective of the colonizer, Driskill utilizes the former as a way of conceptualizing "the Americas." This change in direction, though, is not an inversion, the body coming before the map instead of the opposite. The body of the "I" already is immersed within a mapping of peoplehood, or put another way, the Native speaker's sensation of self-hood (emotional and physical) arises out of an already present sociopolitical field and collective memory of its (ongoing) violation, erasure, and dislocation. The overview provided by the map, then, offers less a unified totality than an accumulation of geographies of communal inhabitance, loss, and survival, opening the possibility for solidarity by positing a resonance between experiences in/of "this land" and other territories—all of which "grow volcanic/with the smoldering hum of bones."

By undoing the series of complexly interlocking dichotomies that help efface ongoing histories of Native occupancy and settler invasion (intimacy vs. violence, local vs. international, past vs. present, personal vs. political, individual vs. collective), the text seeks to refigure the literal, opening the potential for "knowing" differently by rooting that process in an erotics that crosses the boundaries/identities generated by these binaries.

> When your hands travel
> across my hemispheres
> know these lands
> have been invaded before
> and though I may quiver
> from your touch
> there is still a war[26]

Bodies and continents appear inextricable here, frustrating the effort to reduce that relation to metaphor. The confusion/conflation of apparently disparate phenomena operating at discrepant scales works to alter the "you"'s (lover/reader) understanding of both. Seeing the sensual touch between the narrator and hir lover as a moment in the continuing conquest of the Americas changes the meaning of that seemingly personal event, amplifying and making explicit the political and historical dynamics already contained within it. Simultaneously, characterizing the seizure of territory and extension of non-Native jurisdiction over it as invasion/violation of Native bodies—as rape—highlights the ways the abstraction of the map is realized through assault, which is experienced and remembered as communal trauma.[27]

Although Driskill does not deny the possibility of pleasure amidst this persistent pain ("I may quiver"), s/he emphasizes that such moments of what may appear as transcendence are embedded in an ongoing "war," despite settler efforts to declare the violence as merely *history*—the past of conquest supposedly having given way to the peaceful wholeness represented by the map. The narrator observes: "It is not without fear/and memories awash in blood/that I allow you to slip between/my borders/ rest in the warm valleys/of my sovereign body."[28] The lover's "touch" recalls collective "memories" that can be understood only through the kinds of political and territorial identification associated with narratives of invasion and conquest but usually absented from depictions of intimacy. Moreover, the significance of such "borders," and of *sovereignty* itself, shifts through their association with the body. Unlike in the legal geographies of the state—in which land is a thing, national citizenship overrides tribal belonging, and desire must be privatized—peoplehood here is made somatic, lived as a structure of feeling in which sensation and affect are not separable from self-determination, and vice versa.

The text renders the border between the literal and figurative porous in order to push the non-Native "you" toward engaging with forms of Native experience in which sovereignty does not occupy a space separate from that of intimacy and embodiment, in which it is lived viscerally as part of individual selfhood. More than merely poetic figures, references to Native lands indicate the ways felt connection to them persists despite the apparent distance of time and geographies of state-orchestrated dislocation. Reciprocally, such not-quite-metaphors also are an explicit articulation of that sensation of rootedness to non-Natives in order to undo the concepts through which settlers map their relation to Native people, peoplehood, and settler occupancy. The final line reenacts this critical juxtaposition between scales and spheres that has characterized the text's effort to disjoint both the privatizing insulation of intimacy and the imperial abstraction of state jurisdiction and knowledge: "I walk out of genocide to touch you."[29] As opposed to the image of transcendent interracial union with which the poem opens, it closes by forcefully resituating the "you" and the moment of physical contact within a topography of death, implicitly making present the "families" whose decimation shapes the "here" in which these lovers meet. Rather than offering a reproductive futurity that enables a break from the past, this ending indicates that for the narrator the erotics of pleasure cannot be divorced from the unfinished project of conquest and ongoing war in which hir people, and other Indigenous peoples of the Americas, continue to be seen as expendable.

Throughout *Walking with Ghosts*, sexual encounters serve as sites for representing an erotics of indigeneity—an embodied connection to peoplehood and place erased, or specifically targeted for dissolution, within the official discourses of U.S. settler governance (including rhetorics of tribal "self-determination"). The emotions and sensations explored in the poems register a layered structure of feeling that encompasses traditional modes of territoriality and collectivity, the ongoing assault on them by the United States, and the impressions left by both in the flesh as shared memory. Refusing to treat these experiences as merely *personal* or *metaphysical*, Driskill insists on using feeling as a way of remapping (what counts as) politics. Yet the process through which s/he does so is decidedly queer, emphasizing the ways non-normative scenes of desire and pleasure can provide insight into the mechanisms of settler imperialism and the possibilities for forms of collective identification displaced or foreclosed by state logics. The kinds of experience usually designated as properly private within discourses of sexuality become vehicles for illustrating the relation between the imposition of heteronormative ideologies and the disavowal of modes of Native being in which connections with land, tradition, community, and history are lived as intimate parts of selfhood and remembered as such even when foreclosed by settler violence and policy.

Erotics here, then, is not equivalent to *sexuality*, in that the latter presumes the kinds of liberal individualism and distinctions between public and private realms that Driskill rejects. Instead, embodiment operates as a nexus of connection with persons and place in ways that comprise peoplehood, which itself cannot be reduced to bureaucratic structures and cartographic abstractions. Driskill challenges the "sexual values of dominant culture" in ways that seek to make Indigenous nations more inclusive of their queer citizens, but also to trace the role of such values in (dis)figuring possibilities for Native self-determination.[30] Understanding this way of portraying peoplehood, this queer critique of the settler state, as an account of *sovereignty* highlights how Driskill's poetics of pain, sensation, and desire is not merely a metaphor for Native politics, but an effort to reconceptualize what counts as politics—to challenge settler-orchestrated forms of representation and knowledge production that fail to address the contours and experience of Indigenous belonging. In this way, hir poetry explores the (heteronormative) limits of settler law, reclaiming bodily experience for Indigenous articulations of collectivity and place.

Notes

Research for this essay was supported by a New Faculty Grant from the University of North Carolina at Greensboro.

1. Francis Paul Prucha, ed., *Documents of United States Indian Policy*, 3rd ed. (Lincoln: University of Nebraska Press, 2000), 256–59.

2. On the termination program, see Vine Deloria Jr., *Custer Died for Your Sins: An Indian Manifesto* (Norman: University of Oklahoma Press, 1969; repr. 1988); Donald L. Fixico, *Termination and Relocation: Federal Indian Policy, 1945–1960* (Albuquerque: University of New Mexico Press, 1986); Kenneth R. Philp, *Termination Revisited: American Indians on the Trail to Self-Determination, 1933–1953* (Lincoln: University of Nebraska Press, 1999).

3. On rituals of national shame by settler states, see Sara Ahmed, *The Cultural Politics of Emotion* (New York: Routledge, 2004); Elizabeth A. Povinelli, *The Cunning of Recognition: Indigenous Alterities and the Making of Australian Multiculturalism* (Durham, NC: Duke University Press, 2002).

4. Aileen Moreton Robinson, "Introduction," in *Sovereign Subjects: Indigenous Sovereignty Matters,* ed. A. Moreton-Robinson (Crows Nest NSW, Australia: Allen and Unwin, 2007), 4.

5. Raymond Williams, *Marxism and Literature* (Oxford: Oxford University Press, 1977), 130.

6. Ibid., 128.

7. Ibid., 125.

8. Since Driskill has expressed a preference for gender-neutral pronouns, I will use "s/he" and "hir" when referring to Driskill.

9. Qwo-Li Driskill, "Stolen from Our Bodies: First Nations Two-Spirits/Queers and the Journey to a Sovereign Erotic," *SAIL* 16, no. 2 (2004), 51–52.

10. Ibid., 54.

11. Qwo-Li Driskill, *Walking with Ghosts* (Cambridge: Salt, 2005).

12. Ibid., 51–52.

13. Ibid., 56–57. On preremoval Cherokee governance, the conflict with Georgia, and policy surrounding and in the wake of the Indian Removal Act, see Tim Alan Garrison, *The Legal Ideology of Removal: The Southern Judiciary and*

the Sovereignty of Native American Nations (Athens: University of Georgia Press, 2002); William G. McLoughlin, *Cherokee Renascence in the New Republic* (Princeton: Princeton University Press, 1986); Jill Norgren, *The Cherokee Cases: The Confrontation of Law and Politics* (New York: McGraw Hill, 1996); Theda Perdue, *Cherokee Women: Gender and Cultural Change, 1700–1835* (Lincoln: University of Nebraska Press, 1998); Mark Rifkin, *Manifesting America: The Imperial Construction of U.S. National Space* (New York: Oxford University Press, 2009).

14. Daniel Heath Justice, "Beloved Woman Returns: The Doubleweaving of Homeland and Identity in the Poetry of Marilou Awiakta," in *Speak to Me Words: Essays on Contemporary American Indian Poetry*, ed. Dean Rader and Janice Gould (Tucson: University of Arizona Press, 2005), 75.

15. On this broader pattern in U.S. Indian policy, see Mark Rifkin, *When Did Indians Become Straight? Kinship, the History of Sexuality, and Native Sovereignty* (New York: Oxford University Press, 2010).

16. Driskill, *Walking with Ghosts*, 9.

17. Ibid.

18. Ibid.

19. On such baskets and their import, see Marilou Awiakta, *Selu: Seeking the Corn-Mother's Wisdom* (Golden, CO: Fulcrum, 1993); Qwo-Li Driskill, "Doubleweaving Two-Spirit Critiques: Building Alliances between Native and Queer Studies," *GLQ: A Journal of Lesbian and Gay Studies* 16, no. 1–2 (2010): 69–92; Sarah H. Hill, *Weaving New Worlds: Southeastern Cherokee Women and Their Basketry* (Chapel Hill: University of North Carolina Press, 1997).

20. Driskill, *Walking with Ghosts*, 9.

21. On the differentiation of "literal" and "figurative" as part of the expansion of English property holding and New World invasion in the early modern period, see Eric Cheyfitz, *The Poetics of Imperialism: Translation and Colonization from* The Tempest *to* Tarzan (Philadelphia: University of Pennsylvania Press, 1997). On Native poetry's flouting of this distinction, see Eric Gary Anderson, "Situating American Indian Poetry: Place, Community, and the Question of Genre," in *Speak to Me Words: Essays on Contemporary American Indian Poetry*, ed. Dean Radar and Janice Gould (Tucson: University of Arizona Press, 2003), 34–55; Robin Riley Fast, *The Heart as a Drum: Continuance and Resistance in American Indian Poetry* (Ann Arbor: University of Michigan Press, 1999); Justice, "Beloved Woman."

22. Ahmed, *Cultural Politics*, 10.

23. Driskill, *Walking with Ghosts*, 9.

24. Ibid., 10.

25. For discussion of the history and ideological work of map making, and particularly its role in Euro-colonization of the Americas, see Martin Brückner, *The Geographic Revolution in Early America: Maps, Literacy, and National Identity* (Chapel Hill: University of North Carolina Press, 2006); Walter D.

Mignolo, *The Darker Side of the Renaissance: Literacy, Territoriality, and Colonization* (Ann Arbor: University of Michigan Press, 1995); Mark Warhus, *Another America: Native American Maps and the History of Our Land* (New York: St. Martin's Press, 1997).

26. Driskill, *Walking with Ghosts*, 11.

27. On the violation of Native women's bodies as a key technology of settler rule in the United States, see Andrea Smith, *Conquest: Sexual Violence and American Indian Genocide* (Cambridge, MA: South End Press, 2005).

28. Ibid.

29. Ibid.

30. Driskill, "Stolen," 54.

11
Gifts of *Maskihkîy*
Gregory Scofield's Cree Métis Stories of Self-Acceptance

June Scudeler

In "You Can Always Count on an Anthropologist (to Set You Straight, Crooked or Somewhere In-Between)," Métis writer/storyteller/community activist Gregory Scofield describes his struggle to reconcile Cree world-views, particularly the "bestowing of sacred powers,"[1] with multiple genders:

> This embodiment of multiple genders greatly intrigued me, although I found it difficult to understand it in relation to the Cree spiritual world and the teachings I'd been taught. One's sacredness or *pawatew*, the spirit helper who becomes part of one's identity, defines one's lifelong responsibilities, and one's lifelong responsibilities define one's sacredness, one's *pawatew*.[2]

Scofield's quotation illustrates the importance of situating himself in his spiritual traditions in order to accept both his Cree Métis heritage and his sexuality. Writing for Scofield, as for many Aboriginal writers, is *maskihkîy*—medicine—that heals writer, readers, and communities. Scofield's understanding of Cree worldviews means that, while Scofield previously referred to himself as Two-Spirited, he now calls himself gay, because he hasn't been trained in the sacred aspects of an *âyahkwêw*. An essential component of Scofield's stories of self-acceptance is his refusal to be placed into boxes: "most of my writing career has been punctuated by labels such as 'angry,' 'streetwise,' 'Métis,' 'gay,' and 'two-spirited.' It seemed with each new book I was helped into yet another coat of identity, and although there was a certain truth to each one, I found the coats of academics or reviewers, even other Native people, ill-fitting or too restrictive."[3] Through his writing, which involves using Cree words, researching Cree traditions, and communicating with Native people from all walks of life, Scofield is able to forge a set of more flexible self-definitions that avoid the "boxes" that solidify stark binary oppositions, such as white/Aboriginal and gay/Two-Spirited. As Qwo-Li Driskill (Cherokee) emphasizes, Scofield's "poetry cannot be seen as 'Native,'

'Queer,' 'urban,' 'Canadian,'[4] or any of the other words one might use to describe it. His work must be understood within the complexities of overlapping identities."[5] I will investigate how Scofield uses Cree Métis concepts such as *maskihkîy* and *pawatew*, particularly in close readings of examples of his writing, to enable him to accept his sexuality and his Métis ancestry as a natural and integral part of himself. Scofield is fairly fluent in the Cree language, which grounds him in Cree ways of being.[6] Because most Métis have Cree ancestry, Scofield is linked to both his Cree and his Métis ancestors.

Although Métis,[7] the mixed-blood peoples of Canada, along with First Nations and Inuit, are recognized as Aboriginal people under section 35 of the Canadian constitution, there is still a lack of acknowledgment of Métis people, from both non-Native and Native peoples. Scofield was twenty-one before he came to accept his Métis heritage. A Cree elder took him to Back to Batoche Days in Saskatchewan, an annual Métis celebration that features events like fiddling and jigging contests. Because Scofield learned in school that Métis leader Louis Riel was crazy, he wanted to be a full-blooded Cree and not a Halfbreed. Scofield saw himself as "a great chief like Sitting Bull and Red Cloud,"[8] and decided that his adopted Aunty Georgina must be wrong and that he and his Mom Dorothy were "Nay-he-yow-wuk—Crees! After all, we [Scofield and Aunty Georgina] spoke Cree, did beadwork and used Indian medicines."[9] Scofield remembers his Aunty Georgina telling him stories when he was a small boy, stories that "were not meant for TV or books. These were stories that could not be recorded, stories that had to be held and passed around like a newborn baby. These were stories meant to teach a small boy how to use his strength and senses, his awareness and instinct. These were lifetime stories, gifts of *maskihkîy*, medicine."[10] Scofield describes these stories as "thought medicine,"[11] an apt metaphor for a writer. These stories are precious in that they provided Scofield with Cree Métis stories that build a child's sense of self and helped Scofield to accept his Métis heritage.

"Answer for My Brother," from Scofield's first poetry collection *The Gathering: Stones for the Medicine Wheel,* records a conversation with an anonymous interlocutor.[12] Scofield ponders the question, "Who are the Métis?" He knows that the question is a "clever way to get me thinking where is my place."[13] Scofield "writes to heal,"[14] but while there are "volumes" written about Indians, there is "so little written about the Métis because we/are not one or the other but a shaded combination/that is

easier to figure out lumping all of us/together because some Halfbreeds
look like they have a/dark past."[15] The "dark past" to which Scofield
refers is the Métis people's fight against the encroachment of the Canadian government and of settlers in Red River, in what is now Winnipeg, Manitoba, with the formation of a provisional government in 1869
headed by Louis Riel and in 1885 in Batoche, Saskatchewan, under the
military leadership of the renowned buffalo hunter Gabriel Dumont, as
well as Riel. After defeat by the larger forces of the Canadian government (the Métis used rocks as ammunition when their bullets ran out)
in 1885 and the hanging of Riel as a traitor, the Métis scattered and led
lives on the margins, many hiding their identities because of racism and
the prevailing view of Riel. Scofield highlights the false divisions between
First Nations or status Indians and Métis, as Métis dark enough could be
included in treaties while their fair-skinned relatives were written out of
history by passing as white to escape racism. Jo-Ann Episkenew (Métis)
notes that a "significant constituency of Métis were almost impossible
to distinguish from their Indian relatives, much to the dismay of colonial officials charged with the responsibility of negotiating the treaties."[16]
While Scofield acknowledges Métis as a "shaded combination" of Native
and white, he sometimes falls into the "dark equals Indian and light-
skinned equals Métis" binary. Of course, status First Nations as well
as Métis cover the spectrum of light- to dark-skinned. He notes in the
poem that some Métis have a dark past, "which to/outsiders appears an
Indian past & then there are/some so white you wouldn't even think
twice."[17] Scofield's use of this binary, particularly in his earlier poems,
is symptomatic of his yearning to be Cree and not Métis because of the
racism against Métis people. As he accepts his Métis heritage, he no longer finds the binary relevant.

By using gaps on the page in "Answer for My Brother" to highlight
the missing spot in Canadian history into which Métis people should
be written, Scofield shows the lack of understanding from mainstream
Canada as well as other Aboriginal peoples who see the Métis as "being
one or the other," rather than the Métis reality of being a mixture of
cultures. Scofield rewrites history from a Métis perspective:

because greedy land
Grabbers wanted the whole damn country
so whoever looked dark enough got treaty covering up
their tainted blood & their not-so-passable cousins

were sent packing to the backwoods being written
right out of history   except for

Brief mention of our leaders   who were a thorn in the
government's ass   they made it to the N section in the
encyclopedia under the "Northwest Rebellion"[18]
which more or less infers we need to be put into our
proper place
[. . .]
If anything, we are Katipamsoochick[19,20]

The space around "except for" shows that the Métis may have been written out of mainstream Canadian history, but also that Métis people are aware of their own history beyond a "brief mention of our leaders." The last line in the poem proudly asserts that the Métis are Katipamsoochick, which Scofield translates as "the people who own themselves,"[21] the Cree word for the Métis. While there is an inference that Métis people were put in their place, Scofield rewrites history by emphasizing that the Métis own themselves.

Métis writers such as Scofield also write to forge a sense of identity and self-acceptance for Métis people. As Cree/ *nêhiyâw* writer Neal McLeod notes:

The persistence of Cree narrative memory demonstrates the resistance of Cree-speaking peoples in an effort to hold on to their identity despite experiencing the brutalities of English/Canadian colonialism. The narrative memory of Cree-speaking people is also involved in a process of preserving a place in the world—a way of understanding reality. While the pressures of colonialism can crush the collective spirit of a people, it can also solidify resistance and allow people to conceive of an alternate mode of being.[22]

I would argue that McLeod's quotation applies equally well to Métis resistances, particularly for Scofield's work. As Métis researchers Leah Dorion and Darren R. Préfontaine emphasize in *Métis Legacy*, "the dominant theme in Métis history is resistance against coercive power, and to societal stereotypes. . . . When Métis people resisted, it was to ensure their community's survival."[23] Scofield's stories are a way of preserving a Métis place in the world.

Writing by Indigenous peoples, in this instance Cree Métis people, can be a form of resistance. Episkenew emphasizes the importance of stories as a way of healing for Aboriginal peoples: "Over the last three decades, Indigenous peoples have witnessed the healing power of stories as they have begun to reassert their individual and collective narratives."²⁴ More importantly for Scofield's work, Episkenew explains, "everyday stories, *âcimowina,* the stories that are the foundation of contemporary Indigenous literature, although not spiritual, are nevertheless spirit."²⁵ Writing our own stories is powerful *maskihkîy*—medicine—because not only does it educate non-Métis peoples, but more importantly it provides Métis people with a sense of pride in their history. Many Métis people kept their identities secret because of racism, and one of the ways that Métis can connect to their history is through stories by writers such as Scofield, Maria Campbell, and Marilyn Dumont. Writing in this context becomes word *maskihkîy* that heals across the generations and through time, a truly alternate mode of being. Episkenew, like McLeod, sees stories as a form of resistance, as they allow us "to reassemble our collective and individual memories to gain a sense of both personal and collective community control."²⁶ McLeod eloquently describes the place of collective memory in *nêhiyawi-itâpisiniwin,* the Cree viewpoint:

> Collective memory is the echo of old stories that links grandparents with their grandchildren. In the Cree tradition, collective narrative is what puts our singular lives into larger contexts. Old visions echo; the *ancient poetic memory* of our ancestors finds home in our individual lives and allows us to reshape our experience so that we can interpret the world we find ourselves in.
>
> As we find ourselves enmeshed in the trajectories of various stories, we also make contributions to the larger narrative. While we are influenced by the stories of the *kêhtê-ayak* (Old Ones), we also add to the meaning of their stories through our experiences and understanding, and add in small ways to the ancient wisdom.²⁷

Nêhiyawi-itâpisiniwin is a complex idea involving space and time across generations. McLeod's term "ancient poetic memory" is highly applicable to Scofield's work, as he honors both his ancestors and the teachings he received from his Aunty Georgina. Collective memory lives in our bodies through our ancestors' stories; their stories shape the way we view the world. McLeod believes that we are not merely individuals but are linked to a collective memory that includes both our ancestors and also our larger community and our families. Scofield reiterates McLeod's idea of ancient poetic memory: "Even with Native languages, minus their English translations, Native people have always spoken poetry. Native people have always thought in poetic terms. . . . Poetry is reflective of everyday life. It is something that is being spoken on a continual basis. It is something that is being thought on a continual basis."[28] Poetry and ancestral memory are woven together to honor generations. Our ancestors are poetry that live in our own bodies and influence the way we view and understand our contemporary worlds.

Crees have an intricate form of *wâhkotowin,* meaning kinship or the state of being related. *Wâhkotowin* is more extensive than the western conception of kinship, which often focuses on the nuclear family as a starting point. *Wâhkotowin,* like *nêhiyawi-itâpisiniwin,* includes generations past, present, and those yet to come, as well as adopted people, who in some cases can be closer than blood family. Scofield's work ties together his ancestors with his adopted family, such as his Aunty Georgina:

> Georgie verbally adopted me in the Indian way, and from then on I called her *Ne-ma-sis* (my little mother; Aunty). . . . Aunty began to teach me Cree, and I picked it up quickly *as if the words were buried somewhere within me.* She taught me about the old time medicines: how to prepare and use them, what their names were in Cree, the need to be quiet and respectful when I used them. . . . The more Aunty taught me about the medicines and the old-time ways, *the more I felt connected to something.*[29]

Clearly, *nêhiyawi-itâpisiniwin* is a strong force for Scofield in his life and in his writing. The sense of being connected to something larger is palpable in Scofield's writing. Again, it is highly fitting that McLeod uses the term "ancient poetic memory" in his description of *nêhiyawi-itâpisiniwin,* a concept that is highly relevant to Scofield's writing. Scofield has deep connections to Cree spirituality, as he recounts in his memoir *Thunder through My Veins: Memories of a Métis Childhood.* Scofield shares a vision he had in which Grandfather Black Bear

> stood up on his hind legs, and looked deeply into my eyes, and I felt him say to my heart, *Grandson, you have nothing to fear. Your heart is good and you have much work to do.* . . . I awoke with a sacred song in my head. . . . I have been given Bear Medicine—healing medicine— and I honor this medicine by writing. I believe this is what Grandfather Black Bear meant when he said, *"you have much work to do."*[30]

Grandfather Black Bear, the Cree healer and keeper of medicines, enables Scofield to write to heal himself and his communities. Storytelling is *maskihkîy*, medicine that is rooted in his lived experiences of Cree Métis stories, both new and old, on the land and in the city.

Aunty Georgina's teachings grounded Scofield in Cree Métis ontologies that help guide his writing process. In an interview with Linda Richards, Scofield states:

> I very much approach my writing that way and make offerings for my grandmothers and my grandfathers when I write. I make tobacco offerings for them and I ask them to come and sit with me and to give me courage and strength. To write and to be able to be honest and to be able to be reflective. And to be able to touch people. To be able to make medicine. Even out of something bad, to be able to make good medicine out of it. When people read, it's not just the book that they read, it's the medicine behind via the words. That's where the power comes from. That's where the healing comes from.[31]

Scofield not only turns bad medicine into good medicine through his writing but also shares this medicine with his readers. This is part of Scofield's *pawatew*, his responsibility. While Scofield writes as a way of self-healing and self-understanding, it also a political act, in that he shares Métis and *nêhiyâwin* histories and struggles. Furthermore, the awareness of Cree Métis stories and ontologies learned from his Aunty Georgina also affected his journeys to accept his Métis heritage and his sexual identity.

Scofield formerly worried "that being gay had somehow destroyed my credibility in the Native community. I feared my writing would be seen as less credible if I 'came out' and I would bring shame upon myself and those who had mentored me."[32] In the essay "You Can Count," Scofield is now comfortable enough to discuss the politics of sexual identity. He discovers in the *Alberta Elders' Cree Dictionary* that the term *two-spirited* is *nîso achâhkawak*, which "literally translates to 'two spirits' and which if used in a sentence might read, 'The house was haunted by two spirits.'"[33] He goes on to ruminate on the term Two-Spirit:

> How do you translate such a concept, the idea of a third or fourth gender? After all, don't we carry the spirits of our mother and our father, our grandmothers and our grandfathers? Moreover, on a purely biological level, our gender appears to be determined by the

X or Y chromosome. Then again, who really knows what sacred ceremony takes place within the womb? . . . I wondered, are we all genetically built to be doo-dimers? And if so does this mean we're all two-spirited?[34]

Scofield expands the idea of Two-Spiritedness so that the term encompasses not only sexuality, but our very essences. On the surface, Scofield's unpacking of the term *Two-Spirit* seems to contradict the idea of Cree-specific Two-Spiritedness. As mentioned previously, Scofield does not refer to himself as Two-Spirited, because of the term's sacred denotation. While he understands that people find solidarity with labels such as Two-Spirit, he finds the label too personally confining. At the same time, Scofield is proud of his Métis heritage, proving the power of labels to foster a sense of solidarity. Scofield's grappling with identities is a constant theme in his work, a tension that is somewhat mitigated by the use of Cree Métis ontologies. He admits, "still one's sacredness, one's *pawatew*, like sexual identity itself, is not easy to define,"[35] another sign that understanding sacred responsibilities, like sexual identity, is a lifelong process.

Scofield recounts his first encounter with a Cree *âyahkwêw* in a book by a white anthropologist, *The Plains Cree*, by David G. Mandelbaum:

My Cree forerunner was called *ayekkwew*, "neither man nor woman" or "man and woman." It was reported that *Piciw-isk-wew*, which was said to mean "he moves and makes his home/house among women," died from wearing a dress that had been worn by a menstruating woman. He had been killed by the power of the woman's menstrual blood just as the Cree believed a man would have been. Only if he had been born a woman would he have not been harmed.[36]

In his early books of poetry, Scofield used the Cree term *âyahkwêw*,[37] which "loosely translated as a person who has both male and female spirits; also known as Two-Spirited."[38] Mandelbaum's informant, Fine Day from the Little Pine reserve in Saskatchewan, explains that when *a-yahkwew* became sick, a conjuring booth was set up to heal him/her:

Then you could hear the different spirit powers talking. An old man asked them why *a-yahkwew* was sick. "You knew, *a-yahkwew*, that the clothes you put on would hurt you. We try to do everything we can to save you, but we can't. What you call *pawakanak*, spirit helpers— that's us. But we are afraid ourselves of what you have done."

He suffered a long time before he died. He was not old when he died. He had a dress with a picture of a flying porcupine done in quillwork on the back. He had made that himself and never gambled for it. They buried him in this dress.[39]

Of course, the mystery behind this story is why Piciw-isk-wew had worn the woman's dress, as his

death was a direct result of breaking Cree spiritual law[40]: This was, or so it appeared, brought about by his born gender and his male inability to nullify the spiritual power of women. . . . Furthermore, I recall thinking seriously about the idea of two-spiritedness. If the Creator had gifted Piciw-isk-wew with two-spirits, then why had his female power not protected him? . . . Did this mean, therefore, that the idea of two-spiritedness was conceptual rather than spiritual?[41]

Piciw-isk-wew is described as sounding and looking like a man but dressing and staying with the women.[42] His identification with women, however, did not save him/her from wearing the dress.

Two-Spiritedness is described as "cultural constructions of multiple genders (i.e., more than two) and the opportunity for individuals to change gender roles and identities over the course of their lifetimes"[43] and may be partly theoretical, as Two-Spirits can change their gender identification over their lifetimes, a marked contrast to western conceptions of gender. In other words, for Indigenous nations that practiced gender variance, gender was remarkably fluid. For some of the nations that practiced gender variance, Two-Spirits were able to decide their gender roles and change them over a lifetime. However, Piciw-isk-wew's *maskihkîy* was not strong enough to overcome the power of women; disregarding his *pawatew*, his responsibility to uphold Cree sacred law, caused Piciw-isk-wew's death. His/her own spirit helpers were fearful of Piciw-isk-wew's actions; they tell Piciw-isk-wew, "But we are afraid ourselves of what you have done." While an *âyahkwêw's* gender may be fluid, it seems Piciw-isk-wew's maleness was in conflict with the power of women; respecting sacred law and one's *pawatew* supersedes individual actions. Good *maskihkîy* must be shown the proper respect, or it will turn into bad medicine.

As Métis writer and academic Warren Cariou explains in the introduction to the 2009 republished version of *Love Medicine and One Song/ Sâkihtowin-Maskihkiy êkwa Pêyak-Nikamowin,* "reverence, respect and the sacred ... are crucial in the Cree conception of love."[44] Instead of seeing Aboriginal peoples as the victims of sexual abuse, such as in residential schools, *Love Medicine* posits Aboriginal peoples as sexual beings with a precontact history of complex, loving relationships. Scofield describes writing *Love Medicine* as "allowing every dream and desire in relation to love [to come] to life, and for the first time I connected to the unspeakable longing I carried within. ... Through it and the process of writing it, I was finally able to break down the walls of my own internalized homophobia, set free at last the voice of my own spirit."[45]

Cariou explains that love medicine in the Cree tradition is not only a "potion or a particular ritual: it is an entire way of thinking about people's relation with each other and with the world."[46] Cariou emphasizes the importance of responsibility when using love medicine.

> It connects bodily experience with spiritual experience, and it is fundamentally about responsibility as well: our responsibility to each other and to the natural world that is the source of our sustenance. There is also a vital recognition in these poems that love medicine is something that can heal but also something that can be potentially dangerous. In Cree culture, as in many other Indigenous cultures, medicine is something over which humans can never exercise full control. Love medicine can bring many pleasures and benefits, but can also create great suffering if it is used without the proper respect.[47]

The idea of responsibility is again emphasized, both in the use of love medicine and in understanding one's *pawatew*. One cannot expect to receive the benefits of love medicine or of *pawatew* without realizing that misusing these powers results in grave consequences, as evidenced by Piciw-isk-wew. Scofield describes the poems as "medicine-songs" that "come from a sacred place within. I have made tobacco offerings to ask for the help and guidance of The Grandmothers and Grandfathers, and to honour my spiritual processes as well as my Dream-love, to whom the book is dedicated. In doing so, I have asked permission to share him with you, to present him in the most honourable, honest and sacred way I know: to sing my experience of love in both my languages, Cree and English."[48] Scofield's Dream-love is Dean, a former lover who appears in his first three poetry collections and who is a source of both love and torment.

The "Twelve Moons and the Dream," a complex thirteen-poem cycle based on Cree months, chronicles Scofield's relationship with the mysterious Dean, to whom *Love Medicine* is dedicated.[49] Scofield describes Dean "as the source of shadows and songs, my deepest respect and prayers, wherever you may be. Dean, *Ki-sâkihtan!* [I love you!]."[50] *The Gathering* is also dedicated to "D.A., who, like the Medicine Wheel, left behind a mystery." The "Letter to Dean" in the same volume recounts half-forgotten dreams of seeing "you searching for yourself/in the world/of the walking wounded."[51] Scofield confesses that he doesn't understand "the waiting" between Dean and himself: "we will carry on to the unseen end/Perhaps then/We will resume in a free, bloodless space."[52] Dean also appears in *Native Canadiana,* where he is the ghost who appeared "three years ago . . . breathing heat on winter nights."[53] Scofield's relationship with Dean is not idyllic, as Scofield craves

> his touch
> like slivers of glass, soft
> unsuspecting needles
> beckoning
> one perfect drop of crimson
> to the surface.[54]

While Scofield's relationship with Dean is troubled, Dean forms the basis of the desire for a relationship:

> Dean,
> if ever there is love
> between men
> I wish your eyes
> endless moons, my hands
> the ocean
> in which you drown.[55]

Scofield, however, is still grappling both with his love for the absent Dean and with the possibility of love between men: the stark use of "if" at the beginning of the second line poignantly illustrates his doubt.

"Twelve Moons and the Dream" begins with a quotation from an anonymous fourteenth-century mystic, "[f]rom *The Cloud of Knowing:* 'Reconcile yourself to wait in this darkness as long as necessary, but still go on longing after him whom you love. For if you are to feel him in this life, he must always be in this cloud, in this darkness.'"[56] Dean is elusive, the stuff of both nightmares and dreams, darkness and light. In the poem cycle, Dean is intimately tied to the prairie landscape and to Cree Métis traditions. As Cariou explains, the encounters between lovers in *Love Medicine* are not separated from the natural world but have a "spiritual dimension, demonstrating the connectedness of the entire creation, and showing that the lovers are not at all isolated from the animated world that surrounds them."[57] In "*Sâkipakâwi-pîsim/ May/The Budding Moon*," Scofield addresses the moon as *Nôhkom*, or Grandmother, telling her that "in my hands/I see his face/carved from pipestone/fireweed in his eyes."[58] While the month of Sâkipakâwi-pîsim is redolent with "quaking leaves, spruce boughs/green willow and damp moss," Scofield imagines Dean as

> hard earth, a high cliff wall
> I climb and descend
> into secret kivas
> leaving corndust and prayers,
> burn marks etched by my fingers.[59]

This is one of the rare times Scofield references another Indigenous culture. Drawing from Puebloan culture makes Scofield's yearning both familiar and strange. Scofield also posits his love for Dean as covert, as kivas are underground sacred spaces; his love for Dean is both sacred and clandestine.

By *Paskowi-pîsim/July/The Moulting Moon*, Scofield is bereft without his lover; his "sinew-slack drum" is "more silent than the nights."[60] In desperation, he has "skin and veins/to offer anyone, hungry/I have at least these/torn and diluted as they are."[61] Scofield is an empty husk that still holds memories of love. He then wonders "[o]n whose pillow do you lay/your vagrant head?/Whose hands pulled you from my dreams?"[62] Next month, *Ohpahowi-pîsim/The Flying-Up Moon*, Dean has come back, albeit briefly. Instead of being confused about Dean's absence, he can't "name your absence/or its taste"; rather, it is now "a strange language/neither bitter nor sweet."[63] The euphoria of having his lover back has made Scofield forgetful of the pain that Dean has caused him. As befitting the month, he likens Dean to a "heavy-winged bird/ and the bed is a pulse/with the weight of desire."[64] Scofield exclaims, "Finally you've come!/*piko kikway miyonâkwan* [everything is beautiful]."[65] However, all is not perfect with Dean's reappearance, much as Scofield portrays the exhilaration of Dean coming back to him:

> Though this longing is no secret
> you hold it close,

press into me, helpless
against your shame.⁶⁶

While the yearning between Scofield and Dean is not a secret, Dean feels shame about his desire for Scofield but is at the same time overpowered by it. This shame dooms Scofield's relationship with Dean, as it is based on an unwillingness to accept same-sex desire. As much as Scofield yearns for Dean, he will always remain elusive, as Dean has not accepted his same-sex desires, as has Scofield.

Scofield added a new entry to the introduction to the republished version of *Love Medicine*: "Ever so importantly, my deepest love and gratitude to my partner, Mark Ottewell, who continues to walk the road of self-discovery with me, and whose unconditional love is a sacred bundle I carry each and every day. *Nîcimos* [sweetheart] Mark, *Ki-sâkihtan!*"⁶⁷ Again, love is couched in Cree terms. That Scofield refers to Ottewell's love as a sacred bundle shows an acceptance of same-sex love and desire. Instead of about the uncertainty of his relationship with Dean, Scofield now writes of the pleasures and difficulties of being in a long-term mixed-race relationship in "My Husband Goes to War," a poem in his latest book of poetry, *Kipocihkân*.

> My husband goes to war
> With sculpting wax in his hair.
> He will scalp the Cree
> Just to be political. He will
> Hang the proof on his Armani belt.⁶⁸

Ottewell is anxious that Scofield will leave him for "chokecherries and fat/He worries that I am hungry for wild-wîyas [meat]."⁶⁹ Scofield ends the poem with the line: "I am his territory, his discovery,"⁷⁰ a sentiment similar to Qwo-Li Driskill's (Cherokee) lines in "Map of the Americas."

> know these lands
> have been invaded before
> and though I may quiver
> from your touch
> there is still a war⁷¹

As in Driskill's poem, there is a sense of occupation, but also of surrender in "My Husband Goes to War." Scofield doesn't protest that he is Ottewell's territory; rather, it is a way of reassuring Ottewell that

Scofield isn't interested in wild-*wîyas*. But there is another layer to the poem. While white settlers may think Canada is their territory and their discovery, it belongs to Aboriginal peoples; the Métis took up arms to defend our territories. Scofield hasn't completely surrendered. Nevertheless, Scofield does celebrate being in a long-term relationship, especially using Cree Métis ontologies. In "The Return," Scofield describes himself as "heated marrow" as he waits for his lover to return. When Ottewell returns, he lays Scofield "down and your body/is the taste of saskatoons/having ripened."[72] While previously Scofield's marrow was heated, he describes it as congealing like "Wihtikîw/I've eaten you, peyakwâw [once]/nîswâw, nistâw [twice, three times over]/But now I'm hungry/pîmciso, boy [come eat]!"[73]

Wihtikîw is translated as the Cree "legendary eater of humans, the cannibal,"[74] and is a metaphor for gluttony and excess. The *Wihtikîw* is a person that becomes a horrifying monster because he or she committed cannibalism, and although it eats more and more, the *Wihtikîw* is insatiable and never satisfied. McLeod describes *Wihtikîw* as consuming other beings: "The needs of the individual are pressed forward and the needs of the collective are suppressed . . . for me, *Wihtikow* is also a powerful metaphor for greed, the attempt to swallow the light from the sky of the world."[75] The *Wihtikîw* enforces the cannibalism taboo, but it also serves as a caution against selfishness and greed. While Scofield depicts himself as a *Wihtikîw* who has eaten his lover three times and is now ravenous for his lover, the lover is also a *Wihtikîw* as Scofield urges him to come and eat him. They are locked in a cycle of desire and of love in all its destructiveness and coming together.

While Scofield is renowned for his love poetry situated in the prairie landscapes of the Cree and of the Métis, he is also an urban poet, with poems specifically dealing with his experiences as a Native youth worker during the '90s in Vancouver's Downtown Eastside and Granville Street areas.[76] The Downtown Eastside is notorious for its open drug use and run-down single-room occupancy (SRO) hotels. The subtitle of *Native Canadiana: Songs from the Urban Rez* refers to a nickname for Vancouver's Downtown Eastside and surrounding areas. Because it is a poor area, there is a large Aboriginal population; according to the Pivot Legal Society, "the area has a large prevalence of First Nations people: 30 percent of the residents of the Downtown Eastside are indigenous, 10 times higher than the national average."[77] Many First Nations people come from remote reserves and find themselves in the Downtown

Eastside to deal with problems that are often the legacies of the residential school system, such as substance abuse and subsistence sex-trade work. The high incidence of Aboriginal children in care of the British Columbia government, as Scofield remarks, also adds to the large number of Aboriginal peoples in the Downtown Eastside:

> East Hastings Street overflowed with young Native people, many of whom had grown up in foster care. The IV drug use, prostitution, and violence were extreme, as was the alarming rate of HIV infection. . . . Workers such as myself tried our best to help, but it was futile. The kids, even the adults, were so damaged that it was virtually impossible to get them off the street, more ended in suicide, overdose, murder, or AIDS related illnesses. . . . I recall, at first, feeling grateful for being spared the misery of the streets—a reality that could have easily been mine.[78]

Scofield's work and life in the Downtown Eastside and Granville Street areas profoundly influenced both *Native Canadiana* and *The Gathering*. The poems show a frustration with the large numbers of Aboriginal people in the area and with the lack of concrete solutions to addictions and sex-trade work: "I believed that giving out condoms and clean needles, like helping people to get on welfare, was a temporary solution to a long-term problem. And yet I didn't know what the answer was. However, I did know that I wanted to voice these issues and try to make some sort of difference."[79] For Scofield, writing these poems brings light to the stories of Native peoples on the Downtown Eastside, including Two-Spirited/GLBTQ peoples. "Owls in the City" is dedicated to "my *Âyahkwêw* relations . . . back in the 80s/before the plague really hit.":

> What did we know?
> Everything about snagging was easy,
> no one thought beyond the party.
> Today it's worse—
> our *iyiniwak* [people] are dropping
> like rotten chokecherries
> in back alleys or hospitals.
> Even owls have migrated to the city,
> perched on rooftops or clotheslines
> hooting their miserable death chant.[80,81]

Scofield remembers "Donny, Ray, Felicia and Queenie" who "are all sick or dead/or just about."[82] They "slumped together/at the Dufferin/eyeing every white guy/who walked by."[83,84] They are wild-*wîyas* who don't fit into the white gay world.

> Having worked with gay, lesbian and transgendered Native people, I fully understand the need for solidarity and a sense of uniqueness, a defined and supportive place among the dominant white gay male culture. Racism, class discrimination and sexism can be even worse within our own community than they are in general society. Furthermore, the daily burdens of family and ostracism carried by many urban gay/lesbian/transgendered Native people only add to their sense of isolation.[85]

Native Two-Spirit/GLBTQ peoples are discriminated against by gay white male society but also by other Aboriginal peoples. However, discrimination within Aboriginal communities can be even worse. A legacy of colonization is that many Native peoples have lost touch with their tribal-specific Two-Spirit traditions, prompting many people to leave their reserves. While there may be less discrimination now because of organizations like Healing Our Spirit, the Northern Aboriginal HIV/AIDS Task Force, and the Red Roads HIV/AIDS Network in British Columbia, and the Canadian Aboriginal AIDS Network nationally, the remoteness of many of British Columbia's reserves means that services for people with HIV/AIDS are difficult to access. Many move to the city to escape discrimination and to be a part of the Two-Spirit/GLBTQ community. Scofield notes, "So many of our youth were coming down from remote communities . . . and I wanted to try to empower them, to shed light on issues affecting them,"[86] another example of writing as *maskihkîy* and Scofield's responsibility, his *pawatew*.

Scofield ends the poem on a note of celebration by tapping softly on his drum, thinking "how fortunate I am/saved to pull up these *Âyahkwéw* songs/from my still beating heart."[87] Scofield believes what may have saved him from the fate of some of his *Âyahkwêw* relations was that he "was the chicken/of the bunch and/mouthy as any redneck/Because I screamed and hollered/they kept out of my pants."[88] By pulling these songs out of his heart, Scofield both pays tribute to his *Âyahkwêw* relations and expresses a palatable sense of relief that he is alive.

By singing/writing of his experiences as a gay, Métis man, Scofield is honoring Grandfather Black Bear, who told him that he has an important job to do, a part of Scofield's *pawatew*. While Scofield writes to make sense of his own experiences these stories are also *maskihkîy*—life-giving medicine. As Scofield explains:

> My own diligence, both steady and wavering, to accept my Creator-made self, my God-given power, my *pawatew,* is still steeping in my spirit. Until I fully understand the gifts I've been given, I'm grateful for the sight of my two eyes, the ability to create with my two hands. So again, does this make me two-spirited? Perhaps. Perhaps not. I do know, however, that Turtle Island is a place of sacred and not so sacred people, all of us looking for a sense of belonging, a validation of our existence—maybe even a platform to stage our resistance, for whatever reason. One could conclude, I suppose, that these inherent needs are one and the same, an endless step towards self-definition.[89]

Understanding one's *pawatew* is a difficult task, one that is never completely attainable, as *pawatew* is too complex to understand within a lifetime. Scofield writes both to belong to his communities and to resist both Native and non-Native views of Métis peoples. He also portrays the complexities of same-sex relationships. As Cariou stresses, Scofield "has flouted the attempts of critics and reviewers to place hard boundaries around his identity. . . . For Scofield, attempting to stabilize a thing like love—as with personal identity itself—only makes it disappear."[90] While Scofield situates himself within Cree Métis ways of knowing, he repudiates being labeled an *âyahkwêw,* a coat that he refuses to wear, for fear it will be too confining. Even though others try to set Scofield "straight, crooked or somewhere in between," his *pawatew* is to accept himself outside of externally imposed labels and to reach a holistic sense of self.

Acknowledgments

Many thanks to Dr. Sophie McCall and Dr. Deanna Reder (Métis) of Simon Fraser University for providing their suggestions for this essay and for their continued and unflagging support.

Notes

1. Scofield's *Love Medicine and One Song/Sâkihtowin-Maskihkiy êkwa Pêyak-Nikamowin* (1997), was the first volume of erotic poetry published by an Aboriginal writer in Canada. *Love Medicine* predates both Kateri Akiwenzie-Damm's (Anishinaabe) 2003 introduction to her anthology *Without Reservation: Indigenous Erotica* in Canada and Qwo-Li Driskill's formulation in the United States

on the sovereign erotic, making Scofield an essential component of critical inquiry into Two-Spirit/Native GLBTQ issues.

2. Gregory Scofield, "You Can Always Count on an Anthropologist (to Set You Straight, Crooked or Somewhere In-Between)," in *Me Sexy: An Exploration of Native Sex and Sexuality,* ed. Drew Hayden Taylor (Toronto: Douglas and McIntyre, 2008), 162.

3. Ibid., 27–28.

4. While there are Métis in states such as Montana, North Dakota, and Minnesota, Scofield's poetry is firmly rooted in Canadian Métis experiences, particularly of resistance to the Canadian government and encroaching settlers.

5. Qwo-Li Driskill, "Call Me Brother: Two-Spiritedness, the Erotic, and Mixedblood Identity as Sites of Sovereignty in Gregory Scofield's Poetry," in *Speak to Me Words: Essays on Contemporary American Indian Poetry,* ed. Dean Rader and Janice Gould (Tucson: University of Arizona Press, 2003), 223.

6. While Métis people overwhelmingly speak English or French, many speak Cree. Sadly, the Métis language of Michif is endangered.

7. For essays, video, and pictorial information on the Métis, see the Virtual Métis Museum: http://www.metismuseum.ca/.

8. Gregory Scofield, *Thunder through My Veins: Memories of a Métis Childhood* (Toronto: HarperCollins, 1997), 42.

9. Ibid., 65.

10. Scofield, "You Can Count," 164.

11. Ibid., 160.

12. Scofield has identified Dale Awasis, his adopted Cree brother, as the interlocutor in the poem.

13. Gregory Scofield, *The Gathering: Stones from the Medicine Wheel* (Vancouver: Polestar, 1993), 82.

14. Ibid.

15. Ibid.

16. Jo-Ann Episkenew, *Taking Back Our Spirits: Indigenous Literature, Public Policy, and Healing* (Winnipeg: University of Manitoba Press, 2009), 54.

17. Scofield, *Gathering,* 82.

18. Scofield is stressing that Métis prefer the terms *Northwest Resistance* or *1885 Resistance,* which took place in Batoche, Saskatchewan.

19. Scofield used the anglicized spelling of *Cree* in *The Gathering* before switching to Cree orthography. *Katipamsoochick* becomes *katipâmsôchik.*

20. Scofield, *Gathering,* 82–83.

21. Ibid., 91.

22. Neal McLeod, "*nêhiyâwiwin* and Modernity," in *Plain Speaking: Essays on Aboriginal Peoples and the Prairies,* ed. Patrick Douad and Bruce Dawson (Regina, SK: Canadian Plains Research Centre, 2002), 43–44.

23. Leah Dorion and Darren R. Préfontaine, "Deconstructing Métis Historiography," in *Métis Legacy,* ed. Lawrence J. Barkwell, Leah Dorion, and Darren R. Préfontaine (Winnipeg: Pemmican, 2001), 25.

24. Episkenew, *Taking Back Our Spirits,* 11.

25. Ibid., 15.

26. Episkenew, *Taking Back Our Spirits,* 16.

27. Neal McLeod, *Cree Narrative Memory: From Treaties to Contemporary Times* (Saskatoon: Purich, 2007), 11; italics mine.

28. Claire Foster and Sharanpal Ruprai, interview with Gregory Scofield, *Prairie Fire* 24, no. 3 (2001): 47.

29. Scofield, *Thunder,* 43–44; italics mine.

30. Ibid., 9–10.

31. Linda Richards, interview with Gregory Scofield, September 1999, *January Magazine,* http://januarymagazine.com/profiles/scofield.html.

32. Scofield, *Thunder,* 189.

33. Scofield, "You Can Count," 160.

34. Ibid., 160–61.

35. Ibid., 163.

36. Ibid., 165.

37. There are differences in the spellings of Cree words in different authors' works and between Scofield's books. I am using the spellings as the author writes them.

38. Scofield, *Native Canadiana: Songs from the Urban Rez* (Vancouver: Polestar, 1996), 122.

39. David Mandelbaum. *The Plains Cree: An Ethnographic, Historical, and Comparative Study* (Regina, SK: Canadian Plains Research Centre, 1979), 168.

40. Scofield, "You Can Count," 166.

41. Ibid.

42. Ibid.

43. Sabine Lang, "Various Kinds of Two-Spirit People: Gender Variance and Homosexuality in Native American Communities," in *Two-Spirit People: Native American Gender Identity, Sexuality and Spirituality,* ed. Sue-Ellen Jacobs, Wesley Thomas, and Sabine Lang (Chicago: University of Chicago Press, 1997), 103.

44. Warren Cariou, "Introduction," in *Love Medicine and One Song/Sâkihtowin-Maskihkiy êkwa Pêyak-Nikamowin,* Wiarton, ON: Kegedonce, 2009, iii.

45. Scofield, *Thunder,* 194.

46. Cariou, "Introduction," iv.

47. Ibid.

48. Scofield, *Love Medicine,* 3.

49. The 1997 version of *Love Medicine* is also dedicated to Kim, a woman with whom Scofield was involved at this time, before he completely acknowledged his gayness. This dedication is missing from the republished version.

50. Scofield, *Love Medicine*, 4.

51. Scofield, *Gathering*, 58.

52. Ibid.

53. Gregory Scofield, *Native Canadiana*, 93.

54. Ibid., 93.

55. Ibid., 94.

56. Scofield, *Love Medicine*, 41.

57. Cariou, "Introduction," viii.

58. Scofield, *Love Medicine*, 44.

59. Ibid.

60. Ibid., 48.

61. Ibid.

62. Ibid.

63. Ibid., 50.

64. Ibid.

65. Ibid.

66. Ibid.

67. Ibid., 3.

68. Gregory Scofield, *Kipocihkân: Poems New and Selected* (Gibsons, BC: Nightwood Editions, 2009), 136.

69. Ibid., 137.

70. Ibid.

71. Qwo-Li Driskil, *Walking with Ghosts* (Cambridge: Salt, 2005), 11.

72. Gregory Scofield, *Singing Home the Bones* (Vancouver: Polestar, 2005), 82.

73. Ibid., 83.

74. Ibid.

75. Neal McLeod, *Songs to Kill a Wîhtikow* (Regina, SK: Hagios Press, 2005), 8.

76. Scofield also worked with adults, "many of whom were involved with the sex trade" (Scofield, *Thunder*, 190).

77. Pivot Legal Society. "Pivot Legal Society & Vancouver's Downtown Eastside," August 4, 2009, http://www.pivotlegal.org/dtes.htm.

78. Scofield, *Thunder*, 191.

79. Ibid., 192.

80. "In the Cree tradition, owls are believed to be messengers of illness or death" (Scofield, *Singing Home*, 109).

81. Scofield, *Native Canadiana*, 71–72.

82. Ibid., 71.

83. The Dufferin was a well-known gay pub in downtown Vancouver.

84. Scofield, *Native Canadiana*, 71.

85. Scofield, "You Can Count," 161–62.

86. Jennifer David, *Story Keepers: Conversations with Aboriginal Writers* (Owen Sound, ON: Ningwakwe Learning Press, 2004), 36.

87. Scofield, *Native Canadiana,* 72.

88. Ibid., 71.

89. Scofield, "You Can Count," 167.

90. Cariou, "Introduction," vii.

12

The Revolution Is for Everyone

Imagining an Emancipatory Future through Queer
Indigenous Critical Theories

Qwo-Li Driskill, Chris Finley, Brian Joseph Gilley,
Scott Lauria Morgensen

Queer Indigenous peoples boldly choose to love and be true to our
desires, dreaming for moments of emancipation from colonial rule. We
look into a horizon of death to make a life for ourselves, despite the
overwhelming hopelessness that can be part of our lived experiences.
Colonialism, poverty, homophobia, displacement, suicide, and rejection by our families and communities are parts of our lives. This is not
said to perpetuate notions of tragic victimry that so often haunt writing
about Indigenous peoples. Instead, it is said to point out the material
and political conditions that Native GLBQT2 people experience under
colonization, including colonization's accompanying systems of heteropatriarchy, gender regimes, capitalism, ableism, ageism, and religious
oppression. Indigenous queer critiques offer a mode of analysis that
more complexly facilitates an understanding of these entwined systems
so that they can be interrupted.

Colonial oppression is a multibinding system that puts queer and
Two-Spirit Indigenous lives deeply at risk. According to the Centers
for Disease Control, for instance, even though the numbers of HIV and
AIDS diagnoses for American Indians and Alaska Natives in the United
States represent less than 1 percent of the total number of HIV/AIDS
cases reported to CDC's HIV/AIDS Reporting System, "[w]hen population size is taken into account, American Indians and Alaska Natives in
2005 ranked third in rates of HIV/AIDS diagnosis."[1] According to the
U.S. Department of Health and Human Services 1989 report on youth
suicide, "Gay and Lesbian" youth are two to three times more likely to
attempt suicide than other youth, and suicide is the leading cause of
death for GLBT youth.[2] The CDC tracks suicide as the second leading
cause of death for American Indian and Alaskan Native people from ages
fifteen to thirty-four, 1.8 times higher than the national average.[3] Data
compiled by the Bureau of Justice Statistics reveal that "American Indians

were victims of violent crime at about twice the rate of blacks, whites or Asians during 1998," and that Native women have the highest rates of experiencing violence from an intimate partner in the United States.[4] Prison Justice, a Canadian activist organization, highlights stark statistics from 2005–2006: while Aboriginal people make up approximately 4 percent of the Canadian population, they make up 24 percent of admissions into provincial/territorial prison custody, and 18 percent of admissions into federal custody. In Manitoba and Saskatchewan, where Aboriginal people constitute approximately 15–16 percent of the overall population, Aboriginal people make up 71 percent of the Manitoba prison population and 79 percent of the prison population in Saskatchewan.[5]

The story that begins to emerge from these statistics, as limited and problematic as such data might be, is not surprising: queer Indigenous people experience multilayered oppression that profoundly impacts our safety, health, and survival. What also emerges is the reality that our activism and scholarship can't pretend that there are easy fixes. While it is important to engage in activism that interrupts moments of marginalization and oppression, the lived experiences of queer and Two-Spirit Indigenous people show us that we—as Indigenous people, as GLBTQ2 people, as feminists, and as allies in numerous struggles—must engage in long-term, multifaceted, decolonial activism and scholarship that centralize analyses of, and resistance to, heteropatriarchal colonial systems in all of their manifestations.

Implications for Decolonial Activism

Queer Native people do not have the space of a closet to hide our sexualities, since we have been physically, culturally, mentally, and spiritually pathologized and forced into modern representation by the scientific and philosophical discourses of anthropology, history, psychoanalysis, sociology, and medicine. Queer Indigenous people have been under the surveillance of white colonial heteropatriarchy since contact. Since many of the communities we come from are small, the space we have to hide our sexual and political desires is the space of a cupboard, not a closet. The metaphor of the cupboard refers to the marginal spaces allotted to queer Native peoples and the theft of Native lands through the continued occupation of our lands. Declaring "We're here and we're queer" does not mean we get our land back. It does not mean that we can be a part of queer communities. The queer movement does not represent all of what queer Indigenous people desire. Many times coming out means making a choice between being Indigenous—and remaining a part of our communities without discussing or disclosing our queer and/or Two-Spirit identities—and being queer—without a community of other Indigenous people and exoticized by non-Indigenous queer people. Queer indigeneity challenges the very idea of civil rights and exclusionary complaints that grounds the mainstream GLBT movement. Instead, queer and Two-Spirit Indigenous people are going after colonial nation-states and challenging the racist and heterosexist foundation of theft and genocide they support and reproduce. Queer Indigenous critiques do not look for recognition from the nation-state for our pain and suffering because of identities, but seek to imagine other queer possibilities for emancipation and freedom for all peoples. These possibilities are not limited to one vision. As contributors to this collection make clear, there is not a singular queer Indigenous critique.

Considering queer desire as an organizing principle can be very useful to queer Native peoples, because it means we can "get into bed" with many different ideas, peoples, and political ideologies and not just focus on a singular identity politics. This goes along with Denise da Silva's critique of race scholars' focus on exclusionary politics.[6] As she argues, proving people of color have been excluded from being a transparent subject does not challenge the Enlightenment thinking that makes subaltern subjects inferior, inhuman, and subject to violence. This anthology hopes to work along these lines by exposing both the violence and the hope in being an affectable subject that can be transformed, changed, and loved by the world.

Gay marriage is an important queer issue, but as many chapters in this book show, the right for queer Native peoples to be married is only one of many issues facing queer Native peoples today. Debates surrounding gay marriage in Native American nations can provide critiques of Native nationality that mirrors the U.S. nation-state. Usually, tribes who are quick to adopt anti–gay marriage laws—such as the Cherokee Nation and the Navajo Nation—are Native nations that have adopted the heteropatriarchal nation-state model of the settler state. These national formations, while maintaining tribal sovereignty, do not challenge colonialism or the legitimacy of nation-state interference in tribal governance. And while the banning of same-sex marriage in both the Cherokee Nation and the Navajo Nation under the rhetoric of sovereignty is deeply troubling, the mainstream media and conversations within academia have often focused on these cases as examples of homophobia within Indian Country without any mention of the numerous Native nations who have *not* banned same-sex marriage, nor the Coquille Indian Tribe's 2008 law that specifically includes same-sex marriage.[7] Decolonial queer Indigenous activism challenges the authority of the nation-state and the internalized colonization of Indigenous nations, and pushes us to more radical possibilities for decolonial activism that can transform all of our lives.

The Work of Allies

This book creates space for conversations among queer Indigenous peoples to be centered in scholarship. This was the basis on which allies— non-GLBTQ, and non-Indigenous—participated accountably. Much of what contributors write troubles the idea that we can count on identity to be stable, to give us our politics, or to be above critical analysis. This book shows that queer Indigenous critiques remain tied intimately to the lives of people identified as Indigenous and GLBTQ2, but also that they exceed any particular experience to offer a broad critique of settler colonialism and heteropatriarchy to which all people must respond. That said, in context of a politics of alliance, this book's purpose is to call all people linked by the border-crossing potential of queer Indigenous critiques to study their locations in the power relations that these critiques disrupt.

The important work of building alliances is not one that only non-Native and non-GLBTQ2 people must engage in. Within Indigenous GLBTQ2 communities, we must build alliances across differences in order to build stronger decolonial movements. Partially because of the history of Two-Spirit organizations funded by government projects working to reduce HIV transmission rates among Native men who have sex with men, much of the community organizing in the last decade has had an unbalanced focus on men and male-embodied Two-Spirit people. While this is certainly in the process of shifting because of women and female-embodied Two-Spirit people leading organizing and holding women-centered events, much work needs to be done to rebalance gender within our organizations and movements. A decolonial agenda for Indigenous GLBTQ2 people must place the project of interrupting sexism at the center of our work. This means that men within our movements must deeply engage what it means to be anti-sexist allies and activists as part of the work of being Two-Spirit.

Our movements must also recenter ourselves to place transgender and gender non-conforming people and issues at the center of Two-Spirit organizing. While many of us understand that many of the "roles" currently being called "Two-Spirit" are not about sexuality, but about relationships with gender, much of our work ends up conflating *Two-Spirit* with *gay* in ways that often ignore those who should be at the center of our movements: those whose gender identities and expressions fall outside of rigid colonial dichotomies. Further, we must be cautious not to internalize the colonial politics of GLBTQ organizing by understanding that sexuality, like gender, does not exist in rigid binaries. It should come as no surprise to us in our gatherings and organizations that there are people who identify as Two-Spirit and/or queer who have relationships with people of another gender.

Any decolonial movement must work to dismantle the rigid ways of thinking about gender and sexuality that have been imposed upon us, even within Two-Spirit and queer movements, by constantly decolonizing our paradigms. While individuals may choose the term *Two-Spirit* and reject the term *gay*, or choose the term *queer* and reject the term *Two-Spirit*, there is no reason to see any of these identities as in opposition. Individuals may have personal reasons for taking on or rejecting particular identity labels, but identity labels are just that: labels. It is the choice of individuals to embrace or reject any labels that they choose. What we should share in common, however, is a commitment to our communities and to larger decolonial struggles, understanding that colonial heteropatriarchy injures all of us. Decolonial movements of Indigenous GLBTQ2 people that replicate sexism, transphobia, and biphobia in our communities are—in fact—not decolonial at all. We must realize that in order for our projects to be successful in intervening and interrupting oppression, we must become allies to one another in our struggles.

Just as differences among queer Indigenous people must be addressed, so also must those of non-Indigenous and non-GLBTQ people. Our work across these differences as coeditors and contributors has upped the stakes for allies to queer Indigenous criticism. No longer should it be assumed that "empathic" knowledge production will serve to emancipate GLBTQ2 Indigenous people. Rather, the future of scholarship, as mapped in this volume, requires allies to view social, economic, and political realities through the variegated experiences of queer indigeneity. The theories and methodologies we propose intervene not only in current power inequalities but also in assumptions that collapse the experiences of Indigenous GLBTQ2 people and allies. The future of alliance work requires monumental self-reflexivity and a rejection of the universality in liberal knowledge production if we are to work together to challenge the power relations of settler colonialism.

The stakes in allied criticism are well positioned by the methodological shift in Indigenous studies, which centers Indigenous knowledges and anticolonial critiques as a basis for making our claims. In this volume, we centered the histories and knowledges of Indigenous people who are marked or identified as queer and/or Two-Spirit as a basis for what and how we will know. This move calls "straight" Indigenous people to both witness and contribute to work that centers Indigenous queer people and critiques, and to recognize those critiques as a key challenge to sexual colonization. It also calls all non-Indigenous people across gender or sexual identities to center Indigenous knowledges in allied anticolonial work. In this case, it notably calls non-Indigenous queers to challenge how queer friendships or solidarities have elided how colonization still shapes their relationships with Indigenous queer people.

This shift, we hope, decisively displaces non-Native anthropology as a primary basis of knowledge about queer Indigenous lives. We deeply respect efforts by anthropologists to change the discipline by engaging queer Indigenous people as knowledge producers. For instance, Wesley Thomas, a Diné Two-Spirit anthropologist, and Sue-Ellen Jacobs and Sabine Lang as allied non-Native anthropologists, shifted the dominant frame of non-Native anthropology by engaging Two-Spirit organizers. The legacies of that moment of activism by Two-Spirit people inform our work. For instance, Brian Joseph Gilley and Scott Lauria Morgensen responded to their anthropological training as non-GLBTQ2 (Gilley) and non-Indigenous (Morgensen) scholars by centering the self-determined knowledges of queer Indigenous people as a basis for theory: for Gilley, by examining the "sexual survivance" of Two-Spirit men amid the sexual politics of Native communities, and for Morgensen by engaging Two-Spirit organizers' critiques of settler colonialism, notably, in non-Native queer politics. In the future, we argue, non-Indigenous anthropologists and queer studies scholars must recognize that texts on queer indigeneity written by and for non-Indigenous people have been displaced by queer Indigenous critiques. Here, this volume joins other recent collections in which Daniel Heath Justice, Deborah Miranda, James Cox, and Bethany Schneider joined Qwo-Li Driskill, Mark Rifkin, and Lisa Tatonetti in allying across differences to help in changing the terms of scholarship.[8] While many of us have been living this moment for years, academic publications appear, finally, to be catching up. Academic work on queer indigeneity must start in conversation with queer Indigenous criticism, where allies can and must participate by articulating their work through the distinctive theories that arise here.

There are, then, some conversations we hope never to have again; and if we do, we expect them to be accountable to the arguments named here and in other cited texts. For instance, we hope that this collection enables scholars to no longer have to rehearse an intellectual history of the term *Two-Spirit* before beginning any conversation about Two-Spirit and/ or queer Indigenous scholarship. We want future conversations to start from different places. As an example, in queer scholarship and activism, a common suggestion has been that *Two-Spirit* is a dichotomous term that reinforces heteronormative binary sex/gender in Native societies, meaning that it cannot perform queer critique and must be subjected to it. In response, we offer an array of scholarship that shows that queer criticism itself is conditioned by the history of settler colonialism and must account for this. We are uninterested in queer scholars critiquing work based in Two-Spirit or any other Indigenous identity category prior to having centered critiques of settler colonialism in the world and in their lives and claims.

The essays performing queer Indigenous criticism in this volume show that settler colonialism is the historical, institutional, and discursive root of heteronormative binary sex/gender systems on stolen land. In this reading, to interrogate heteronormativity *is* to critique colonial power, which then necessarily intersects the work of decolonization pursued by queer Indigenous people. Our contributors further argue that both subject-focused and subjectless critiques work in queer Indigenous criticism to shatter colonial heteropatriarchy as a basis for Indigenous people's lives. The critique of colonial heteropatriarchy occurs when reclaiming traditions through *asegi, takatapui, fa'afafine,* Two-Spirit, or other identities, just as it does when scholars do not seek out identities but instead investigate how Indigenous *peoples* were queered by colonization, so that all Indigenous people today are called to question heteronormativity as part of decolonization. These subject-focused and subjectless critiques are not the same, but they also are not in opposition to one another in queer Indigenous criticism. Each informs queer Indigenous critiques in denaturalizing and challenging heteronormativity as a colonial project. Thus, like "subjectless" queer Indigenous critiques, any Two-Spirit or other Indigenous critique that reclaims traditional gender and sexuality also is critically queer, for unlike normative queer theory, each marks and disrupts colonial power as a condition of *all* hetero-normative *and* queer claims on stolen land, and challenges other queer critiques to offer a decolonial response.

Implications for Our Futures

In Native studies, "the community" is often a privileged and idealized site of study or place to return to our mythic and unsullied histories. Yet the construction of the idea of "community" often creates a false binary between activist and academic discourses. Activist scholarship can remain rooted in grassroots political movements and simultaneously recognize that academia *is* a community in which activist work should take place. We should not devalue the importance of having an academic intellectual community where we organize and debate the importance of Foucault, Da Silva, Butler, and Puar to our work. We should not be ashamed of our participation in academia or our desire to be part of this community. As Malea Powell and Andrea Smith argue, this work is part of building intel-lectual alliances as activism.[9] The building of scholarship and activism in academic communities does not foreclose participation in nonacademic communities, nor does it exclude nonacademics from participating in this community. Our political and familial commitments can lead us to better scholarship and support for our academic work. Intellectual activ-ism in the academy makes an important contribution to political change. Placing ourselves in an academic community also means we have to be ethically, socially, and politically accountable to one another. An anthol-ogy is a community in itself. As editors, we learned much from working together as well as from working with the contributors and the University of Arizona Press. We produced the intellectual work of this anthology as a community and political organizing tool. We hope activists, scholars, Native community members, and tribal government workers and offi-cers read this book and deeply engage the ideas presented here.

The work of belonging to, challenging, and transforming "the com-munity" long has been modeled by Indigenous women activists, who include Indigenous feminist theorists linking activist and academic work. Kim Anderson and Joanne Barker argue that in Canada, marking patri-archy *as* a colonial effect of the Indian Act led Aboriginal Women's

Movement activists to critique Indigenous communities for adopting patriarchy as a stand-in for "tradition."[10] Such work joined the efforts of Indigenous women to reassert traditional women's leadership, as when Haudenosaunee women such as Patricia Monture-Angus called for change in their nations as a method of collective empowerment.[11] The recent publication of Native feminist collections in *Wicazo sa Review* and *American Quarterly* announces a new moment in Native studies, when Indigenous feminists are making the field a more critical site for the study of colonialism by centering gender and sexuality in its theories and methodologies.[12] Our hope as a collective is that Indigenous feminist critiques will guide emerging work in queer Indigenous studies. Critically studying heteropatriarchy and colonization bridges their intertwined histories with the ways that we inherit them in everyday life. In the process we learn both how power defines us and how we engage power creatively in resistance. We take inspiration from Indigenous feminism in assisting the renewed participation and leadership in Indigenous communities of people of all gender identities, who work daily to shift colonization's heteropatriarchal legacies while changing minds and building solidarities for new action.

Our future, as this volume's introduction argues, is an imagining. What are the possibilities for the future of queer/Two-Spirit Indigenous activisms? What kind of world do we want to live in? What do we have to say about Indigenous issues often not considered "queer," such as language revitalization, land redress, environmental justice, and prison abolition? How can these issues be rearticulated through Indigenous queer critiques? Certainly, this isn't just part of imagining a future. GLBTQ2 Indigenous people are already engaged in these struggles. Many Two-Spirit people see their participation in activism or their work as teachers, counselors, caregivers, and community health activists as part of fulfilling their "traditional" roles in their communities. What would it mean for non-GLBTQ2 Indigenous people to acknowledge this, and to see GLBTQ2 people and critiques of colonial heteropatriarchy as central to decolonization and community well-being? What would it mean for Indigenous communities to not simply tolerate GLBTQ2 people, but to see our concerns, our activism, and our work as integral to the survival and resistance of Indigenous communities? What does a queer decolonization of our homelands, bodies, and psyches look like?

At least some of the answers are located in the imagining of GLBTQ2 Indigenous artists. Queer Native art, literature, and film have been, for several decades, theorizing queer and Two-Spirit Indigenous critiques and building places for us through their imaginings. As demonstrated in *Sovereign Erotics: A Collection of Two-Spirit Literatures*, the sister book of creative writing accompanying this anthology of critical scholarship, queer artistic expression is an important method of survival for queer Native peoples and of engagement with peoples outside their experience. The Métis resistance leader Louis Riel is credited with saying, "My people will sleep for one hundred years; when they awake it will be the artists who give them their spirit back." We should engage these artists, both to support their livelihoods and to critically interpret the maps they produce of their versions of queer indigeneity. Artists are the visionaries leading us to a bright future, to mourning the past in productive ways, and to sensuously stunning us in the present. Through this artistic activism, Indigenous queer and Two-Spirit people can reclaim our spirits. And through an unapologetic critique of colonial heteropatriarchy, we can continue to commit revolutionary acts in our scholarship, our practices, our activism, and our imaginations.

Notes

1. Centers for Disease Control and Prevention, "HIV/AIDS among American Indians and Alaska Natives," http://www.cdc.gov/hiv/resources/Factsheets/aian.htm.

2. Marcia R. Feinleib, ed. *Report on the Secretary's Task Force on Youth Suicide*, vol. 3, *Prevention and Interventions in Youth Suicide* (U.S. Department of Health and Human Services, Public Health Service, Alcohol, Drug Abuse, and Mental Health Administration, 1989), 110.

3. Centers for Disease Control and Prevention. "Suicide: Facts at a Glance," http://www.cdc.gov/ViolencePrevention/suicide/index.html.

4. U.S. Department of Justice Statistics. "Differences in Rates of Violent Crime Experienced by Whites and Blacks Narrow: American Indians Are the Most Victimized By Violence," http://bjs.ojp.usdoj.gov/content/pub/press/vvr98pr.cfm.

5. Prison Justice, "Prison Facts and Statistics," http://www.prisonjustice.ca/politics/facts_stats.html.

6. Denise Ferreira da Silva, *Toward a Global Idea of Race* (Minneapolis: University of Minnesota Press, 2007).

7. Bill Graves, "Coquille Same-Sex Marriage Law Takes Effect," *Oregon Live*, http://www.oregonlive.com/news/index.ssf/2009/05/coquille_samesex_marriage_law.html.

8. Daniel Heath Justice and James H. Cox, eds., "Queering Native Literature, Indigenizing Queer Theory," *Studies in American Indian Literature* 20,

no. 1 (2008); Daniel Heath Justice, Mark Rifkin, and Bethany Schneider, eds., "Sexuality, Nationality, Indigeneity," *GLQ: A Journal of Lesbian and Gay Studies* 16, no. 1–2 (2010); Qwo-Li Driskill, Daniel Heath Justice, Deborah Miranda, and Lisa Tatonetti, eds., *Sovereign Erotics: A Collection of Two-Spirit Literatures* (Tucson: University of Arizona Press, forthcoming).

9. Malea D. Powell, "Down by the River, or How Susan La Flesche Picotte Can Teach Us about Alliance as a Practice of Survivance," *College English* 67, no. 1 (2004): 38–60; Andrea Smith, *Native Americans and the Christian Right: The Gendered Politics of Unlikely Alliances* (Durham, NC: Duke University Press, 2008).

10. Kim Anderson, *A Recognition of Being: Reconstructing Native Womanhood* (Toronto: Second Story Press, 2000); Joanne Barker, "Gender, Sovereignty, Rights: Native Women's Activism against Social Inequality and Violence in Canada," *American Quarterly* 60, no. 2 (2008).

11. Patricia Monture-Angus, *Thunder in My Soul: A Mohawk Woman Speaks* (Black Point, NS: Fernwood, 1995).

12. Mishuana Goeman and Jennifer Nez Denetdale, eds., "Native Feminisms: Legacies, Interventions, and Sovereignties," *Wicazo Sa Review* 24, no. 2 (2009); Andrea Smith and J. Kehaulani Kauanui, eds., "Forum: Native Feminisms without Apology," *American Quarterly* 60, no. 2 (2008).

Works Cited

Archival Collections

Alexander Turnbull Library, Wellington, New Zealand, MS-Papers
British Library
Church Missionary Society Archives, Birmingham University

Secondary Sources

Ahmed, Sara. *The Cultural Politics of Emotion.* New York: Routledge, 2004.
Alfred, Taiaiake. *Wasase: Indigenous Pathways of Action and Freedom.* University of Toronto Press, 2005.
Allen, Paula Gunn. "Beloved Women: Lesbians in American Indian Cultures." *Conditions: Seven* 3, no. 1 (1981): 67–87.
———. *The Sacred Hoop: Recovering the Feminine in American Indian Traditions.* Boston: Beacon Press, 1986.
———. *The Woman Who Owned the Shadows.* San Francisco: Spinsters Ink, 1983.
Altman, Dennis. "Globalization and the International Gay/Lesbian Movement." In *Handbook of Lesbian and Gay Studies,* edited by Diane Richardson and Steven Seidman, 415–25. London: Sage, 2002.
Anderson, Eric Gary. "Situating American Indian Poetry: Place, Community, and the Question of Genre." In *Speak to Me Words: Essays on Contemporary American Indian Poetry,* edited by Dean Radar and Janice Gould, 34–55. Tucson: University of Arizona Press, 2003.
Anderson, Kim. *A Recognition of Being: Reconstructing Native Womanhood.* Toronto: Second Story Press, 2000.
Anguksuar, Richard LaFortune. "A Postcolonial Colonial Perspective on Western [Mis]Conceptions of the Cosmos and the Restoration of Indigenous Taxonomies." In *Two-Spirit People: Native American Gender Identity, Sexuality, and Spirituality,* edited by Sue-Ellen Jacobs, Wesley Thomas, and Sabine Lang, 217–23. Urbana: University of Illinois Press, 1997.
Anthropological Research Group on Homosexuality. "A.R.G.O.H. Charter." *Anthropological Research Group on Homosexuality* 2, no. 1 (1980): 3–4.
Anzaldúa, Gloria. *Borderlands/La Frontera: The New Mestiza.* San Francisco: Aunt Lute Books, 1987.

Arrizón, Alicia. *Queering Mestizaje: Transculturation and Performance*. Ann Arbor: University of Michigan Press, 2006.

Aspin, Clive, and Jessica Hutchings. "Reclaiming the Past to Inform the Future: Contemporary Views of Maori Sexuality." *Culture, Health and Sexuality* 9, no. 4 (2007): 415–27.

Aspin, Clive, Paul Reynolds, Keren Lehavot, and Jacob Taiapa. "An Investigation of the Phenomenon of Non-Consensual Sex among Maori Men Who Have Sex with Men." *Culture, Health and Sexuality* 11, no. 1 (2009): 35–49.

Audre Lorde Project. "About the Audre Lorde Project." *Missive*, June 1997, 2.

Awiakta, Marilou. *Selu: Seeking the Corn-Mother's Wisdom*. Golden, CO: Fulcrum, 1993.

Barker, Joanne. "Gender, Sovereignty, Rights: Native Women's Activism against Social Inequality and Violence in Canada." *American Quarterly* 60, no. 2 (2008): 259–66.

Belich, James. *Making Peoples: A History of New Zealanders*. Wellington: Allen Lane/Penguin Press, 1996.

Benedict, Ruth. *Patterns of Culture*. Boston: Houghton Mifflin, 1934.

Bentley, Trevor. *Captured by Maori: White Female Captives, Sex and Racism on the Nineteenth-Century New Zealand Frontier*. Auckland: Penguin Books, 2004.

Berlant, Lauren. *The Queen of America Goes to Washington City*. Durham, NC: Duke University Press, 1997.

Binney, Judith. "'Whatever Happened to Poor Mr Yate? An Exercise in Voyeurism.'" *New Zealand Journal of History* 9, no. 2 (1975): 111–25.

Brant, Beth, ed. *A Gathering of Spirit: Writing and Art by North American Indian Women*. Rockland, ME: Sinister Wisdom, 1984.

Brant, Beth. *Mohawk Trail*. Ithaca, NY: Firebrand Books, 1985.

Brooks, Lisa. "Afterword." In *American Indian Literary Nationalism*, edited by Jace Weaver, Craig Womack, Robert Allen Warrior. Lincoln: University of Nebraska Press, 2006.

———. "Digging at the Roots: Locating an Ethical, Native Criticism." In *Reasoning Together*, edited by The Native Critics Collective, 234–264. Norman: University of Oklahoma Press, 2008.

Brown, Lester B., ed. *Two-Spirit People: American Indian Lesbian Women and Gay Men*. New York: Harrington Park Press, 1997.

Brückner, Martin. *The Geographic Revolution in Early America: Maps, Literacy, and National Identity*. Chapel Hill: University of North Carolina Press, 2006.

Bruyneel, Kevin. *The Third Space of Sovereignty: The Postcolonial Politics of U.S.–Indigenous Relations*. Minneapolis: University of Minnesota Press, 2007.

Burns, Marjorie. "J.R.R. Tolkien: The British and the Norse in Tension." *Pacific Coast Philology* 25, no. 1/2 (November 1990): 49–59.

Burns, Randy. "Preface." In *Living the Spirit: A Gay American Indian Anthology*, edited by Will Roscoe. New York: St. Martin's Press, 1988.

Butler, Judith. *Gender Trouble: Feminism and the Subversion of Identity*. New York: Routledge, 1990.

———. *Undoing Gender*. New York: Routledge, 2004.

Cairos Collective. "Founding Matrons & Patrons." *Color Life!* June 28, 1992, 32.

Callender, Charles, and Lee Kochems. "The North American Berdache." *Current Anthropology* 24, no. 4 (1983): 443–70.

Cannon, Martin. "The Regulation of First Nations Sexuality." *Canadian Journal of Native Studies* 18, no. 1 (1998).

Cariou, Warren. "Introduction." In *Love Medicine and One Song/Sâkihtowin-Maskihkiy êkwa Pêyak-Nikamowin*. Wiarton, ON: Kegedonce, 2009.

Centers for Disease Control and Prevention. "HIV/AIDS among American Indians and Alaska Natives." http://www.cdc.gov/hiv/resources/Factsheets/aian.htm.

———. "Suicide: Facts at a Glance." http://www.cdc.gov/violenceprevention/pdf/Suicide-DataSheet-a.pdf.

Champagne, Duane. *Social Change and Cultural Continuity among Native Nations*. Lanham, MD: Alta Mira, 2007.

Chatterjee, Piya. *A Time for Tea: Women, Labor, and Post/Colonial Politics on an Indian Plantation*. Durham, NC: Duke University Press, 2001.

Cheyfitz, Eric. *The Poetics of Imperialism: Translation and Colonization from The Tempest to Tarzan*. Philadelphia: University of Pennsylvania Press, 1997.

Chow, Rey. *The Protestant Ethnic and the Spirit of Capitalism*. New York: Columbia University Press, 2002.

Chrystos. *Fugitive Colors*. Vancouver: Press Gang, 1995.

———. *Not Vanishing*. Vancouver: Press Gang, 1988.

Colley, Ann C. *Robert Louis Stevenson and the Colonial Imagination*. Aldershot, UK: Ashgate, 2004.

Colson, Charles, with Anne Morse. "The Moral Home Front." *Christianity Today* 48 (October 2004): 152.

———. "Societal Suicide." *Christianity Today* 48 (June 2004): 72.

Contreras, Sheila Marie. *Bloodlines: Myth, Indigenism, and Chicana/o Literature*. Austin: University of Texas Press, 2008.

Cook-Lynn, Elizabeth. "The American Indian Fiction Writers: Cosmopolitanism, Nationalism, the Third World and First Nation Sovereignty." In *Why I Can't Read Wallace Stegner and Other Essays: A Tribal Voice*, 78–99. Madison: University of Wisconsin Press, 1996.

———. "American Indian Intellectualism and the New Indian Story." In *Natives and Academics: Researching and Writing about American Indians*, edited by Devon Mihesuah, 111–38. Lincoln: University of Nebraska Press, 1998.

Cook-Lynn, Elizabeth. "Who Stole Native American Studies?" *Wicazo Sa Review* 12 (Spring 1997): 9–28.

Coulthard, Glen. "Subjects of Empire: Indigenous Peoples and the 'Politics of Recognition' in Canada." *Contemporary Political Theory* 6, no. 4 (2007): 437–60.

David, Jennifer. *Story Keepers: Conversations with Aboriginal Writers.* Owen Sound, ON: Ningwakwe Learning Press, 2004.

Davis, Angela Y., and Neferti X. M. Tadiar, eds. *Beyond the Frame: Women of Color and Visual Representation.* New York: Palgrave Macmillan, 2005.

Deloria, Vine Jr. *Custer Died for Your Sins: An Indian Manifesto.* 1969. Reprint, Norman: University of Oklahoma Press, 1988.

Denetdale, Jennifer Nez. "Carving Navajo National Boundaries: Patriotism, Tradition, and the Diné Marriage Act of 2005." *American Quarterly* 60, no. 2 (2008): 289–94.

———. "Chairmen, Presidents, and Princesses: The Navajo Nation, Gender, and the Politics of Tradition." *Wicazo Sa Review* 21, no. 1 (Spring 2006): 9–28.

Dening, Greg. *Islands and Beaches: Discourse on a Silent Land: Marquesas 1774–1880.* Chicago: Dorsey Press, 1980.

Deschamps, Gilbert. "We Are Part of a Tradition: A Guide on Two-Spirited People for First Nations Communities." Toronto: 2-Spirited People of the 1st Nations, 1998.

Dorion, Leah, and Darren R. Préfontaine. "Deconstructing Métis Historiography." In *Métis Legacy,* edited by Lawrence J. Barkwell, Leah Dorion, and Darren R. Préfontaine, 13–37. Winnipeg: Pemmican, 2001.

Driskill, Qwo-Li. "Call Me Brother: Two-Spiritedness, the Erotic, and Mixed-blood Identity as Sites of Sovereignty and Resistance in Gregory Scofield's Poetry." In *Speak to Me Words: Essays on Contemporary American Indian Poetry,* edited by Janice Gould and Dean Rader, 223–34. Tucson: University of Arizona Press, 2003.

———. "Doubleweaving Two-Spirit Critiques: Building Alliances between Native and Queer Studies." *GLQ: A Journal of Lesbian and Gay Studies* 16, no. 1–2 (2010): 69–92.

———. "Stolen from Our Bodies: First Nations Two-Spirits/Queers and the Journey to a Sovereign Erotic." *Studies in American Indian Literatures* 16, no. 2 (2004): 50–64.

———. *Walking with Ghosts.* Cambridge: Salt, 2005.

Eng, David L., Judith Halberstam, José Esteban Muñoz. "Introduction: What's Queer about Queer Studies Now?" In *What's Queer about Queer Studies Now?* edited by D. L. Eng, J. Halberstam, and J. E. Muñoz. Durham, NC: Duke University Press, 2005.

Episkenew, Jo-Ann. *Taking Back Our Spirits: Indigenous Literature, Public Policy and Healing.* Winnipeg: University of Manitoba Press, 2009.

Epple, Carolyn. "Coming to Terms with Navajo Nádleehí: A Critique of Berdache, 'Gay,' 'Alternate Gender,' and 'Two-Spirit.'" *American Ethnologist* 25, no. 2 (1998): 267–90.

Fast, Robin Riley. *The Heart as a Drum: Continuance and Resistance in American Indian Poetry.* Ann Arbor: University of Michigan Press, 1999.

Feeling, Durbin. *Cherokee–English Dictionary.* Dallas: Southern Methodist University, 1975.

Feinleib, Marcia R., ed. *Report on the Secretary's Task Force on Youth Suicide.* Vol. 3: *Prevention and Interventions in Youth Suicide.* U.S. Department of Health and Human Services, Public Health Service, Alcohol, Drug Abuse, and Mental Health Administration, 1989.

Fergusson, David M., L. John Horwood, Elizabeth M. Ridder, and Annette L. Beautrais. "Sexual Orientation and Mental Health in a Birth Cohort of Young Adults." *Psychological Medicine* 35, no. 7 (2005): 971–81.

Fixico, Donald L. *Termination and Relocation: Federal Indian Policy, 1945–1960.* Albuquerque: University of New Mexico Press, 1986.

Ford, Clellan, and Frank Beach. *Patterns of Sexual Behavior.* New York: Harper, 1951.

Foster, Claire, and Sharanpal Ruprai. Interview with Gregory Scofield. *Prairie Fire* 24, no. 3 (2001): 42–48.

Foster, Morris W. *Being Comanche.* Tucson: University of Arizona Press, 1991.

Foster, Tol. "Of One Blood: An Argument for Relations and Regionality in Native American Literary Studies." In *Reasoning Together,* edited by The Native Critics Collective, 265–302. Norman: University of Oklahoma Press, 2008.

Foucault, Michel. *The History of Sexuality.* Vol. 1: *An Introduction.* New York: Vintage Books, 1978.

———. *The History of Sexuality.* Vol. 2: *The Use of Pleasure.* Harmondsworth, Middlesex: Penguin, 1990.

Fregoso, Rosa Linda. *meXicana Encounters: The Making of Social Identities on the Borderlands.* Berkeley: University of California Press, 2003.

Garrison, Tim Alan. *The Legal Ideology of Removal: The Southern Judiciary and the Sovereignty of Native American Nations.* Athens: University of Georgia Press, 2002.

Gay American Indians (comps.). *Living the Spirit: A Gay American Indian Anthology.* Edited by Will Roscoe. New York: St. Martin's Press, 1988.

Gilley, Brian Joseph. *Becoming Two-Spirit: Gay Identity and Social Acceptance in Indian Country.* Lincoln: University of Nebraska Press, 2006.

———. "Making Traditional Spaces: Cultural Compromise at Two-Spirit Gatherings in Oklahoma." *American Indian Culture and Research Journal* 28, no. 2 (2004): 81–95.

———. "Two-Spirit Powwows and the Search for Social Acceptance in Indian Country." In *Powwow: Origins, Significance, and Meaning,* edited by Eric Lassiter, 224–40. Lincoln: University of Nebraska Press, 2005.

Gilson, R. P. *Samoa 1830 to 1900: The Politics of a Multi-Cultural Community.* Melbourne: Oxford University Press, 1970.

Glasier, Anna, A. Metin Gülmezoglu, George P. Schmid, Claudia Garcia Moreno, and P.F.A. Van Look. "Sexual and Reproductive Health: A Matter of Life and Death." *Lancet, Sexual and Reproductive Health* (October 2006): 11–23.

Gluckman, Laurie K. *Medical History of New Zealand Prior to 1860.* Christchurch: Whitcoulls, 1976.

Goeman, Mishuana, and Jennifer Nez Denetdale, eds. "Native Feminisms: Legacies, Interventions, and Indigenous Sovereignties." *Wicazo Sa Review* 24, no. 2 (2009): 9–187.

Gopinath, Gayatri. *Impossible Desires.* Durham, NC: Duke University Press, 2005.

Gould, Janice. *Beneath My Heart: Poetry.* Ithaca, NY: Firebrand Books, 1990.

Goulet, Jean-Guy A. "The 'Berdache'/'Two-Spirit': A Comparison of Anthropological and Native Constructions of Gendered Identities among the Northern Athapaskans." *Journal of the Royal Anthropological Institute* n.s. 2, no. 4 (1996): 683–701.

Gracewood, Jolisa. "Sometimes a Great Ocean: Thinking the Pacific from Nowhere to Now & Here." *Hitting Critical Mass: A Journal of Asian American Cultural Criticism* 5, no. 1 (special issue, Spring 1998): 1–28.

Grahn, Judy. *Another Mother Tongue: Gay Words, Gay Worlds.* Boston: Alyson, 1984.

Gramsci, Antonio. *Selections from the Prison Notebooks.* 12th ed. Translated by Quintin Hoare and Geoffrey Nowell Smith. New York: International, 1971.

Grande, Sandy. *Red Pedagogy.* Lanham, MD: Rowman and Littlefield, 2004.

Graves, Bill. "Coquille Same-Sex Marriage Law Takes Effect." *Oregon Live.* http://www.oregonlive.com/news/index.ssf/2009/05/coquille_samesex_marriage_law.html.

Green, Rayna. "The Pocahontas Perplex: The Image of Indian Women in American Culture." *Massachusetts Review* 16, no. 4 (1975): 698–714.

———. "The Tribe Called Wannabee." *Folklore* 99, no. 1 (1988): 30–55.

Harjo, Joy, and Poetic Justice. "A Postcolonial Tale." In *Letter from the End of the Twentieth Century.* Boulder: Silver Wave Records, 1997.

Herdt, Gilbert. "The Dilemmas of Desire: From 'Berdache' to 'Two-Spirit.'" In *Two-Spirit People: Native American Gender Identity, Sexuality and Spirituality,* edited by Sue-Ellen Jacobs, Wesley Thomas, and Sabine Lang, 276–283. Chicago: University of Illinois Press, 1997.

———. "Introduction: Third Sexes and Third Genders." In *Third Sex, Third Gender,* edited by Gilbert Herdt. New York: Zone Books, 1993.

———. *Same Sex, Different Cultures: Exploring Gay and Lesbian Lives.* Oxford: Westview Press, 1997.

Hill, Sarah H. *Weaving New Worlds: Southeastern Cherokee Women and Their Basketry.* Chapel Hill: University of North Carolina Press, 1997.

Hobsbawm, Eric. "Introduction: Inventing Traditions." In *The Invention of Tradition,* edited by Eric Hobsbawm and Terence Ranger. Cambridge: Cambridge University Press, 1983.

International Indigenous People's Summit. The Toronto Charter: Indigenous People's Action Plan on HIV/AIDS 2006. Toronto: International Indigenous People's Summit, 2006.

Jacobs, Sue-Ellen. "Is the North American Berdache Merely a Phantom in the Imagination of Western Social Scientists?" In *Two-Spirit People: Native American Gender Identity, Sexuality and Spirituality,* edited by Sue-Ellen Jacobs, Wesley Thomas, and Sabine Lang, 21–43. Chicago: University of Illinois Press, 1997.

Jacobs, Sue-Ellen, Wesley Thomas, and Sabine Lang, eds. *Two-Spirit People: Native American Gender Identity, Sexuality, and Spirituality.* Urbana: University of Illinois Press, 1997.

Jacobs, Sue-Ellen, Wesley Thomas, and Sabine Lang. "Introduction." In *Two-Spirit People: Native American Gender Identity, Sexuality, and Spirituality,* edited by S.-E. Jacobs, W. Thomas, and S. Lang. Urbana: University of Illinois Press, 1997.

James, Beverly, and Kay Saville-Smith. *Gender, Culture and Power.* Auckland: Oxford University Press, 1989.

Journal of the Polynesian Society. "The Samoan Story of Creation: A Tala." *Journal of the Polynesian Society* 1, no. 3 (1892): 164–89.

Justice, Daniel Heath. "Beloved Woman Returns: The Doubleweaving of Homeland and Identity in the Poetry of Marilou Awiakta." In *Speak to Me Words: Essays on Contemporary American Indian Poetry,* edited by Dean Rader and Janice Gould, 71–81. Tucson: University of Arizona Press, 2005.

———. *Dreyd: The Way of Thorn and Thunder, Book 3.* Wiarton, ON: Kegedonce Press, 2007.

———. *Kynship: The Way of Thorn and Thunder.* Wiarton, ON: Kegedonce Press, 2005.

———. *Our Fire Survives the Storm: A Cherokee Literary History.* Minneapolis: University of Minnesota Press, 2006.

———. *Wyrwood: The Way of Thorn and Thunder, Book 2.* Wiarton, ON: Kegedonce Press, 2006.

Justice, Daniel Heath, and James H. Cox, eds. "Queering Native Literature, Indigenizing Queer Theory." *Studies in American Indian Literature* 20, no. 1 (2008): xiii–xiv.

Justice, Daniel Heath, Mark Rifkin, and Bethany Schneider, eds. "Sexuality, Nationality, Indigeneity." *GLQ: A Journal of Lesbian and Gay Studies* 16, no. 1–2 (2010).

Kairaiuak, Larry. Addressing Two-Spirits in the American Indian, Alaskan Native and Native Hawaiian Communities. Oakland, CA: National Native American AIDS Prevention Center, 2002.

Katz, Jonathan. *Gay American History: Lesbians and Gay Men in the USA*. New York: Thomas Crowell, 1976.

Kenny, Maurice. "Papago." *Gay Sunshine: A Journal of Gay Liberation* 29/30 (1976): 23.

———. "Tinselled Bucks: An Historical Study of Indian Homosexuality." *Gay Sunshine: A Journal of Gay Liberation* 26/37 (1975/76): 15–17.

———. "United." *Gay Sunshine: A Journal of Gay Liberation* 26/27 (1975/76): 17.

Kilpatrick, Jack F., and Anna G. Kilpatrick. *Walk in Your Soul: Love Incantations of the Oklahoma Cherokees*. Dallas: Southern Methodist University, 1965.

Kroeber, Alfred L. "Psychosis or Social Sanction?" *Character and Personality* 8, no. 3 (1940): 204–15.

Lang, Sabine. *Men as Women, Women as Men*. Austin: University of Texas Press, 1998.

———. "Various Kinds of Two-Spirit People: Gender Variance and Homosexuality in Native American Communities." In *Two-Spirit People: Native American Gender Identity, Sexuality and Spirituality*, edited by Jacobs, Sue-Ellen, Wesley Thomas, and Sabine Lang, 100–118. Chicago: University of Chicago Press, 1997.

Low, Nicola, Nathalie Broulet, Yaw Adu-Sarkodie, Pelham Barton, Mazeda Hossaihn, and Sarah Hawkes. "Global Control of Sexually Transmitted Infections." *Lancet: Sexual and Reproductive Health* (October 2006): 77–92.

Mageo, Jeannette Marie. *Theorizing Self in Samoa: Emotions, Genders, and Sexualities*. Ann Arbor: University of Michigan Press, 1998.

Masters, Catherine. "Top Bishop's Vision: A World without Gays." *New Zealand Herald*, June 5, 2004.

Matautia-Hartson, Phineas. *Community Legal Research Paper: Fa'afafine in Australia*. Sydney: 2005.

Mayer, Sophie. "This Bridge of Two Backs: The Two-Spirit Erotics of Anthology/Documentary/Community." *Studies in American Indian Literature* 20, no. 1 (2008): 1–26.

McColl, P. "Homosexuality and Mental Health Services." *British Medical Journal* 308, no. 6928 (1994): 550–51.

McLeod, Neal. *Cree Narrative Memory: From Treaties to Contemporary Times*. Saskatoon: Purich, 2007.

———. "*nêhiyâwiwin* and Modernity." In *Plain Speaking: Essays on Aboriginal Peoples and the Prairies*, edited by Patrick Douad and Bruce Dawson, 35–53. Regina, SK: Canadian Plains Research Centre, 2002.

———. *Songs to Kill a Wîhtikow*. Regina, SK: Hagios Press, 2005.

Mandelbaum, David G. *The Plains Cree: An Ethnographic, Historical, and Comparative Study*. Regina, SK: Canadian Plains Research Centre, 1979.

McLoughlin, William G. *Cherokee Renascence in the New Republic*. Princeton: Princeton University Press, 1986.

McMullin, Dan Taulapapa. "The Passive Resistance of Samoans to U.S. and Other Colonialisms." In *Sovereignty Matters: Locations of Contestation and Possibility in Indigenous Struggles for Self-Determination,* edited by Joanne Barker, 109–22. Lincoln: University of Nebraska Press, 2005.

Mead, Margaret. *Coming of Age in Samoa: A Psychological Study of Primitive Youth for Western Civilisation.* New York: William Morrow, 1928.

———. *Sex and Temperament in Three Primitive Societies.* New York: William Morrow, 1935.

Medicine, Beatrice. "Changing Native American Roles in an Urban Context *and* Changing Native American Sex Roles in an Urban Context." In *Two-Spirit People: Native American Gender Identity, Sexuality, and Spirituality,* edited by Sue-Ellen Jacobs, Wesley Thomas, and Sabine Lang, 145–56. Urbana: University of Illinois Press, 1997.

Mignolo, Walter D. *The Darker Side of the Renaissance: Literacy, Territoriality, and Colonization.* Ann Arbor: University of Michigan Press, 1995.

Ministry of Health. "Sexual and Reproductive Health Strategy." Wellington: Ministry of Health, 2001.

Miranda, Deborah. *The Zen of La Llorona.* Cambridge: Salt, 2005.

Monture-Angus, Patricia. *Journeying Forward.* Halifax: Fernwood, 1999.

———. *Thunder in My Soul: A Mohawk Woman Speaks.* Halifax: Fernwood, 1995.

Moraga, Cherríe. *The Last Generation: Prose and Poetry.* Boston: South End Press, 1993.

Moraga, Cherríe, and Gloria Anzaldúa, eds. *This Bridge Called My Back: Writings by Radical Women of Color.* 2nd ed. New York: Kitchen Table Women of Color Press, 1983.

Morgensen, Scott Lauria. "Activist Media in Native AIDS Organizing: Theorizing the Colonial Conditions of AIDS." *American Indian Culture and Research Journal* 35, no. 2 (2008): 35–56.

———. "Arrival at Home: Radical Faerie Configurations of Sexuality and Place." *GLQ: A Journal of Lesbian and Gay Studies* 15, no. 1 (2009): 67–96.

———. *Spaces between Us: Queer Settler Colonialism and Indigenous Decolonization.* Minneapolis: University of Minnesota Press, 2011.

———. "Settler Homonationalism: Theorizing Settler Colonialism within Queer Modernities." *GLQ: A Journal of Lesbian and Gay Studies* 16, no. 1–2 (2010): 105–31.

Morley, David. *Home Territories: Media, Mobility and Identity.* New York: Routledge, 2000.

Muñoz, José Esteban. *Disidentifications: Queers of Color and the Performance of Politics.* Minneapolis: University of Minnesota, 1999.

Murray, D.A.B. "Who Is Takatapui? Maori Language, Sexuality and Identity in Aotearoa/New Zealand." *Anthropologica* 45, no. 2 (2003): 233–44.

Nanda, Serena. *Neither Man nor Woman: The Hijras of India*. Belmont, CA: Wadsworth, 1990.

Norgren, Jill. *The Cherokee Cases: The Confrontation of Law and Politics*. New York: McGraw Hill, 1996.

Obertino, James. "Barbarians and Imperialism in Tacitus and *The Lord of the Rings*." *Tolkien Studies* 3 (2006): 117–31.

Owlfeather, M. (Clyde M. Hall). "Children of Grandmother Moon." In *Living the Spirit: A Gay American Indian Anthology*, edited by Will Roscoe. New York: St. Martin's Press, 1988.

Pahe, Erna. "Speaking Up." In *Living the Spirit: A Gay American Indian Anthology*, edited by Will Roscoe. New York: St. Martin's Press, 1988.

Parker, Richard G., Regina M. Barbosa, and Peter Aggleton, eds. *Framing the Sexual Subject: The Politics of Gender, Sexuality and Power*. Berkeley: University of California Press, 2000.

Perdue, Theda. *Cherokee Women: Gender and Cultural Change, 1700–1835*. Lincoln: University of Nebraska Press, 1998.

Perez, Emma. *The Decolonial Imaginary: Writing Chicanas into History*. Bloomington: Indiana University Press, 1999.

———. "Queering the Borderlands: The Challenges of Excavating the Invisible and Unheard." *Frontiers: A Journal of Women's Studies* 24, no. 2–3 (2003): 122–31.

Perez, Hiram. "You Can Have My Brown Body and Eat It, Too." *Social Text* 23, (Fall–Winter 2005): 171–91.

Phillips, Kim M., and Barry Reay. "Introduction," In *Sexualities in History: A Reader*, edited by K. M. Philips and B. Reay. New York: Routledge, 2002.

Philp, Kenneth R. *Termination Revisited: American Indians on the Trail to Self-Determination, 1933–1953*. Lincoln: University of Nebraska Press, 1999.

Pivot Legal Society. "Pivot Legal Society & Vancouver's Downtown Eastside." August 4, 2009. http://www.pivotlegal.org/dtes.htm.

Povinelli, Elizabeth A. *The Cunning of Recognition: Indigenous Alterities and the Making of Australian Multiculturalism*. Durham, NC: Duke University Press, 2002.

———. *The Empire of Love: Towards a Theory of Intimacy, Genealogy, and Carnality*. Durham, NC: Duke University Press, 2006.

Powell, Malea D. "Down by the River, or How Susan La Flesche Picotte Can Teach Us about Alliance as a Practice of Survivance." *College English* 67, no. 1 (2004): 38–60.

Pratt, Mary Louise. *Imperial Eyes: Travel Writing and Transculturation*. London: Routledge, 1992.

Prison Justice. "Prison Facts and Statistics." http://www.prisonjustice.ca/politics/facts_stats.html.

Prucha, Francis Paul, ed. *Documents of United States Indian Policy*. 3rd ed. Lincoln: University of Nebraska Press, 2000.

Puar, Jasbir. *Terrorist Assemblages: Homonationalism in Queer Times.* Durham, NC: Duke University Press, 2007.

Ramirez, Renya. *Native Hubs: Culture, Community and Belonging in Silicon Valley and Beyond.* Durham, NC: Duke University Press, 2007.

Rearick, Anderson. "Why Is the Only Good Orc a Dead Orc? The Dark Face of Racism Examined in Tolkien's World." *Modern Fiction Studies* 50, no. 4 (2004): 861–75.

Reddy, Gayatri. *With Respect to Sex.* Chicago: University of Chicago Press. 2005.

Remafedi, Gary, Simone French, Mary Story, Michael D. Resnick, and Robert Blum. "The Relationship between Suicide Risk and Sexual Orientation: Results of a Population-Based Study." *American Journal of Public Health* 88, no. 1 (1998): 57–60.

Richards, Linda. Interview with Gregory Scofield. *January Magazine,* September 1999. http://januarymagazine.com/profiles/scofield.html.

Rifkin, Mark. *Manifesting America: The Imperial Construction of U.S. National Space.* New York: Oxford University Press, 2009.

———. "Romancing Kinship: A Queer Reading of Indian Education and Zitkala-Sa's *American Indian Stories.*" *GLQ: A Journal of Lesbian and Gay Studies* 12, no. 1 (2006): 27–59.

———. *When Did Indians Become Straight? Kinship, the History of Sexuality, and Native Sovereignty.* New York: Oxford University Press, 2011.

Robinson, Aileen Moreton. "Introduction." In *Sovereign Subjects: Indigenous Sovereignty Matters,* edited by Aileen Moreton-Robinson. Crows Nest NSW, Australia: Allen and Unwin, 2007.

Robson, Andrew E. *Prelude to Empire: Consuls, Missionary Kingdoms, and the Pre-Colonial South Seas Seen Through the Life of William Thomas Pritchard.* Vienna: Transaction, 2004.

Roscoe, Will. *Changing Ones: Third and Fourth Genders in Native North America.* New York: St. Martin's Press, 1998.

———. "How to Become a Berdache: Towards a Unified Analysis of Gender Diversity." In *Third Sex, Third Gender: Beyond Sexual Dimorphism in Culture and History,* edited by Gilbert Herdt. New York: Zone Books, 1993.

———. "Native North American Literature." In *The Gay and Lesbian Literary Heritage,* edited by Claude Summers, 513–17. New York: Henry Holt, 1995.

———. *Queer Spirits: A Gay Men's Myth Book.* Boston: Beacon Press, 1995.

———. *The Zuni Man-Woman.* Albuquerque: University of New Mexico Press, 1991.

Rosebury, Brian. "Race and Ethnicity in Tolkien's Works." In *The J.R.R. Tolkien Encyclopedia: Scholarship and Critical Assessment,* edited by Michael D. C. Drout, 555–57. New York: Routledge, 2006.

Ross, Luana. *Inventing the Savage.* Austin: University of Texas Press, 1998.

Routledge, Gregory E. "Futurist Fiction & Fantasy: The Racial Establishment." *Callaloo* 24, no. 1 (2001): 236–52.

Rowell, Ron. "HIV Prevention for Gay/Bisexual/Two-Spirit Native American Men: A Report of the National Leadership Development Workgroup for Gay/Bisexual/Two-Spirit Native American Men." Oakland, CA: National Native American AIDS Prevention Center, 1996.

Rush, Andrea Green. "Models of Prevention: Minnesota American Indian AIDS Task Force." *Seasons: Newsletter of the National Native American AIDS Prevention Center* (1989): 4–5.

Sahlins, Marshall. *Islands of History*. Chicago: University of Chicago Press, 1985.

Said, Edward. *Orientalism*. London: Routledge and Kegan Paul, 1978.

Saldana-Portillo, Maria Josefina. *The Revolutionary Imagination in the Americas and the Age of Development*. Durham, DC: Duke University Press, 2003.

Sale, Kirkpatrick. *The Conquest of Paradise*. New York: Plume, 1990.

Salmond, Anne. *The Trial of the Cannibal Dog: Captain Cook in the Southern Seas*. Auckland: Penguin Books, 2003.

Schultz, Jack M. *The Seminole Baptist Churches of Oklahoma: Maintaining a Traditional Community*. Norman: University of Oklahoma Press, 2000.

Scofield, Gregory. *The Gathering: Stones from the Medicine Wheel*. Vancouver: Polestar, 1993.

———. *Kipocihkân: Poems New and Selected*. Gibsons, BC: Nightwood Editions, 2009.

———. *Love Medicine and One Song/Sâkihtowin-Maskihkiy êkwa Pêyak-Nikamowin*. Wiarton, ON: Kegedonce, 2009.

———. *Native Canadiana: Songs from the Urban Rez*. Vancouver: Polestar, 1996.

———. *Singing Home the Bones*. Vancouver: Polestar, 2005.

———. *Thunder through My Veins: Memories of a Métis Childhood*. Toronto: HarperCollins, 1997.

———. "You Can Always Count on an Anthropologist (to Set You Straight, Crooked or Somewhere In-Between)." *Me Sexy: An Exploration of Native Sex and Sexuality*, edited by Drew Hayden Taylor, 160–68. Toronto: Douglas and McIntyre, 2008.

Sears, Vickie. *Simple Songs*. Ithaca, NY: Firebrand Books, 1990.

See, Sarita Echavez. *The Decolonized Eye: Filipino American Art and Performance*. Minneapolis: University of Minnesota Press, 2009.

Silva, Denise Ferreira da. *Toward a Global Idea of Race*. Minneapolis: University of Minnesota Press, 2007.

Silverstein, Michael. "Shifters, Linguistic Categories, and Cultural Description." In *Meaning in Anthropology*, edited by Keith H. Basso and Henry A. Selby, 11–55. Albuquerque: School of American Research, University of New Mexico Press, 1976.

Simpson, Audra. "On Ethnographic Refusal: Indigeneity, 'Voice' and Colonial Citizenship." *Junctures* 9 (2007): 67–80.

Skegg, Keren, Shyamala Nada-Raja, Nigel Dickson, Charlotte Paul, and Sheila Williams. "Sexual Orientation and Self-Harm in Men and Women." *American Journal of Psychiatry* 160, no. 3 (2003): 541–46.

Smith, Andrea. *Conquest: Sexual Violence and American Indian Genocide.* Cambridge, MA: South End Press, 2005.

———. "Heteropatriachy: A Building Block of Empire." *Solidarity*, http://www .solidarity-us.org/node/736.

———. "Heteropatriarchy and the Three Pillars of White Supremacy: Rethinking Women of Color Organizing." In *The Color of Violence: Incite Women of Color against Violence,* edited by INCITE Women of Color Against Violence, 66–73. Boston: South End Press, 2006.

———. *Native Americans and the Christian Right: The Gendered Politics of Unlikely Alliances.* Durham, NC: Duke University Press, 2008.

Smith, Andrea, and J. Kehaulani Kauanui, eds. "Forum: Native Feminisms without Apology." *American Quarterly* 60, no. 2 (2008): 241–315.

Smith, Andrea, and J. Kehaulani Kauanui. "Native Feminisms Engage American Studies." *American Quarterly* 60, no. 2 (2008): 241–49.

Smith, Linda Tuhiwai. *Decolonizing Methodologies: Research and Indigenous Peoples.* New York: Zed Books, 1999.

Sophia, Paula. "Women Marry in the Cherokee Nation." *Gayly Oklahoman,* March 16, 2005.

Spivak, Gayatri. *A Critique of Postcolonial Reason.* Cambridge: Harvard University Press, 1999.

Stair, Rev. John B. *Old Samoa, or Flotsam and Jetsam from the Pacific Ocean.* London: 1897.

Stannard, David. *American Holocaust.* Oxford: Oxford University Press, 1992.

Stevenson, Winona. "'Ethnic' Assimilates 'Indigenous': A Study in Intellectual Neocolonialism." *Wicazo Sa Review* 13 (Spring 1998): 33–51.

Stoler, Ann. *Carnal Knowledge and Imperial Power: Race and the Intimate in Colonial Rule.* Berkeley: University of California Press, 2002.

———. *Race and the Education of Desire.* Durham, NC: Duke University Press, 1995.

Sturm, Circe. *Blood Politics.* Berkeley: University of California Press, 2002.

Tadiar, Neferti. "Manila's New Metropolitan Form." *difference: A Journal of Feminist Cultural Studies* 5, no. 3 (1993): 154–78.

Tatonetti, Lisa. "The Emergence and Importance of Queer American Indian Literatures, or, 'Help and Stories' in Thirty Years of *SAIL*." *Studies in American Indian Literature* 19, no. 4 (2007): 143–70.

Taylor, Diana. *The Archive and the Repertoire: Performing Cultural Memory in the Americas.* Durham, NC: Duke University, 2003.

Te Awekotuku, Ngahuia. "Maori: People and Culture." In *Maori Arts and Culture*, edited by Arapata T. Hakiwai, Roger Neich, Mick Pendergrast, and Dorota C. Starzecka. Auckland: David Bateman, 1996.

Teaiwa, Teresia. "Reading Paul Gauguin's *Noa Noa* with Epeli Hau'ofa's *Kisses in the Nederends*: Militourism, Feminism and the 'Polynesian' Body." In *Inside Out: Literature, Cultural Politics, and Identity in the New Pacific*, edited by Vilsoni Hereniko and Rob Wilson, 249–64. Lanham, MD: Rowman and Littlefield, 1999.

Teuton, Christopher. "Theorizing American Indian Literature: Applying Oral Concepts to Written Traditions." In *Reasoning Together*, edited by The Native Critics Collective. Norman: University of Oklahoma Press, 2008.

Thomas, Wesley, and Sue-Ellen Jacobs. "'. . . And We Are Still Here': From *Berdache* to Two-Spirit People." *American Indian Culture and Research Journal* 23, no. 2 (1999): 91–107.

True, Jacqui. "Fit Citizens for the British Empire? Classifying Racial and Gendered Subjects in 'Godzone' New Zealand." In *Women out of Place: The Gender of Agency and the Race of Nationality*, edited by Brackette F. Williams, 103–28. New York: Routledge, 1996.

Turner, George, L.L.D. *Samoa a Hundred Years Ago and Long Before*. London: 1884.

UNAIDS. *2006 Report on the Global Aids Epidemic*. New York, NYC: UNAIDS, 2006.

U.S. Department of Justice Statistics. "Differences in Rates of Violent Crime Experienced by Whites and Blacks Narrow: American Indians Are the Most Victimized by Violence." http://bjs.ojp.usdoj.gov/content/pub/press/vvr98pr.cfm.

Valentine, David. "I Went to Bed with My Own Kind Once": The Erasure of Desire in the Name of Identity. *Language and Communication* 23, no. 2 (2002): 123–38.

van Griensven, Frits, Peter H. Kilmarx, Supaporn Jeeyapant, Chomnad Manopaiboon, Supaporn Korattana, and Richard A. Jenkins. "The Prevalence of Bisexual and Homosexual Orientation and Related Health Risks among Adolescents in Northern Thailand." *Archives of Sexual Behavior* 33, no. 2 (2004): 137–47.

Vance, Carole. "Anthropology Rediscovers Sexuality: A Theoretical Comment." In *Culture, Society and Sexuality: A Reader*, edited by Richard R. Parker and Peter Aggleton. London: UCL Press, 1999.

Vernon, Irene S. *Killing Us Quietly: Native Americans and HIV/AIDS*. Lincoln: University of Nebraska Press, 2001.

Vizenor, Gerald. *Manifest Manners: Narratives on Postindian Survivance*. Lincoln: University of Nebraska Press, 1999.

Wallace, Lee. *Sexual Encounters: Pacific Texts, Modern Sexualities*. Ithaca: Cornell University Press, 2003.

Warhus, Mark. *Another America: Native American Maps and the History of Our Land.* New York: St. Martin's Press, 1997.

Warner, Michael. "Introduction." In *Fear of a Queer Planet,* edited by M. Warner. Minneapolis: University of Minnesota Press, 1993.

Warren, Karen. "A Feminist Philosophical Perspective on Ecofeminist Spiritualities." In *Ecofeminism and the Sacred,* edited by Carol Adams, 119–32. New York: Continuum, 1993.

Warrior, Robert Allen. "Native Critics in the World: Edward Said and Nationalism." In *American Indian Literary Nationalism,* edited by Jace Weaver, Craig Womack, Robert Allen Warrior. Albuquerque: University of New Mexico Press, 2006.

———. *Tribal Secrets: Recovering American Indian Intellectual Traditions.* Minneapolis: University of Minnesota Press, 1994.

Weaver, Jace. "Splitting the Earth: First Utterances and Pluralist Separatism." In *American Indian Literary Nationalism,* edited by Jace Weaver, Craig Womack, Robert Allen Warrior. Albuquerque: University of New Mexico Press, 2006.

———. *That the People Might Live: Native American Literatures and Native American Community.* New York: Oxford University Press, 1997.

Weaver, Jace, Craig Womack, Robert Allen Warrior, eds. *American Indian Literary Nationalism.* Lincoln: University of Nebraska Press, 2006.

Weeks, Jeffrey. *Against Nature: Essays on History, Sexuality and Identity.* London: Rivers Oram Press, 1991.

———. *Sexuality.* New York: Routledge, 1986.

———. "Sexuality and History Revisited." In *Sexualities in History: A Reader,* edited by Kim M. Phillips and Barry Reay. New York: Routledge, 2002.

Weston, Kath. "Lesbian/Gay Studies in the House of Anthropology." *Annual Reviews in Anthropology* 22 (1993): 339–67.

———. *Long, Slow Burn: Sexuality and Social Science.* New York: Routledge, 1998.

WeWah and BarCheeAmpe. "500 Years of Survival and Resistance." *Buffalo Hide* 2, no. 1 (1992): 16–17.

———. "New Movement for Two Spirits." *Buffalo Hide* (Early Spring 1991): 5.

Whitehead, Harriet. "The Bow and the Burden Strap: A New Look at Institutionalized Homosexuality in Native North America." In *Sexual Meanings: The Cultural Construction of Gender and Sexuality,* edited by Sherry Ortner and Harriet Whitehead. Cambridge: Cambridge University Press, 1981.

Wickberg, Daniel. "Homophobia: On the Cultural History of an Idea." *Critical Inquiry* 27, no. 1 (2000): 42–57.

Wichstrom, Lars, and Kristinn Hegna. "Sexual Orientation and Suicide Attempt: A Longitudinal Study of the General Norwegian Adolescent Population." *Journal of Abnormal Psychology* 112, no. 1 (2003): 144–51.

Williams, Herbert W. *A Dictionary of the Maori Language.* Wellington: A. R. Shearer, Government Printer, 1971.

Williams, Raymond. *Marxism and Literature.* Oxford: Oxford University Press, 1977.

Williams, Walter L. *The Spirit and the Flesh: Sexual Diversity in American Indian Culture.* Boston: Beacon Press, 1986.

Wilson, Waziyatawin Angela. *Remember This!* Lincoln: University of Nebraska Press, 2005.

Womack, Craig. "The Integrity of American Indian Claims (or, How I Learned to Stop Worrying and Love My Hybridity)." In *American Indian Literary Nationalism,* edited by Jace Weaver, Craig Womack, Robert Allen Warrior. Lincoln: University of Nebraska Press, 2006.

———. *Red on Red: Native American Literary Separatism.* Minneapolis: University of Minnesota Press, 1999.

———. "A Single Decade: Book-Length Native Literary Criticism between 1986 and 1997." In *Reasoning Together,* edited by The Native Critics Collective. Norman: University of Oklahoma Press, 2008.

Wright, Matthew. *Illustrated History of New Zealand.* Auckland: Reed, 2004.

Yolen, Jane. "Introduction." In *After the King: Stories in Honor of J.R.R. Tolkien,* ed. Martin H. Greenberg, xii–ix. New York: Tor Books, 1994.

About the Contributors

Clive Aspin is Maori and his tribal affiliation is Ngati Maru. He was born in Waiuku and grew up on his tribal land of Hauraki. Today he lives in Sydney, Australia, but he maintains strong connections to his ancestral land of Aotearoa/New Zealand. Through his travels, Clive has had intimate experience of some of the major events of the late twentieth century, and these have helped to shape his understanding of sexuality, sexual behavior, and cultural expression. He has a strong interest in the intersection of sexuality and cultural identity and is particularly interested in historical expressions of sexuality as they were understood and articulated by his ancestors. His research interests have focused on providing answers that will contribute to enhanced health and well-being of Indigenous people and other marginalized groups. He is committed to ensuring that the voices of Indigenous people are heard in a way that will lead to significant Indigenous community development throughout the world.

Qwo-Li Driskill is a Cherokee queer/Two-Spirit writer, scholar, and performer. S/he is the author of *Walking with Ghosts: Poems* and is currently Assistant Professor in the Department of English at Texas A&M University.

Michelle Erai, originally from Whangarei, Aotearoa/New Zealand, graduated from Victoria University, Wellington, with a BA in Sociology and Women's Studies, and with an MA (Applied) in Social Science Research. After several years working as a contract researcher, Michelle relocated to the United States, where she completed a PhD in the History of Consciousness (with a parenthetical notation in Feminist Studies), University of California, Santa Cruz. Michelle held a UC Office of the President's Post-doctoral Fellowship and accepted an appointment to Women's Studies, UC Los Angeles. In addition to her academic work, Michelle cofounded Incite! Women of Color Against Violence and is involved with Amokura: A Family Violence Prevention Initiative, governed by the seven northernmost Maori tribes in Aotearoa. Currently writing her first book, *Civilizing Images: Colonial Violence and the Visual Interpellation of Māori Women*, Michelle's research interests include: postcolonial feminist theories, visual culture, indigenous feminisms, violence, historiography, and the Pacific. Michelle's tribal affiliations are with Ngapuhi, Ngati Whatua, and Ngati Porou.

Chris Finley is a queer Native feminist finishing her PhD in American Culture at the University of Michigan in 2011. The title of her dissertation is: "Bringing 'Sexy Back' and Out of Native Studies' Closet: Sexualized Images of Native Peoples in American Culture." She is a member of the Colville Confederated Tribes located in what is now called Washington State. Finley's work deals specifically with decolonizing sexualized cultural images of Native peoples by showing a strong connection between colonizing discourses of Native peoples to heteropatriarchy and how Native peoples internalize and reproduce these discourses in our communities and in our systems of tribal governance.

Brian Joseph Gilley is Associate Professor of Anthropology and Director of the First Nations Education and Culture Center at Indiana University, Bloomington. He is the author of *Becoming Two-Spirit* (2006, University of Nebraska Press).

Dan Taulapapa McMullin is a Samoan painter and poet, from the U.S. Territory of American Samoa, which is on the United Nations List of Nations to be Decolonized. He is currently teaching a seminar on contemporary art of Oceania at University of California, Irvine. His paintings and sculptures were exhibited at the Permanent Forum for Indigenous Peoples at the United Nations in New York, at the Bishop Museum in Honolulu, and at Pacific Islander–operated galleries in Aotearoa, including Okaioceanikarts Gallery, McCarthy Gallery, and Fresh Gallery Otara. He received a Poets&Writers Award from The Writers Loft, and a Best Short Film Award from the Rainbow Film Festival of Honolulu. He was Artist-in-Residence at the De Young Museum in San Francisco in 2010, and a solo exhibition of his work was displayed at the Gorman Museum at University of California, Davis, in January 2011. He can be reached at and his artwork can be viewed at www.taulapapa.com.

Scott Lauria Morgensen is Assistant Professor in the Department of Gender Studies and the Graduate Program in Cultural Studies at Queen's University, where he teaches courses in antiracism/critical race studies, Indigenous studies, queer studies, and feminist methodologies. He is the author of *Spaces between Us: Queer Settler Colonialism and Indigenous Decolonization* (University of Minnesota Press, 2011). His writing appears in such journals as *GLQ, Women and Performance, Signs,* and *American Indian Culture and Research Journal,* and in numerous anthologies in queer studies, feminist studies, and Indigenous studies.

Mark Rifkin is an assistant professor in the English Department at the University of North Carolina Greensboro, where he teaches Native American literature. He is the author of *Manifesting America: The Imperial Construction of U.S. National Space* and *When Did Indians Become Straight? Kinship, the History of Sexuality, and Native Sovereignty,* and he is a coeditor of *Sexuality, Nationality,*

Indigeneity: Rethinking the State at the Intersection of Native American and Queer Studies.

June Scudeler (Métis) is completing her PhD in English at the University of British Columbia. Her dissertation, "'Âyahkwêw's Lodge': Cree and Métis GLBTQ2 Literature," will use the work of Cree and Métis writers such as Gregory Scofield and Tomson Highway to investigate how theories and stories of the erotic, Native American literary nationalism, and GLBTQ2 peoples intersect to form a body of work that asserts a decolonial resistance. She is on the Board of the Vancouver Métis Community Association and worked as a policy analyst at United Native Nations, an Aboriginal political organization that represents urban Aboriginal peoples in BC. Her other interests include Romantic and Gothic literatures and popular culture.

Andrea Smith teaches in Media Studies at UC Riverside.

Lisa Tatonetti is an associate professor of English and American Ethnic Studies at Kansas State University, where she studies, teaches, and publishes on Two-Spirit literatures and Native literatures. She is coeditor, together with Qwo-Li Driskill, Daniel Heath Justice, and Deborah Miranda, of *Sovereign Erotics,* a forthcoming collection of queer Native writing. She has essays forthcoming in *Sherman Alexie: A Collection of Critical Essays,* ed. Jan Roush and Jeff Berglund (University of Utah Press), and *Strawberries in Brooklyn: Maurice Kenny, Mohawk Poet,* ed. Penelope Kelsey (New York: SUNY Press) and has published in the recent special issue of *GLQ,* "Sexuality, Nationality, Indigeneity" (16, no. 1–2), as well as in *Studies in American Indian Literatures, Studies in American Fiction, Western Literature,* and *MELUS.* She is currently working on a book project that maps the rise and importance of contemporary Two-Spirit literature.

Index

feminism, 31; Chicana, 140–41; Indigenous, 15, 40; and sovereignty, 8–9
Field, Phillip, 92
Finley, Chris, 43
First Nations, 192; in urban areas, 203–4
Fitzgerald, James, 73
Foucault, Michel, 31, 34

Gabbard, Mike, 91
GAI. *See* Gay American Indians
Gathering of Spirit, A (Brant), 156
Gay American Indians (GAI), 135–36, 140, 142, 143, 156
Gay Games, 93
gays: Cherokee identity as, 106–7
Gay Sunshine (journal), 155–56
gender, 1, 9, 11, 23, 31, 38, 190, 215; diversity of, 123, 124–29, 166–67; Native histories of, 134–35
gendered space: Pacific as, 68–69
gender systems/roles, 12, 20, 59, 123, 127; Cherokee, 98–99, 103–4, 105, 111n1; Cree, 196–98; Native, 36–37; Samoan families, 81–82, 83–84; Two-Spirit terminology and, 13–14
genocide, 48; indigeneity and, 50–51
Gopinath, Gayatri, 50, 51–52
Gould, Janice, 157
Green, Rayna, 34–35, 50–51

Hall, Clyde M., 135
Harris, Curtis, 136
health: in New Zealand, 71–72
heteronormativity, 19, 39, 61, 130, 217; and heteropatriarchy, 33–34; queer theory and, 43–44
heteropatriarchy, 9, 39, 58, 59, 99; colonial, 21–23, 36, 143, 214, 217–19; land and, 34–35; and sexuality, 33–34
histories, 5, 21; colonial, 20, 67–68; Métis, 191–93

HIV/AIDS, 117–18, 211
HIV/AIDS programs, 136, 137, 142, 205
homophobia, 16, 38, 114, 116, 125, 127, 139, 214
homosexuality: Maori, 115, 116; in Samoa, 85–86, 87, 90, 93
hub: diaspora and, 52
hybridity, 55; and queerness, 52–53

identities, 21, 112n13, 173; Indigenous GLBTQ2, 2, 3, 4; Native, 49, 50, 51; native critiques, 6–7; and place, 175–77; queer, 99–100; queer culture and, 46–47; settler colonialism and, 147–48; sexual, 123, 197–99; sexuality and, 11–12, 113; takutapui, 118–19; tribal, 7–8; Two-Spirit, 10–11, 12–13, 14, 98, 100–102, 129–30, 133, 134–35, 136–37, 145–46; U.S. census, 97–98
immigration: to New Zealand, 72–73
Indian Act (Canada), 218–19
Indian hating, 51
Indian Territory, 175, 176, 177, 179
indigeneity, 60–61, 141, 159, 186, 213; appropriation of, 51–52; genocide and, 50–51; in *Lord of the Rings*, 163–64
Indigenous People's Task Force, 137
inequalities of desire, 124
intellectualism: sovereignty and, 19–20

Justice, Daniel Heath: *The Way of Thorn and Thunder*, 158, 162–63, 164–69

Kairaiuak, Larry, 137
Kenny, Maurice, 155, 156
knowledge(s), 5, 7, 49; Indigenous, 3, 4, 8, 9–10, 20, 216; Maori transmission of, 115–16
Kororareka, 69

Two-Spirit movement, 126–27, 214; literary studies, 157–58, 161–62; scholarship, 215–17

Two-Spirit people, 1, 126–27, 132, 149–50n2; acceptance of, 110–11, 128–29; Cherokee, 97, 98–99, 100–103, 107–8, 109; community roles of, 103–5; Cree concept of, 196–98; distinctiveness of, 136–37; identity as, 10–11, 98, 129–30; in literatures, 14–15; non-native narratives of, 138–41; organizing, 133, 134, 141–45, 215; positionality of, 123–24; queer politics and, 145–49; traditional culture and, 16–17, 127–28; use of term, 3, 12–14, 15–16, 17–18; in Vancouver, 204–5

2 Spirits, 137

"United" (Kenny), 155, 156
urban population, 203–4

Vancouver: First Nations people in, 203–4
Vancouver Native Cultural Society, 135
violence, 59, 162, 212; of conquest, 36, 66; of dispossession, 175–76, 181–82; of forced assimilation, 160–61; against GLBTQ2, 159–60

Wakefield, Edward, 72
Walking with Ghosts (Driskill), 186; themes in, 158–62, 174–75
Warner, Michael, 47
Warren, Karen, 58
Warrior, Robert, 45
Way of Thorn and Thunder, The (Justice), 158, 162–63; decolonization, 168–69; on erotic sovereignty, 167–68; gender diversity in, 166–67; nationalism in, 165–66; Tolkein comparisons in, 164–65
WeWah and BarCheeAmpe, 136–37, 142
whaling, 66–67, 69
Whitikiw, 203
Williams, Walter, 139
Wings of Wadaduga, On the, 106, 110, 112n9
women, 34, 35, 76; convict, 66, 67; Maori, 70, 74–75

Yate, Mr., 114–15
"You Can Count" (Scofield), 196–97

Zoccole, Art, 137
Zuni Man-Woman, The (Roscoe), 126, 139–40
Zuni Nation, 12, 140